RELIGION AND HUMAN FLOURISHING

RELIGION AND HUMAN FLOURISHING

Adam B. Cohen

Editor

BAYLOR UNIVERSITY PRESS

Cover and book design by Kasey McBeath
Cover image by Paweł Czerwiński, Unsplash

Hardcover ISBN: 978-1-4813-1285-1
Library of Congress Control Number: 2020017776

This volume came out of a conference on religion and human flourishing sponsored by the Templeton Foundation, conducted at Harvard University in 2018. Attending scholars represented world-renowned universities, including Yale, Notre Dame, UC Santa Barbara, Oxford, Arizona State University, University of British Columbia, University of Texas, Harvard, Chapman, Cambridge, Hope College, and Baylor, as well as the London-based think tank Perspectiva. Attendees of the conference have all made profound contributions to the academic study of religion, and we are honored to present their essays in this volume. The Templeton Foundation also provided funding that supported this volume.

Printed in the United States of America on acid-free paper with a minimum of thirty percent recycled content.

CONTENTS

II

III

CONTRIBUTORS

Adam B. Cohen is a professor of psychology at Arizona State University. His research examines how religious differences function as cultural differences and suggests that religion is profoundly influential in shaping self-construal and strongly affects intergroup relations. He is an author of *Generating Generosity in Catholicism and Islam: Beliefs, Institutions, and Public Good Provision.*

Matthew Croasmun is associate research scholar and director of the Life Worth Living Program at the Yale Center for Faith and Culture and lecturer in humanities at Yale College. He is author of *The Emergence of Sin: The Cosmic Tyrant in Romans* and co-author with Miroslav Volf of *For the Life of the World: Theology That Makes a Difference.*

Celia Deane-Drummond is a senior research fellow and the inaugural director of *Laudato Si'* Research Institute at Campion Hall, University of Oxford. Her research, writing, and teaching focus on constructive systematic and moral theology in their relation to the biological and human sciences. She is the author of *Theological Ethics through a Multispecies Lens: The Evolution of Wisdom, Volume 1.*

Christopher G. Ellison is the Dean's Distinguished Professor of Social Science and a professor of sociology at The University of Texas at San Antonio. His work looks at the role of religious involvement in mental and physical health and well-being, religion, and family life, and the role of religion in the lives of

African Americans and Latino Americans. He is an editor of *Religion, Families, and Health: Population-Based Research in the United States.*

Laurence R. Iannaccone is professor of economics and director of the Institute for the Study of Religion, Economics, and Society at Chapman University. His research publications apply economic theory to the study of church participation, conversion, extremism, and other aspects of religion and spirituality.

Sriya Iyer is a University reader in economics at the University of Cambridge. She has used the tools of economics to offer insights into one of the most religiously diverse countries in the world in her book *The Economics of Religion in India.*

Byron R. Johnson is Distinguished Professor of the Social Sciences and professor of sociology at Baylor University where he is also the founding director of Baylor's Institute for Studies of Religion. He is a leading authority on the scientific study of religion, the efficacy of faith-based organizations, domestic violence, and criminal justice and an author of *The Quest for Purpose: The Collegiate Search for a Meaningful Life.*

Dominic D. P. Johnson is professor of international relations at the University of Oxford. His research focuses on the role of cognitive psychology, evolutionary biology, and religion in human conflict and cooperation behavior. His most recent book is *God Is Watching You: How the Fear of God Makes Us Human.*

Ryan McAnnally-Linz is the associate director of the Yale Center for Faith and Culture and a lecturer in humanities at Yale College. He has written in multiple fields, including systematic theology and humanities education.

David G. Myers is a Hope College psychology professor and coauthor of introductory and social psychology texts. His writings also have related psychological science to happiness, intuition, and faith.

Jonathan Rowson is the director of the London-based Perspectiva, a new research institute seeking to highlight the importance of the connections between systems, souls, and society in a range of complex problems. He is the author of *Spiritualise: Cultivating Spiritual Sensibility to Address 21st Century Challenges* and *The Moves That Matter: A Chess Grandmaster on the Game of Life.*

Azim F. Shariff is Canada 150 Research Chair in Moral Psychology at the University of British Columbia (UBC) where he is also an associate professor of psychology and director of UBC's Center for Applied Moral Psychology. His work focuses on the intersection of morality with religion, cultural attitudes, and social and technological trends. He is the author of more than fifty scientific papers.

Tyler J. VanderWeele, Ph.D., is the John L. Loeb and Frances Lehman Loeb Professor of Epidemiology at the Harvard T. H. Chan School of Public Health and the founding director of the Human Flourishing Program at Harvard University. His research concerns methodology for distinguishing between association and causation in observational studies as well as the empirical study of the determinants of human flourishing and of religion as a social determinant of health. He is an author of *Explanation in Causal Inference.*

Miroslav Volf is the Henry B. Wright Professor of Theology at the Yale Divinity School and the founding director of the Yale Center for Faith and Culture. He is the author of *Flourishing: Why We Need Religion in a Globalized World.*

Harvey Whitehouse holds a statutory chair in social anthropology and is the director of the Centre for the Study of Social Cohesion at the University of Oxford. A founder of the interdisciplinary cognitive science of religion field, he has published three books on "modes of religiosity" and is currently completing a new work on the subject, *The Ritual Animal: Imitation and Cohesion in the Evolution of Social Complexity.*

INTRODUCTION

Adam B. Cohen

It is fair to say that people in times not too long past looked to religion as the chief indicator of their flourishing. They might ask their priest or rabbi or imam, or they might look to religious texts or to their religious communities to see if they were living their lives in the right ways. If not, they might have been encouraged to lead a more religious life, so as to flourish more. But time has marched on, and we no longer take it for granted that religion can help us flourish, or can tell us what it means to flourish. Today more than ever we might move religion to the sidelines, or even consider whether religion is detrimental to our flourishing.

Religion may have consequences for humanity at multiple levels, from the health or well-being of individuals to relationships within and among groups to the development and maintenance of social institutions to cultural evolution. What is the relation of religion to flourishing? Can religion help us to flourish or tell us whether we are flourishing, or does religion interfere with our flourishing?

These are deep and nuanced questions, which bear careful theological and philosophical thought, and careful empirical examination. This volume undertakes to determine the quality of evidence for and against claims that religion contributes to human flourishing.

The essays in the present book grew out of a conference organized as part of the Humble Approach Initiative, funded by the JTF and conference held at Harvard in Nov–Dec of 2018. The participants gathered to discuss the broad question of religion's relationship to human flourishing, and the diversity of thought they represent is readily obvious

1

in the diversity of approaches on display in their essays. The contributors generally hold that religion is causally consequential—whether positively or negatively—at each of level of analysis from the very small to the very large. But their essays show that there are gaps in our knowledge and point to the kinds of theoretical and empirical research initiatives that would have potential to provide definitive answers to a range of important questions.

If we are to talk about religion and flourishing, one of the first things we need to figure out is how to even frame these questions, theologically and philosophically. All faith traditions claim for their systems of belief goals and intrinsic goods that can be incompatible with self-interest. Religious definitions of health and wholeness may be broader than those of the secular world. Research that takes seriously uniquely religious aspects of human flourishing as desired outcomes may be needed as well as ever greater methodological rigor in future investigations of causal connections. Not least, this volume considers how theological and philosophical perspectives might shape such future research as well as how such research might benefit religious communities.

The first section of the book takes up these foundational theological and philosophical questions.

Of course, to proceed with our inquiry we should establish what precisely is meant by "flourishing" ("religion" is not necessarily a settled term either, but for our purposes the broad sense of faith traditions will serve). This definitional groundwork is laid by Miroslav Volf in "Meanings and Dimensions of Flourishing: A Programmatic Sketch." Volf aims to clarify the meaning of flourishing by integrating three perspectives from Western tradition, arguing that a flourishing life is a life that is being *led well* (agency), that *goes well* (circumstances), and that *feels right* (emotions).

Next, Celia Deane-Drummond, in "Virtues, Vices, and the Good Life: A Theologian's Perspective on Compassion and Violence," further takes up the basic philosophical and theological question of human flourishing's meaning. As a Roman Catholic theologian, she is most interested in cultural change toward values that encourage rather than inhibit the good life, understood as the common good, so meaning the good for all and the good for each.

Jonathan Rowson, in "*Status Viatoris* and the Path Quality of Religion: Human Flourishing as a Sacred Process of Becoming," asks how we might conceive of the relationship between our ultimate societal ends and our available institutional means, in ways that help clarify how we should live. He introduces a theoretical and empirical research initiative (what does it mean to grow as a person and why does it matter for society?), highlights some little understood individual differences (e.g., mental complexity and levels of maturation) that are not often taken into account in the context of flourishing, and introduces a way of thinking (constructive-developmental) that is unhelpfully dispersed across myriad forms of scholarship and practice.

Rounding out the section on conceptual foundations, Dr. Tyler VanderWeele, in "Spiritual Well-Being and Human Flourishing: Conceptual, Causal, and Policy Relations," situates the question of whether religion contributes to flourishing across a number of different levels: the individual, different communities, competing notions of the good, and the final end of the human person.

The next section of the book turns to the empirical dimension and encompasses perspectives ranging from anthropology to biostatistics to evolutionary biology to psychology. The scholars represented here consider whether we can ever say that membership in faith communities is not only tethered to but also responsible for personal weal, and ponder whether a decades-long attempt to use the tools of social science to investigate how religion functions at various stages of life has brought us any closer to understanding how religious belief and practice produce spiritual capital on which people can draw in times of exigency and crisis. As a set, these chapters clarify what individual differences and environmental variables (whether related to neighborhoods or nation states) we need to take into account in advancing claims that religion is causally consequential when it comes to flourishing, which in turn raises the question of whether we have the right theoretical models and enough empirical work over long enough periods to examine causal influences.

The first few chapters take quite a distal approach, informed by evolutionary views of religion. Professor Harvey Whitehouse, in a chapter entitled "Religion and Human Flourishing in the Evolution of Social Complexity," explains that religion has undoubtedly contributed to the evolution of social complexity. Specifically, the role of religious rituals in the rise of civilization has implications for human flourishing.

Following nicely on Whitehouse's work on ritual, Dominic Johnson writes on "The Next Generation: Evolutionary Perspectives on Religion and Flourishing." Professor Johnson argues that religious beliefs and behaviors pose an evolutionary puzzle because they are costly; however, there are material benefits that can exceed these costs, resulting in net benefits overall. He further proposes that the costs themselves can in fact represent the benefit, via signaling; consequently, religion has (in the past) and may continue (today) to contribute to human "flourishing," as measured by Darwinian fitness (survival and reproductive success).

The next two chapters focus on religion, trust, and prosociality—issues which are often proposed to have helped in the cultural evolution of religion. In "Religion's Role in Building Trust," I show that people from different religious groups trust one another to a surprising extent, and that "costly signals" of religion increase trust, even between people who are from different religions.

Professor Azim Shariff then poses the question of "Religion's Contribution to Prosociality." Shariff provides an overview of a meta-analysis on religion and prosociality, considering both self-reported and objective measures of prosocial behaviors, whether there is evidence for causality, and whether religious prosociality is parochial.

The third and final section of the book follows in the empirical mold by moving to more sociological and economic levels of analysis. Chapters 9–12 focus on religion and flourishing in terms of health and well-being at the individual and group levels. Chris Ellison begins with "Religion's Contribution to Population Health: Key Theoretical and Methodological Considerations." Ellison has three main objectives: (1) to provide a cursory review of some key elements of the literature; (2) to outline some of the key explanatory pathways or mechanisms via which religion may influence health and well-being; and (3) to identify several important directions for further exploration that will help to clarify whether, and to what extent, religion actually influences health and well-being.

Next, Dr. Byron Johnson, in "Offender-Led Religious Movements: Identity Transformation, Rehabilitation, and Justice System Reform," looks to offender-led religious movements in prison as a concrete example of how faith and wellness can relate. He shows that these movements have the capacity to provide participants a strong identity, an alternative moral framework, and a set of embodied practices that emphasize virtue and character development.

Closing this unit, David Myers draws out "Some Big-Data Lessons" from religion and human flourishing. Myers presents evidence that helps determine whether religious engagement is associated with misery, or the good life; greed, or prosocial generosity of time and money; self-serving pride and bigotry, or virtues such as humility and forgiveness; stress and illness, or health and longevity; happiness and life satisfaction, or repression and depression. Big data from varied sources reveal a curious *religious engagement paradox*: religious engagement correlates *negatively* with human flourishing across aggregate levels (when comparing more versus less religious countries or American states), and *positively* across individuals (especially within relatively more religious places).

With Professor Myers' wrestling with varying levels of analysis as a basis, the two penultimate chapters bring economic perspectives to bear on religion and flourishing. Larry Iannaccone, in "Smart and Spiritual: The Coevolution of Religion and Rationality," argues that a capacity for sacred stories represents a biologically grounded capacity for being fascinated, entertained, and persuaded—all vital elements in economic exchange. "Sacredness" here suggests the capacity's ability to extend our sense of reality beyond that which we perceive as natural, normal, and strictly material, and must be capable of transcending (and thereby constraining and reshaping) our rational, self-interested impulses.

From a more particular economic vantage, Dr. Sriya Iyer explores "The Economics of Religion in Developing Countries." Iyer reports on research which examined how religious organizations provide and change their religious and nonreligious services in response to the competition for adherents and inequality. This study draws on the first Indian economic survey of religious organizations, called the India Religion Survey, between 2007 and 2010, which focused on various organizations' welfare service provision. Iyer further develops a theoretical economic framework drawing upon industrial organization and game theory to argue that the strength of religious beliefs may be related to economic inequality, religious competition, and nonreligious service provision.

As a concluding reflection on the entire project, Azim Shariff reflects "On Balance" on whether religion promotes—and detracts—from flourishing. Shariff takes seriously the possibility that the degree to which religion positively contributes to human flourishing is only one side of an important question. After summarizing what the social scientific research says about both the positive and negative effects of religion, Shariff discusses the challenge of weighing these various features to draw a balanced conclusion about whether, and how, religion contributes to human flourishing.

Given all the cross-disciplinary richness on display here—theological and philosophical conceptualization; empirical observation of biological and social relations; individual, societal, and economic levels of analysis; and overall careful reflection on the positive and negative effects of religion on flourishing—we all hope that this book will have broad appeal, to both academics and nonspecialists. Scholars and lay people alike are interested in religion, and many more still are interested in how to lead a good and meaningful life—how to flourish. The rigorous science, and impact on popular culture, of the positive psychology movement attest to this. The collaborative undertaking represented by this book will further attest to the perennial importance of the questions of religious belief and the pursuit of the good life, and hopefully become a standard for further exploration of such questions. Seldom has such an impressive group of scholars come together to take a nuanced approach to a complex question with such intellectual alacrity. The significance of the book is in its collecting and synthesizing the work of all these scholars, so anyone (in or outside the academy) interested in religion and flourishing has access to a much broader and deeper overview than would be possible if the study were produced from within a singular disciplinary silo. Whatever we may determine about the role of religion in human existence, it is certain that flourishing necessitates community; it is fitting that this exploration reflects just that.

MEANINGS AND DIMENSIONS OF FLOURISHING

A Programmatic Sketch

Miroslav Volf, Matthew Croasmun, Ryan McAnnally-Linz

I

One of the major challenges in the current research about human flourishing—about the good life, happiness, well-being, the true life, the life worth living, and other designations under which the topic is discussed—is lack of agreement on what we mean by "flourishing" and its many near synonyms. The disagreement is not surprising. For there is no way to determine "objectively" what it would mean for human beings to flourish. The reasons for this are many, but first among them is that flourishing is a normative idea; it names what kind of beings humans *ought to be* and provides the orienting criteria—the "tables of value," to use Friedrich Nietzsche's phrase—for what they *ought to desire* and how they *ought to live.*

Given the normative character of human flourishing, it follows that the sciences have both an indispensable and limited role in helping clarify what we mean by "flourishing." For no amount of knowledge about what was, what is, and what is likely to be can determine what *ought* to be. Various sciences can and should *inform* our reflection on the meaning of flourishing, but they cannot set its basic meaning. They must, rather, assume it. When it comes to flourishing, the main role of the sciences is to enlighten us about human behavior (in a given culture) and identify the most effective means by which we can come to flourish in the way we have on other grounds (or no grounds at all) determined that we ought to.

If we were to give up on privacy and allow all data about us to be collected—all our correspondence and other interactions, data about our health, the history of our purchases, all the books we've read and comments about them we've made, etc.—a complex algorithm would be able to come up with an exceptionally accurate account of our behavior, even know us in many regards better than we know ourselves; it would fairly reliably predict what we would do in many situations. But the one thing it wouldn't be able to tell us is what we *ought to do*. The algorithm could tell us what we actually desire and what we find desirable, even what we aspire to find desirable, but it couldn't tell us what we *ought to desire*. The same is true of science.

To get clarity on the meaning of flourishing, we need to engage not so much in scientific research as in philosophical and religious reflection. The great philosophers—from Socrates to Simone Weil—present us with the most rigorous forms of reflection on the meaning of flourishing. The great religious traditions—from Hinduism and Judaism to Christianity and Islam—offer the most enduring communities of living and attentive reflecting about alternative visions of flourishing. And of course, traditions that fall somewhere in between religion and philosophy, like Buddhism and Confucianism, do so as well. These diverse traditions have long been the main sources of our visions of flourishing life. They remain relevant even, and perhaps especially, in a modern world in which visions of the good life have been privatized and are often embraced as changing individual "dreams."[1]

II

If we cannot derive visions of flourishing from the results of scientific research, what reasons do we have to embrace any of them? Most would agree that such visions, whether explicitly or implicitly held, are essential to human life. Some would argue that since they, ultimately, set goals for human action, their importance only increases with the exponential growth in knowledge and technology.[2] But the need to have them in general is not a sufficient reason to embrace any one of them in particular. One option would be to say that all accounts of who human beings ought to be and what kinds of tables of value they should embrace are arbitrary. But then the best we could do would be to accept a kind of new polytheism of ultimate goals, a tension-laden pantheon of countless private and national gods.[3] The unhappy marriage of science, which uses reason to pursue truth but cannot set human purposes, and myth, which articulates a vision into which human beings should stretch themselves but is devoid of reason, would then be our best option.

Advocates of the world religions and great philosophical traditions that emerged through axial transformations were never satisfied with a polytheism of values.[4] As they saw it, visions of human flourishing and the accounts of the self, social relations, and the good upon which they rest, involve truth claims that can be rationally evaluated. They believed that the marriage of "mythos" and "logos" could be a happy one.[5] Especially in recent decades, religious scholars and philosophers have developed sophisticated procedures to assess rationally the comparative epistemic advantages of rival versions of flourishing life and the interpretations of reality associated with them.[6]

None of us can stand outside of these rival visions of flourishing, even as we try to survey the landscape of contending visions and assess them. What follows is our proposal, as Christian theologians, of how best to frame the theological and philosophical reflection required to ground our research into—and pursuit of—flourishing life. We begin by articulating a three-part formal structure for visions of flourishing. We then illustrate each of the three aspects by considering thinkers who have placed just one of them at the center of their visions of flourishing. Finally, we sketch (in very broad strokes) an integrated vision of flourishing within our particular religious tradition by constructively engaging the theology of St. Paul.

While we expect that some aspects of the formal structure we propose will be useful as a heuristic through which to understand and compare different visions of flourishing across religious and philosophical traditions, it will also become apparent that this formal structure serves us well in our constructive work as Christian theologians. We invite others, working within other traditions, to offer revisions to our proposed formal structure, or, indeed, replacements for it that are more genial to their work articulating their own visions of flourishing.[7]

III

Our proposal builds on Nicholas Wolterstorff's argument in *Justice: Rights and Wrongs*.[8] Wolterstorff writes in opposition to a tradition of thought that is concerned mainly with the quality of humans as agents—their acts, practices, and virtues. He argues for a vision of the good life in which humans show up also as *patients*—"patient" being used here in the ancient sense of being affected. Humans are bearers of rights, he argues, and therefore certain things are owed to them; receiving what is owed to them, and not just doing what they ought to do, is essential to their flourishing. Leading life well is not all there is to flourishing. Life going well matters too.

Our proposal is an expansion of Wolterstorff's: we flourish when, in addition to leading life well (agency) and life going well (circumstances), life also *feels right* to us (affect). It is predicated on the belief that emotions, such as joy or sorrow, are neither merely active (produced by the agent) nor merely passive (a reaction to some outside stimulus) but are activo-passive. As we experience an emotion, we are, in one undivided experience, both affected and active: we are, in a particular way, actively relating to the way "objects" affect us. Even more, emotions partly contribute to the construction of the objects that affect us, to their appearing to us *as* objects of a particular kind.

Life led well refers to the "agential" dimension of the flourishing life, to the good conduct of life—from right thoughts and right acts to right habits and right virtues. *Life going well* refers to the "circumstantial" dimension of the flourishing life, to the desirable circumstances of life—be they natural (like fertile, uncontaminated land), social (like friendships or the absence of war), or personal (like certain kinds of genes or a well-functioning body). *Life feeling as it should* is about the "affective" dimension of the flourishing life, about "happiness" (or contentment or joy), empathy, and the like.

FIG. 1.1 THREE DOMAINS OF FLOURISHING: AGENCY, EMOTIONS, AND CIRCUMSTANCES.[9]

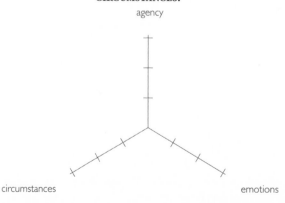

agency

circumstances   emotions

IV

In acquainting ourselves with these three aspects of flourishing, it may be helpful to consider three thinkers that see the whole of flourishing life largely through the lens of just one aspect. Our account of each will be brief and insufficiently nuanced; its purpose here is to illustrate an option and cast the three aspects in sharp relief so as to make evident their distinction from one another.

Let the ethics of ancient Stoics, people like the emperor Marcus Aurelius, serve as an example of an account of flourishing, or the good and true life, understood primarily as a matter of agency, as life being led well. The possession and exercise of virtue, they argued, is not just necessary for flourishing, but sufficient as well. Flourishing human beings are self-sufficient. Reliance on external goods would make a person dependent and therefore detract from their flourishing. Though health and wealth are to be preferred to sickness and poverty, people can be virtuous and therefore happy even if they don't get what they prefer. The Stoic relation to emotions was more nuanced than their relation to external goods like health and wealth. Though they viewed most "passions" negatively, as reflecting and reinforcing undue investment in things outside of one's control, they insisted that certain "good passions," including joy, will be by-products of the virtuous life. The flourishing life is preponderantly one of virtuous agency, not of positive feeling (which, in a strictly limited form, flows out of virtuous agency) or adequate external goods (which, strictly speaking, are irrelevant).

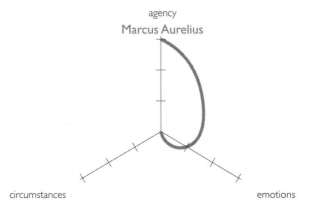

FIG. 1.2 STOIC PRIORITY OF AGENTIAL FLOURISHING.

FIG. 1.3 MARXIAN PRIORITY OF CIRCUMSTANTIAL FLOURISHING.

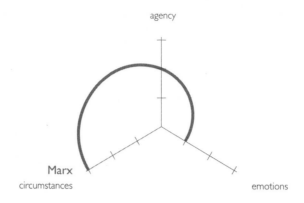

Let the economic and social theory of a modern thinker, Karl Marx, serve as an example of an account of flourishing understood primarily as life going well—or, rather, let one plausible, though perhaps not the most compelling, interpretation of Marx serve as such.[10] The communist society is primarily one of right technological, economic, and political circumstances. True, the revolution will bring about a transformation of moral agency; human beings will no longer treat either themselves or others as mere means and will engage in free, creative activities while their individual and communal interests coincide. But the revolution will neither come about mainly through moral critique and corresponding political engagement (as the utopian socialists argued), nor will life in the postrevolutionary society, at the basic level, depend on the virtue and moral agency of individuals. The transformation of circumstances, brought about by historical processes, is sufficient for the flourishing of all; "moral" behavior and appropriate affective states will follow.

Let Mustapha Mond, a fictional character from Aldous Huxley's dystopia *Brave New World*, serve as the spokesperson for an account of flourishing understood as life feeling right.[11] With the help of social engineering, biotechnology, and pharmacology, people will be conditioned and the world arranged in such a way as to get "rid of everything unpleasant" and make everyone happy:[12] all people "get what they want" and they "never want what they can't get."[13] There is no need for moral effort, as "there's no such a thing as divided allegiance" and "you're so conditioned that you can't help doing what you ought to do."[14] Mustapha Mond's own agency is utterly subservient to the realization and maintenance of a kind of world that makes all of each

FIG. 1.4 PRIORITY OF FLOURISHING EMOTIONS.

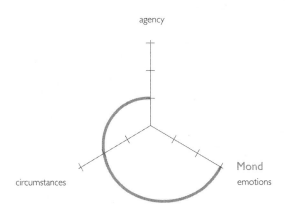

person's experiences only pleasant. In Mond, one can recognize a realization of the vision of Jeremy Bentham, who begins *An Introduction to the Principles of Morals and Legislation* (1789) with the statement "Nature has placed mankind under the governance of two sovereign masters, pain and pleasure. They alone point out what we *ought to* do and determine what we *shall* do."[15]

Marcus, Marx, and Mond are each exemplars of ways of thinking about the flourishing life. We sketched each from the perspective of its core content, identifying in it the dominant dimension of flourishing: agency in Stoicism, circumstances in Marxism, and emotions in Utilitarianism. But accounts of flourishing generally spell out not just the core content of flourishing but also ways to achieve flourishing life. They are about both a vision and the journey into it, about a goal and the means of its realization. Often the goal and the means match. But sometimes they don't. The match is tight in Stoicism: moral agency is the goal and moral agency is the means. In the version of Marxism we presented above, the means and ends correspond as well: historical processes, driven by development of productive forces, bring about revolutionary change of circumstances, which is the core content of flourishing life. But there is a pronounced discrepancy between the goal and the means in Utilitarianism: a certain selfless kind of agency (embodied in *Brave New World* by Mustapha Mond) is the necessary means by which all reach the goal of the good life, whose core content is pleasure and therefore differs markedly from the means.

V

Advocates of the ways of thinking about flourishing represented here by Marcus, Marx, and Mond are involved in intense debates, and the debates internal to each way of thinking can be more intense than the debates among them. We don't need to wade into these debates here, except to note that from our perspective, for all their merits, these accounts of flourishing life are each one-sided. As we mentioned earlier, our contention is that a plausible account of flourishing life *needs to integrate all three of the dimensions of flourishing life around which these visions are organized.*

Even more, though each of the three dimensions of flourishing has its own integrity, the relationship between them is *not merely additive.* It's not as if each dimension were a leg in some three-legged good life stool, such that, though you need all three legs to sit comfortably, each leg bears part of your weight separately. The relationship between the three dimensions of flourishing is also *perichoretic*, to use analogously a term that has its original home in theological reflection on God. Each aspect often partly contains the other two. Take, for example, friendship as an aspect of life going well. Arguably, the love of a few significant other people is among the most significant circumstances of a flourishing life. But we cannot have friends unless we actively relate to them *as* friends; friendship requires an exercise of our agency. Inversely, relating to someone as friend doesn't itself create a friendship if they don't want to reciprocate and we are acted upon as their friends. And relating to another person as a friend isn't merely doing the things a friend does but letting oneself be affected by friends so as to rejoice when they rejoice and mourn when they mourn. Though we can plausibly categorize friendship as a circumstance of life, it emerges from the interrelation of all three aspects of flourishing. Or consider the example of an emotion like joy. Joy is not simply an internal psychological state. I rejoice *over something*, and that means: (a) that a slice of the world has to be worthy of joy as an emotional response to it and (b) that I have to construe it as such (which opens up the possibility of appropriate and inappropriate rejoicing). An experience of genuine joy is an interweaving of life going well (circumstances worthy of rejoicing), life being led well (rightly construing circumstances as worthy of rejoicing), and life feeling right (the emotional state itself).

VI

To flesh out the content of the formal structure of the flourishing life—the content of each dimension and the perichoretic relation between them—we turn to a vision of flourishing in the tradition we know the best: the Christian faith. More specifically, we offer a sketch based on the texts of the first Christian theologian, the apostle Paul.[16]

Paul summarizes the flourishing life in his definition of the kingdom of God—the whole created world at home in having become the home of God—in Romans 14:17: "The Kingdom of God is not food and drink but righteousness, peace, and joy in the Holy Spirit." Flourishing life is more than the meeting of the human animal's material needs, but it does not exclude these. It requires, in addition, construing these basic necessities as *gifts* rather than mere *things*, part of the network of relations that is the kingdom or home of God—relations among God, all humans, and all living things.

If the substance of flourishing life is not to be found in the basic material needs of life, where should we look instead? Paul points to the unity of our agency (*righteousness*—life in conformity to the law of love), our circumstances (*peace*—both material abundance and rich relationships), and our emotions (*joy*—the signature emotion of flourishing life). These three are not independent of one another, but rather each in its fullness includes some aspect of the others. Love as agency is only ever fully at home in a *world of love* (circumstance) and is cold unless discharging duties toward those we love has the *warmth* of longing and care (emotion). True peace entails not just a dynamic order of life-enhancing circumstances, but feeling at peace (emotion) and living peaceably (agency). Finally, joy in full bloom is not just a matter of individual *feeling*; it requires opening oneself to joy in both actively construing the world or some aspect of it as worth rejoicing over and letting oneself be "taken into" joy (agency); and it culminates in a *state* of joy, a social space marked by joy into which one might enter (circumstance).[17]

While all three dimensions are equally requisite, they do not equally demand our allegiance; love takes priority, as we will see shortly. Moreover, because we live in a world marked by suffering and oppression, love often takes the form of sacrifice. There are times when we ought to choose to sacrifice genuine circumstantial and affective goods of our own for the sake of the flourishing of all. Under such conditions, all our agency will be qualified by the need to help those who suffer oppression, exclusion, or misfortune and will therefore include an element of sacrifice. Similarly, because we live in a world that is not fully flourishing, there are circumstances over which it would be perverse to rejoice; we are to mourn with those who mourn (Rom 12:15), even as, in light of

FIG. 1.5 THE PERICHORETIC RELATIONSHIP BETWEEN FLOURISHING AGENCY, CIRCUMSTANCES, AND EMOTIONS IN THE THEOLOGY OF THE APOSTLE PAUL.

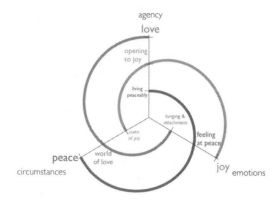

God's goodness and the primordial goodness of the world, we rejoice always (Phil 4:4).

Finally, all three of these are not possessions of independently self-actualized human beings, but rather markers of a life flourishing in relationship to the divine; each and all three together are, as Romans 14:17 insists, only fully ours *"in the Holy Spirit."*

The perichoretic structure of the relations among the three dimensions of flourishing means that we can view the whole content of the flourishing life by properly construing one aspect. The entirety of the world as the home of God can be described as the world of love, the world of peace, or the world of joy. Still, what creates and sustains the world properly described in each of these ways is God's love, which Paul suggests in describing righteousness, peace, and joy as being "in the Holy Spirit," who is the Spirit of divine love. The agency of divine love, therefore, has primacy. Correspondingly, the human work of receiving that divine love in faith by relating to God and to the world as gift and of being an active instrument of divine love has primacy.

VII

Flourishing, we have said, is a normative idea. Normative ideas are, by and large, matters of contention. Consequently, we have no doubt that even the rather sparse, formal claim we have made here—that a plausible account of flourishing requires the integration of three distinguishable dimensions—will meet with resistance and critique. Our hope is not that it will be universally accepted but that it will advance the conversation and deepen our understanding of the most important question of our lives.

References

Bellah, Robert N., and Hans Joas. 2012. *The Axial Age and Its Consequences.* Cambridge, Mass.: The Belknap Press of Harvard University Press.

Bentham, Jeremy. 1970. *An Introduction to the Principles of Morals and Legislation.* Edited by J. H. Burns and H. L. A. Hart. Oxford: Clarendon.

de Benoist, Alain. 2018. *On Being a Pagan.* Translated by John Graham. North Augusta, S.C.: Arcana Europa.

Harari, Yuval Noah. 2018. *21 Lessons for the 21st Century.* New York: Spiegel & Grau.

Huxley, Aldous. 2014. *Brave New World.* New York: HarperCollins.

MacIntyre, Alasdair. 1988. *Whose Justice? Which Rationality?* Notre Dame, Ind.: University of Notre Dame Press.

———. 1990. *Three Rival Versions of Moral Enquiry.* Notre Dame, Ind.: University of Notre Dame Press.

Rosa, Hartmut. 2019. *Resonance: A Sociology of Our Relationship to the World.* Translated by James C. Wagner. Cambridge: Polity.

Volf, Miroslav. 2016. *Flourishing: Why We Need Religion in a Globalized World.* New Haven: Yale University Press.

———. 2019. "Religion in 2068: Humanity and What Matters Most in the Age of Artificial Intelligence." The Landon Saunders Lecture on the Human Being as the Nexus of World and Faith, Lipscomb University, Nashville, Tenn. Filmed February 2019. YouTube video, 1:36:07. https://www.youtube.com/watch?v=FJo2IJrlKDE.

Volf, Miroslav, and Matthew Croasmun. 2019. *For the Life of the World: Theology That Makes a Difference.* Grand Rapids: Brazos Press.

Wolterstorff, Nicholas. 2007. *Justice: Rights and Wrongs.* Princeton: Princeton University Press.

———. 2019. *Religion in the University.* New Haven: Yale University Press.

2

VIRTUES, VICES, AND THE GOOD LIFE

A Theologian's Perspective on Compassion and Violence

CELIA DEANE-DRUMMOND

Starting Points: Religion, Theology, and Human Flourishing

Seeking and finding a clear evidential basis for human flourishing is a task more properly assigned to the natural and human sciences.[1] However, that does not necessarily mean that theological analysis and moral theology are redundant in this exploration, or that theological reflection cannot benefit from engagement with these sciences. The first and perhaps most basic question, which is also an obvious philosophical and theological one, is what does human flourishing mean? To say that religion or religions promote or deny that flourishing depends on how it is understood and its internal appropriation within a community and not just its assessment by outside observers. Where that community is religious it becomes rather harder for "outsiders" to understand internal meanings and potential benefits. I am defining religion as a structured social organization in which (a) there is a shared affective experience, usually in relation to immaterial goods, (b) specific beliefs are accepted and agreed upon and held to

19

be true by the majority of its members, and (c) there is usually an organized structure relating to that particular belief or set of beliefs. Note that in terms of origin (a) may appear prior to (b) or (c), which is why habitually some will describe themselves as being "spiritual" but not having any particular "religious" affiliation. Such distinctions are important when considering the origin of religious belief, since that affective capacity did not necessarily initially show clear signs of traces of collective religious practice in the evolutionary record. In addition, averages across large-scale groups do not do justice to the wide variety of interpretations within a given community and what some scholars have called "thick" descriptions of human relationships that are missed out when analysis of flourishing is according to procedural or contractual agreements.[2] Distinctions between "inside" and "outside" become much less clear once an ethnographic perspective tries to understand and think alongside those communities.

The point I am trying to make is that any one academic discipline is limited, especially when it comes to arriving at firm conclusions about the meaning of human flourishing and its particular relationship to religious beliefs, as it will be set by the particular methodologies and background assumptions within that discipline as to what that flourishing or religious beliefs mean and how they can be measured. For example, flourishing in religious terms could be about *giving up* certain goods, an ascesis, as much as acquiring more, but that ascesis is for the sake of what are perceived to be higher goals of perfection and ultimate satisfaction. The task of theology in this case will be to help interpret the reasons behind such practices and enable a richer understanding of its meaning and significance. Theology, just like any scientific discipline, will have internal debates about what is the most reasonable and convincing argument, and that will also vary between different traditions and even within the same tradition. While it is possible for a theologian not to participate personally in religious belief, many definitions of theology assume that a theologian is a religious believer and so understands how a particular community works from within. The good life, for a theologian, is by definition that which is related in a primary sense to God and neighbor, where understanding the meaning of what God either is or is not like becomes integral to the theological task. Although Frederick Nietzsche declared that God was "dead," belief in God has not waned, but rather continued to influence contemporary culture in what Charles Taylor has described as a postsecular age.[3] While science and social science more often than not analyze varieties of "religion" and its particular belief systems, theology is concerned to understand and unravel human meaning as it has been carried in traditional sources, but now appropriated and interpreted for new contexts.

Moral Evolution: A Test Case in Dialogue

The research area that has most interested me in the last five years or so that is most relevant to the theme of human flourishing is what some scholars have called *moral evolution*. As a Roman Catholic theologian, I am most interested in cultural change toward values that encourage rather than inhibit the good life, understood as the common good, so meaning the good for all and the good for each. In the classic theological tradition these values are known as the virtues, which are defined as habits of mind leading to positive actions for the good that can be acquired through family or community education or, in some cases, understood as being infused by the work of divine grace. At the same time the opposing habits to virtues, vices, work against the good. Understanding those vices is *also* part of the theological task as it helps to clarify what their tendencies are, how to overcome them, and, therefore, how to become more virtuous. Although virtue and vice tend to be understood as individual character traits, their action is relevant to the functioning of the community as a whole, and therefore impinges on collective action.

But where did such virtues and vices begin to be expressed in human history? Does tracing their origin give any clues about their meaning and significance? Deep time, evolutionary history, can, I suggest, shed light on this problem in a way that is constructive for the theological task and illuminating for an understanding of human flourishing. Not all theologians or philosophers would, of course, welcome such a move, since they resist naturalistic interpretations of ethics in favor of constructive approaches that are understood to operate through alternative frameworks such as principled reasoning, or even divine commands, that are not simply emergent from evolutionary models. Such critiques give due warning for theologians entering this debate not to reduce ethical theory to naturalistic accounts or assume that evolutionary arguments provide a full explanatory framework for the emergence of either morals or a religious sense. Paying attention to specific dispositions also impact on the task of evolutionary anthropology as much as theology. Analysis of different virtues and vices in evolutionary terms can move archeological discussion away from a simple consideration of morphological differences toward reflection on the most probable mental lives of early hominins.

Compassion in the evolutionary record has a stronger evidential basis than other virtues, though in my own research with evolutionary anthropologist Agustín Fuentes we have explored the possibility of a shift in the human capacity for wisdom in early hominin evolution.[4] Other specific virtues that are both relevant to moral theology and address the theme of human flourishing include justice, humility, generosity, and gratitude, to name just a few.[5] An exploration of the evolutionary roots of different vices is also significant, since understanding how and in what sense they have arisen enables a richer and deeper insight into what makes us human and therefore how humanity may be able to overcome such tendencies and take positive steps toward human flourishing. For theology stories of origin are relevant to stories about the future or eschatology, so in the case of human flourishing, knowledge of evolutionary anthropological theories is also relevant to its task.

Rather than take all the different possible virtues and vices, I will illustrate my point by referring in a little more detail to two that are mirror behavioral images of each other in that they are both about individual *and* collective action for good and ill, namely, compassion and violence. Both are interesting in that both have arguably very deep evolutionary roots. They are also highly significant both from a religious and theological perspective. While I cannot do full justice to either in such a short essay, my purpose is to illustrate some of the ways in which scientific discussion about both of these attributes in alignment with theological reflection on the topics can be fruitful for further deliberations on what it means to flourish. Trying to understand the drive to love others opens up interesting philosophical and theological questions about the psychology of love and its evolution. Social and natural scientists, through research on empathy and compassion, have focused on what are arguably the prerequisite capacities for fully developed love. Theologians, on the other hand, are more likely to parse out distinctions in what it means to love in terms of mercy, charity, friendship, and passion.

The Roots of Compassion

Pity, sympathy, empathy, and compassion are often muddled in the literature, both ancient and modern, which makes it even harder to appraise the relationships between them. Martha Nussbaum's definitions of empathy and compassion are particularly clear and are useful as a baseline, so empathy is "an imaginative reconstruction of another person's experience without any particular evaluation of that experience."[6] Further, "compassion is a painful emotion occasioned by the awareness of another person's undeserved misfortune."[7] The more specific judgment that a person is in distress, also accompanied by a desire to do something about it, is a judgment of *compassion* rather than empathy. Nussbaum is not claiming that this is *all there is* to compassion, but that compassion, when it overcomes negative emotions such as disgust, envy, and shame, entails judgment. Ethnographic research that defines empathy as including a desire to help seems similar to compassion in Nussbaum's definition. Often psychologists will use the term "empathy" inclusive of an active or even cognitive component, so that it comes much closer to the definition of compassion used by Nussbaum above.

Penny Spikins and her colleagues have done some fascinating work on the possible reconstruction of psychological emotions in the prehistory of the *Homo* lineage.[8] The most common attitude among anthropologists, Spikins claims, is to ignore all emotions in human prehistory on the basis that they are far too hard to detect. What kind of archeological evidence might point to changes in the mental lives of these early humans? Spikins believes that while this research is fraught with difficulties, it is still possible to create a reasonable narrative about what may have been the case. Spikins believes that it is long-term *compassion* that is the most distinctly human characteristic that marks out humans from our primate cousins. She defines compassion as motivation to act in a way that is evolutionary advantageous.[9] Spikins seems to define compassion as "caring deeply for each other."[10]

I will use just one illustrative example to show the kind of evidential base used to support her claims:

> The most well-known early example of long-term support for an incapacitated individual comes from KNM-ER 1808, a female *Homo ergaster* dated to around 1.5 mya. . . . Examinations of the skeletal remains of this individual have led to suggestions that she was suffering from hypervitaminosis A, a disease caused by excessive intake of vitamin A.[11]

These symptoms can be tracked in the human remains through reduction in bone density and the development of coarse bone growths. The symptoms for sufferers are known from contemporary medical studies to include "abdominal pain, nausea, headaches, dizziness, blurred vision, lethargy, loss of muscular coordination and impaired consciousness."[12]

This pathology would have taken many months to develop, which shows that the caretaking in this case must have been long term as the individual could not have survived on their own without the intensive care of others. The point is that this requires *long-term* and *sustained* care of a type that has not yet been found in primates not in the *Homo* lineage.

The right judgment of compassion, and in this sense, the channeling of empathy toward moral rather than immoral ends, requires the ability to navigate complex relationships successfully. Thomas Aquinas was well aware of this in his treatment of the moral virtues interpreted as the correct alignment of concupiscible and irascible appetitive powers to reason.[13] Empathy and compassion are not used in the *Summa Theologiae*, rather, Thomas uses the terms "charity" and *misericordiae*, a term that when translated into English means variously compassion, pity, and mercy. Where *misericordiae* denotes being so affected that it leads to action on behalf of the other, it can refer to compassion; when *misericordiae* means removal of another's pain through forgiveness of harm, it is best translated as *mercy* given by the one who forgives. Robert Miner—in a helpful article considering the place of *misericordiae* in Thomistic thought and focusing on the questions in the *Summa Theologiae* on charity—interprets compassion as "the affect that Thomas regards as a necessary but not sufficient condition for mercy as a human virtue."[14] In other words, mercy is the developed virtue, even if compassion is its precondition.

The relation between empathy and compassion is analogous to that between compassion and mercy, in that mercy cannot exist without compassion, but compassion alone is insufficient for *misercordiae* as virtue. Thomas's placing of his question on mercy in the middle of the section on the acts and effects of charity, which itself is placed in the central section on charity, leads Miner to conclude that "mercy lies at the very center of Thomas' treatment of charity."[15] It is worth dwelling on the specific way Aquinas refers to *misericordiae* in relation to God's acts, since this also gives some indication of its overall importance. In speaking of divine omnipotence, he claims: "Then again, as we have seen, the carrying out of divine mercy is at the root of all God's works. We are entitled to nothing except on the basis of what has come from God in the first place as sheer gift."[16] It seems to me that there is no reason why *misericordiae* cannot have connotations of both compassion and mercy here, given that it is at the root of God's acts, and given that *misericordiae* is also elemental to God's love, for *amor* is the sole reason for God's *miseretur*.[17] This becomes even clearer in the passage where Thomas claims:

> Above all *misericordiae* is to be attributed to God, nevertheless in its effect, not in the affect of feeling. By way of explanation we note that a person is called *misericors* because he has a heart with misery, and is affected with sadness for another's plight as though it were his own. He identifies himself with the other, and springs to the rescue; this is the effect of *misericordiae*.[18]

Aquinas then explains that to feel sad about another's plight is not a divine attribute, but rather God is capable of driving out every kind of defect. The movement from identification with another and then springing to action is exactly the trajectory expected for empathy and compassion working together. In other words, the narrower meaning of mercy understood simply as forgiveness of sins does not seem to apply in this context. Further, as Gregory Peterson has pointed out, drawing on the empirical work of contemporary research in psychology,[19] this is suggestive of empathy as positive and not just negative in its emotional state.[20]

In the second book of the *Summa*, Thomas cites Augustine when he identifies the close identification between mercy and compassion: "since mercy is compassion for another's wretchedness, mercy is properly shown to another and not to oneself."[21] *Misericordia* is "heartfelt *compassio* for another's *miseriae*, a *compassio* that drives us to do what we can to help him."[22] He then goes on to discuss the play on words between the Latin for *misericordiae* and *miseriae*. Mercy also includes one of the judgments that Nussbaum names for compassion, namely that of non-desert. So, mercy is "strictly speaking . . . compassion for the misery of another."[23]

It is through the movement of *misericordiae* beyond sensing the pain of the other toward action that is regulated by right reason that shows *misericordiae* is a moral virtue, rather than simply an emotion.[24] There is no doubt in Aquinas' mind that while charity is the virtue that unites humanity to God, the greatest virtue with respect to our neighbor is that of mercy: "Of all the virtues which have to do with our neighbor, however, *misericordiae* is the greatest, even as its acts surpasses all others, for to relieve the wants of another is, as such, the function of someone higher and better."[25] While the last phrase implies superiority for the one showing the compassion, this should not imply pride or condescension in that giving, but rather indicates the person is closer to God. For by showing *misericordiae* this "is a sacrifice more acceptable to God."[26] He goes further in saying that *misericordiae* "sums up the Christian religion as to outward activities," but at the same time, the inward affection of charity, which unites the believer to God, is "something which outweighs both love and mercy for our neighbors."[27]

The Roots of Warfare

It seems obvious from this discussion so far that at least the intention of religious piety is to find ways to foster greater acts of compassion and mercy by believers toward others, rather than the opposite. Aquinas analyzes warfare and other forms of organized violence as one of the vices opposed to charity. Discussion as to which is more fundamentally part of human nature, a tendency toward violence or that toward peacemaking, has a long history of debate back to the tussle in political philosophy between Thomas Hobbes and Jean-Jacques Rousseau in the seventeenth century about the basic state of nature. In evolutionary theory, the focus is on the origins of *organized* violence and the extent to which it either has a relatively recent cultural history or deeper biological roots. Charles Darwin believed that human warfare has evolutionary advantages for the successful tribe, leading to enhanced innovation in weaponry, sagacity, and cooperation.[28] His views have influenced subsequent generations of biologists. He believed warfare also promoted other moral qualities such as courage, faithfulness, and sympathy. Accordingly, warfare is portrayed in a positive light for both the moral and social qualities that it promoted. Anthropologists at the turn of the century became much more skeptical, believing that universal explanations failed to do justice to the complexity and variability of different societies. An anthropology of the "peaceful savage" followed that was a mirror image of Darwin's original views.[29]

While there are some risks in using data from contemporary work among hunter-gatherers to project into the distant past, ethnographic analysis can be part of a suite of related lines of evidence. Anthropologist Bruce Knauft, for example, worked among the Gebusi community in south-central Papua New Guinea and found that much of the conflict arose in the context of illnesses believed to have arisen from sorcery by suspected sorcerers who are then subject to torture and communal cannibalism.[30] Stalking, mutilation, a slow and lingering death, and consumption of victims under the banner of assault sorcery are reported among Amerindians in highlands of Guyana, Venezuela, and Brazil.[31] The motivation for killing is often related to desire for revenge or a deterrent against potential aggressors.[32] The particular way in which the victims' bodies are treated either by cannibalism or other practices is culturally prescribed, highly emotionally charged, and inclusive of specific symbolic rituals.

Does religion, or some forms of it, therefore express a form of cultural violence by supporting violent practice? Those "purple" passages in the Hebrew Bible that seem to justify brutal violence toward others under the banner of divine commands are more often than not avoided by modern biblical commentators. Secular theorists are rather less squeamish and, as a result, have drawn on religious texts to argue that religious belief proactively encourages warfare and violence rather than the opposite. Evolutionary psychologists Yael Sela, Todd Shackelford, and James Liddle, for example, argue that religious practices and norms "lower the threshold for violence" and "explicitly promote and conveniently justify violent actions."[33] For them the basic motivation for violence is tied into evolutionary theories of sexual selection and parental investment. Aggressive tendencies in men are interpreted in evolutionary terms as a desire for social status and greater reproductive success, while long parental investment means the risk of cuckoldry is greater, and violent reactions follow. The role of religious motivation is interpreted through these lenses, so violence arising as a result of partner infidelity is given a religious boost, as are threats to status. Importantly, explicit religious beliefs that promote such reactions are interpreted as carrying evolutionary beneficial advantages for those that hold such views.

How is this God of violence perceived by contemporary theological scholarship? In general, there are two broad approaches among biblical scholarship. One approach tends to neutralize the text by trying to understand incitation to violence as aberrant to an overall message promoting God's love and peace making.[34] An alternative approach admits to such passages, but then argues that the New Testament has reversed such portrayals of God as being illusionary and based on sinful cultural biases.[35] Classic texts were prepared to be more intermediary in their arguments. Thomas Aquinas' discussion on war is embedded in his discussion on the ten vices that are opposed to charity, including the vices of hatred, spiritual apathy, envy, discord, contentiousness, schism, brawling, sedition, and scandal. War is thus one of the vices that are opposed to charity.[36]

The first question that Aquinas addresses is whether war is a sin. Against that view he pitches Augustine's perspective that soldiering as such was not banned in the New Testament, rather soldiers were commanded not to take advantage of their position in doing "violence" and be content with their pay.[37] Conditions attached to war include having it associated in the first place with sovereign authority, protection of the commonweal against foreign attack and in the interests of peacemaking. Secondly, the cause of the war needs to be just, citing Augustine, who claimed that it "avenged wrongs." And thirdly, the long-term intention of such war is to promote the good and avoid evil.[38] Repressing evil, supporting the good, and avoiding cruelty are all conditions under which war needs to be waged. Those who fight in wars for any other motivation apart from a "zeal for justice" are considered sinful. Clerics and priests, however, could not be involved directly in warfaring since their role is always to be dedicated to a higher good.[39] In other instances, Aquinas discusses how courage is elicited in the context of warfare, either in a military context or more local situations of bravery in conflict.[40]

What is particularly interesting is the way that Aquinas interlaces warfare as being bound up with peacefare, believing that underlying warmongering is a desire for a situation or peace that more closely matches their hopes. This is particularly clear in the following passage:

> Even those who are bent on wars and dissentions are really only desiring a peace, which, in their eyes, they do not possess. For, as we have said, it is not peace if a man agrees with another against what he himself prefers. And so by war people try to upset such agreement, for they find the peace somehow defective, and their intention is to arrive at a peace in which nothing that conflicts with their own desires will be found. This is why a people at war seek by war to arrive at a peace which will be more perfect than before.[41]

In this argument he is suggesting that there are ways to rationalize war and that those rationalizations relate to an overall desire to maintain peace. Thomas was, it seems, in matters of war, a realist. Albert the Great noted that the temptation to sin is very strong and is only with great difficulty avoided in war.[42] Those who have never experienced war are likely to view warmongering as counter to peace rather than being coincident with it in the way that Aquinas claims. However, his views are consistent with evolutionary anthropology that finds war and cultural justification, including religious justification, intricately bound together. It is important that Aquinas resists any use of cruelty and torture in war, even though he seemed to permit deception. So, where power is exercised violence and coercion can only be used to the extent to which "principles of justice permit, whether by way of fighting enemies or of punishing malefactors."[43] If, on the other hand, leaders use their power to take away property in a way "contrary to justice," then they commit "robbery" and are "bound to make restitution."[44] When the condition of war is not according to norms of justice, then those engaged in it are bound by the obligation to make restitution. Extortionate demands or pillage in the course of war are also not permitted. Similar conditions surround the use of subterfuge in war. While Aquinas allows some deception where it is warranted as part of a war that is just, it is deception that follows certain conditions. Telling lies or giving promises that are not kept are always wrong, even with an enemy. However, deliberately disguising or deliberately concealing one's intention in a way that tricks the enemy is permissible.[45] His conclusion that such actions are not really "deception" in the true sense relates to his view that complete openness would show up an undisciplined will. Concealing operational orders from the enemy is therefore particularly significant. He also specifically notes how the Old Testament Law resists moderation in victory, so harming women and children or cutting down trees is not permissible.[46] Aquinas' accommodation of war within his theological treatise may have been related to his own experience of territorial wars, which also impacted on his own family members. Most notable in this respect was the war that led to the downfall of the Hohenstaufens and Charles of Anjou taking power in Naples. Those on the emperor's side included two of his brothers up to his father's death, when they switched sides and supported the pope. The emperor executed one of his brothers.[47] Such qualifications need to be set within Aquinas' overall characterization of war as a vice opposed to charity. It seems to suggest, therefore, that while Aquinas was prepared to admit to the reality of war and set limits on it, at root it could not have a fundamental religious justification.

Preliminary Conclusions

The goal of human flourishing for Christian theology has generally focused on the perfection of a virtuous life, rather than just acquisition of material goods. I do not want to give the false impression that theologians are not concerned with material goods. For example, economic and political analysis would be part of an analysis of structures of society according to norms of well-worked-out deliberations on different forms of justice that contribute to human flourishing. But the point is that the material goods alone are not the end point in consideration of the good life and can even detract from those higher spiritual goals.

Different natural and social sciences, including moral psychology and evolutionary anthropology, are important tools in order to understand the biological and cultural roots of those tendencies toward moral action or its opposite. Moral evolution makes much more sense if it is teased out into specific tendencies to act in particular ways that are clearly defined.[48] I have chosen for this chapter to focus on characteristics that have a particularly deep evolutionary history, namely, those toward compassion and violence. In theological discussion of compassion, the most original aspect of theological reflection relates to the need for mercy. That capacity also has relevance in the context of tendencies toward violence and specifically human capacities for cruelty and warfare. Although there are purple passages in the Bible that portray God as a violent punitive God, thus providing justification for all kinds of horrendous practices, such interpretations fail to consider both biblical hermeneutics and more nuanced discussion of just war theories. Overall, unraveling the drive toward *peacefare*, which seems to be synchronous in early evolutionary history with warfare, is an area to which theological reflection can contribute and reinforce.

References

Aquinas, Thomas. 1965. *Summa Theologiae*. Vol. 42, *Courage* (2a2ae. 123–140). Translated by P. G. Walsh. London: Blackfriars.

———. 1966. *Summa Theologiae*. Vol. 5, *God's Will and Providence* (1a. 19–26). Translated by Thomas Gilby. London: Blackfriars.

———. 1968. *Summa Theologiae*. Vol. 23, *Virtue* (1a2ae. 55–67). Translated by W. D. Hughes. London: Blackfriars.

———. 1969. *Summa Theologiae*. Vol. 29, *The Old Law* (Ia2ae. 98–105). Translated by David Bourke. London: Blackfriars.

———. 1972. *Summa Theologiae*. Vol. 35, *Consequences of Charity* (2a2ae. 34–46). Translated by Thomas R. Heath. London: Blackfriars.

———. 1974a. *Summa Theologiae*. Vol. 34, *Charity* (2a2ae. 23–33). Translated by R. J. Batten. London: Blackfriars.

———. 1974b. *Summa Theologiae*. Vol. 38, *Injustice* (2a2ae. 63–79). Translated by Marcus Lefébure. London: Blackfriars.

Boyd, Gregory. 2017. *The Crucifixion of the Warrior God. Interpreting the Old Testament Violent Portraits of God in the Light of the Cross*. Vol. 1, *The Cruciform Hermeneutic*. Minneapolis: Fortress Press.

Darwin, Charles. 2004. *The Descent of Man: Selection in Relation to Sex* [1871]. Edited by Adrian Desmond and James Moore. London: Penguin Classics.

Deane-Drummond, Celia. 2017. "Empathy and the Evolution of Compassion: From Deep History to Infused Virtue." *Zygon* 52, no. 1: 258–78.

———. 2019. *Theological Ethics through a Multispecies Lens: The Evolution of Wisdom, Volume 1*. Oxford: Oxford University Press.

Deane-Drummond, Celia, and Agustín Fuentes, eds. 2017. *The Evolution of Human Wisdom*. Lanham, Md.: Rowman and Littlefield/Lexington Books.

Deane-Drummond, Celia, Agustín Fuentes, and Neil Arner. 2016. "The Evolution of Morality: Three Perspectives." *Philosophy, Theology and the Sciences* 3, no. 2: 115–51.

Evans, John H. 2018. *Morals Not Knowledge: Recasting the Contemporary U.S. Conflict between Religion and Science*. Oakland: University of California Press.

Heath, Thomas. 1972. "Appendix 2: War." In Aquinas, *Summa Theologiae*, vol. 35, *Consequences of Charity* (2a2ae. 34–46), translated by Thomas R. Heath. London: Blackfriars.

Kim, Nam C., and Mark Kissel. 2018. *Emergent Warfare in Our Evolutionary Past*. New York: Routledge.

Klimecki, Olga M., Suzanne Leiberg, Matthieu Ricard, and Tania Singer. 2014. "Differential Pattern of Functional Brain Plasticity after Compassion and Empathy Training." *Social Cognitive and Affective Neuroscience* 9, no. 6: 873–79.

Knauft, Bruce. 2011. "Violence Reduction among the Gebusi of Papua New Guinea—and across Humanity." In *Origins of Altruism and Cooperation*, edited by Robert Sussman and C. Robert Cloninger, 203–25. New York: Springer.

Martens, Elmer A. 2015. "Toward an End to Violence: Hearing Jeremiah." In *Wrestling with the Violence of God: Soundings in the Old Testament*, edited by M. Daniel Carroll and J. Blair Wilgus, 133–50. Winona Lake, Ind.: Eisenbrauns.

Mead, Margaret. 1940. "Warfare is Only an Invention, Not a Biological Necessity." *Asia* 1, no. 8: 402–5.

Miner, Robert. 2015. "The Difficulties of Mercy: Reading Thomas Aquinas on Misericordia." *Studies in Christian Ethics* 28, no. 1: 70–85.

Nussbaum, Martha. 2001. *Upheavals of Thought: The Intelligence of Emotions*. Cambridge: Cambridge University Press.

Peterson, Gregory. 2017. "Is My Feeling Your Pain Bad for Others? Empathy as Virtue versus Empathy as Fixed Trait." *Zygon* 52, no. 1: 232–57.

Sela, Yael, Todd Shackelford, and James Liddle. 2016. "A Moral Guide to Depravity: Religiously Motivated Violence and Sexual Selection." In *The Evolution of Morality*, edited by Todd K. Shakelford and Ranald D. Hansen, 197–216. Cham, Switzerland: Springer International.

Spikins, Penny. 2015. *How Compassion Made Us Human: The Evolutionary Origins of Tenderness, Trust and Morality.* Barnsley: Pen and Sword Books.

Spikins, Penny A., Holly E. Rutherford, and Andy P. Needham. 2010. "From Homininity to Humanity: Compassion from the Earliest Archaics to Modern Humans." *Time and Mind* 3, no. 3: 303–25.

Taylor, Charles. 2007. *A Secular Age.* Cambridge, Mass.: Harvard University Press.

Whitehead, Neil. 2002. *Dark Shamans: Kanaima and the Poetics of Violent Death.* Durham: Duke University Press.

3

STATUS VIATORIS AND THE PATH
QUALITY OF RELIGION

Human Flourishing as a Sacred Process of Becoming

JONATHAN ROWSON

Does religion contribute to human flourishing? The answer seems to be a mixture of yes, it depends, let's hope so, not always, and define your terms. The analytical difficulty with the question is that the validity of the answer depends entirely on how we operationalize the two capacious and contested concepts—religion and flourishing—and thereby frame their relationship. While it may be possible to give an empirically valid answer by making the terms ontologically commensurate and epistemically relatable, for instance reducing religion to metrics of church attendance, and flourishing to, for instance, longevity or perhaps self-reports of subjective well-being, this kind of empirical achievement comes at great theoretical cost. The risk is that we may unwittingly answer the question affirmatively while simultaneously denaturing its meaning and undermining why it is being asked.

The question is deliciously important, however, and I have focused on what seems to matter most within it, namely: How might we best conceive of the relationship between one of our ultimate societal ends (flourishing) and one of our established institutional means (religion) in ways that help to clarify how we should live? My answer is that flourishing derives its substantive meaning from an implicit idea of human growth that needs to be rendered more explicit in order for religion's essential role in supporting flourishing to become clear. In what follows, I focus on the *path quality* of flourishing and religion's role in illuminating the path and helping us to walk it.

The experience of flourishing manifests in many ways, but it is often grounded in forms of human growth and development directed by normative ends, social support, and spiritual sensibility.[1] For the purposes of the question at hand, I introduce a theoretical and empirical research initiative (what does it mean to grow as a person and why does it matter for society?), highlight some little understood individual differences (e.g., mental complexity and levels of maturation) that are not often taken into account in the context of flourishing, and introduce a way of thinking (constructive-developmental) that is fundamental to the relationship between religion and flourishing but unhelpfully dispersed across myriad forms of scholarship and practice. The idea that human flourishing should be viewed as a bio-psycho-social-spiritual process of becoming is offered as a theological and philosophical perspective that might shape future research. The issue at hand is not primarily academic for me, however. I believe a richer appreciation for our scope to not merely change but *grow* may be necessary to shape social and political thinking about educational reform in the context of our ecological crisis.[2]

I

Flourishing risks being an ambiguous honorific term like "thriving" or "prosperity," but it has intellectual dignity and spiritual resonance because it illuminates the normative significance of human maturation. Flourishing is easily conflated with pleasure or success or happiness; but what seems most distinctive and intriguing about the idea of flourishing is a not a sensation or a state of mind but a particular kind of process, namely the cultivation of joy in the lifelong process of *becoming*. At its heart, flourishing is a process of spiritual growth characterized by an evolving, maturing relationship to psychological and existential motion, including recurring experiences of loss and change and the sense that one's work is never quite done. An eloquent expression of this idea comes from German Catholic philosopher Joseph Pieper in his extended meditation *On Hope*:

> Pastoral melodramatics have robbed the reference to man as "a pilgrim upon this earth" and of his earthly life as a pilgrimage of its original significance and virility as well as its effectiveness. It no longer clearly mirrors the reality it is intended to convey. . . . To be a *viator* is to be on the way. The *status viatoris* then is the condition or state of being on the way. . . . [This] is not to be understood in a primary and literal sense of a designation of place. It refers to the innermost structure of created nature. It is the inherent "not yet" of the finite being.[3]

We are all *status viatoris*, on-the-way, and the contribution of religion is to illuminate that way and support us as we experience and traverse it. In a pertinent lecture, the former archbishop of Canterbury, Rowan Williams, offered four main perspectives that characterized the religious relationship to flourishing, and he explicitly framed it as a process of maturation. First, there is a realization that we do not have to be our own origin, unfolding insight into "the illusion of self-creation," and, in a Christian context, "Yielding not to an alien will, but to an affirming source." Second, there is scope to become less subject to our passions and more aware of how they can lead us astray. Religion takes us beyond what Williams calls "an uncritical affirmation of the ego, and the positioning of the ego in a state of rivalry and conflict." Third, religious sensibility gives rise to a qualitatively different relationship to time, which is not viewed as a commodity for acquisition, but a complex gift, "the medium in which we grow and move forward but also constructively return and literally 're-source' ourselves." Fourth, the acceptance of mortality. Building on the work of Ernest Becker, Williams remarks that awareness of death reminds us that "every project we are engaged in is limited. . . . It is the denial of death that takes us back to the pathologies of power."[4] In each of these four sensibilities, there is an implicit developmental journey; we move from a callow freedom to a mature freedom through a commitment to see ourselves more clearly.

In Buddhism, the Four Noble Truths can be seen as what Stephen Batchelor calls four ennobling truths; we should *fully know* dukkha (suffering), *relinquish* craving, *experience* cessation or nirvana, and *live* the eightfold path. The contention is that Westerners typically think of truths as tenets to believe in, rather than descriptions of experience that elicit different kinds of spiritual injunction. While western Buddhism tends to place nirvana, "the truth of cessation," as the goal, the Buddha's original teachings frame nirvana as more like a glimpse of a different kind of experience that motivates us to seek a new form of life. That new life is the eightfold path, through which our daily task is to strive toward right view, right thinking, right mindfulness, right speech, right action, right diligence, right concentration, right livelihood; where "right" is to be understood as an increasingly wise relationship to reality. The same point arguably applies to any form of religious and spiritual experience, which serves not just as insight, but also as inspiration to keep us on felicitous paths. Moreover, Batchelor emphasizes that while we think of a path as getting from A to B, in the Buddha's time it was much more about setting off into uncertainty with only minimal sources of orientation, a way to live life as a rewarding question, fully open to experience.[5]

There are many more relevant religious reference points, including James Fowler's stages of faith development, but the central point is not so much that religion can describe flourishing. The more subtle point is that religion may be *required* to help make sense of the moral and spiritual significance of a range of other (biological, philosophical, psychological, sociological, political) perspectives on the process of becoming. Moreover, religion may be placed to offer the institutional and community rituals and practices necessary to support the unfolding of such processes over time.

II

In the positive psychology literature, "flourishing" is a form of well-being that amounts to an updated version of the Aristotelian conception of *eudaimonia* (literally "good spirit"), which is grounded in virtue ethics (*arete*) and juxtaposed with hedonic well-being (pleasure). In this sense the question of flourishing is not so much a matter of subjective experience, but which forms of life are most worth living. For something to flourish, our *status viatoris* needs a positive direction, which makes the question of what it means to grow in virtue a shared societal inquiry about the kinds of good life we seek to make possible—those are the kinds of questions religion is for.

Relatedly, social psychologist Mihaly Csikszentmihalyi and Kevin Rathunde coauthored an extraordinary essay in 2014 called "The Development of the Person: An Experiential Perspective on the Ontogenesis of Psychological Complexity." They reflect on what it means to be a person and argue that psychological complexity is "the central dimension" to personhood, and that this complexity evolves over the life cycle. The argument is structured by asking what it means to live well and age well and what kind of person we would like to be in our latter years. It then works backwards toward the kinds of opportunities, challenges, and experiences we might need to become that kind of person. They argue that a particular kind of intrinsic value lies at the heart of human development, namely the experience of "flow"—deeply rewarding absorption in a task where our skill level and challenge level are well matched. By seeking out challenges we increase our mental complexity and thereby grow rather than merely change.

There are several models of "mental complexity," but perhaps the richest philosophical perspective is outlined in an the opening chapter of *The Evolving Self* by Harvard psychologist Robert Kegan, where he details "the unrecognized genius of Jean Piaget." Piaget's purported genius is relatively unrecognized because he is thought of as a developmental psychologist, but his work is about the nature of "life" as such. Open systems biology was the inspiration for his genetic epistemology (study of the origins of knowledge), and many models of human development today, for instance Kurt Fischer's, examine the mind as a dynamic nonlinear system as a result.[6] Piaget studied the nature of conceptual schemas (the concepts and categories we use to structure experience) and the processes of assimilation (experience recognized according to existing schemas) and accommodation (refining schemas to better process and act upon experience) and equilibration (a rebalancing of one's perception at a more complex and inclusively meaningful level). Piaget's principal loyalty was to the ongoing conversation between the individuating organism and the world, regardless of whether he was studying a mollusk or a child. As Kegan puts it: "This eternal conversation is panorganic; it is central to the nature of all living things."

This "conversation" between organism and world is marked by periods of dynamic stability followed by periods of instability and qualitatively new balances or truces. The guiding principle of such a truce, the point that is always at issue and is renegotiated in the transition to each new balance, is this: what, from the point of view of the organism, is composed as "object" and what is "subject." The question always is: "To what extent does the organism differentiate itself from (and so relate itself to) the world?"

Kegan accepts that when seen biologically, this process of differentiation and reintegration, assimilation and accommodation seems uninspiring. It is the business of protozoa, coleus plants, and elephants as well as of human beings. And yet, "this evolutionary motion is the prior (or grounding) phenomenon in personality; that this process or activity, this adaptive conversation, is the very source of, and the unifying context for, thought and feeling; that this motion is observable, researchable, intersubjectively ascertainable; that this understanding is crucial to our being of help to people in pain; and that unlike other candidates for a grounding phenomenon, this one cannot be considered arbitrary or bound over to the partialities of sex, class, culture, or historical period." Kegan goes on to argue that this experience may be the source of our emotions themselves. "Loss and recovery, separation and attachment, anxiety and play, depression and transformation, disintegration and coherence-all may owe their origins to the felt experience of this activity, this motion to which the 'emotion' refers."[7]

The point here is that this process, which sounds like a dry cognitive matter or a kind of back office administration, is actually the defining feature of how we make sense of world and therefore central to what it means to be human. It has even been argued that Piaget helps to make sense of why Jesus uses parables in the gospels of Mark, Matthew, and Luke. As Foster and Moran put it: "Jesus' use of unexpected behavior, moral dilemmas, and exaggerated responsibilities *disequilibrated* his listeners. Without the disruption of their current schemes, the radical new concepts he wished to teach, such as grace, forgiveness, and love of one's enemies, might have been rejected"[8] (my italics).

III

The idea of human growth that helps make sense of flourishing can therefore be seen as biological and psychological and spiritual, but crucially it is also sociological and political. For instance, false consciousness—not being able to accurately perceive reality because our perception of it is subtly manipulated by powerful forces beyond our control—is a barrier to flourishing. In this respect, the critical theorist Theodor Adorno speaks of overcoming "the ontology of false conditions," and sociologist Zygmunt Bauman famously described our present condition by saying: "Never have we been so free, never have we felt so powerless." Political scientist Stephen Eric Bronner highlights why such matters are essential to a fuller view of flourishing: "At stake is the substance of subjectivity and autonomy: the will and ability of the individual to resist external forces intent upon determining the meaning and experience of life."[9]

Postliberal ideas of positive freedom in political theory (e.g., Patrick Deneen; John Milbank) are also important because they highlight not merely what we need to become free *from*, for instance state coercion, ambient advertising, or ideology, but more importantly what we are free to *become* in terms of our character and our virtue. Religion is critical here. Positive freedom refers to the freedom to flourish informed by substantive claims about the nature of reality, the purpose of human life, and the nature of the good society.

In contrast, negative freedom is the prevailing ideal within most forms of modern liberalism; the freedom to live almost entirely as one chooses, where one's vision of the good is a private choice, and we are not beholden to shared substantive ideals beyond minimalist legal ethics and prevailing social norms. In the context of a range of collective action problems, including our inability to address ecological challenges, democratic deconsolidation, technological imperialism, and socially corrosive inequality, relying on negative freedom as a sufficient basis for human flourishing seems foolhardy and naïve. In recent lectures on political economy, Jeffrey Sachs has explicitly argued that the purpose of the economy should be about human flourishing and the cultivation of virtue, and that policy should be designed around that objective.[10]

There are many other theorists of human growth, including Lawrence Kohlberg, Carol Gilligan, Michael Commons, and Bill Torbert, and there are many fields of inquiry that intersect with theories of human growth that are beyond our scope here. For instance, Whitehead's process-relational philosophy offers an account of becoming in the context of a unifying vision of reality as a whole, including God, who is the only one who has the strength and ability to be open to every single experience in the world.[11] Without suggesting every process philosopher has the same view of the divine, it is worth noting how Piaget reflected on reading the French process philosopher Henri Bergson when he was still a teenager, as recorded in his autobiography: "The identification of God with life itself was an idea that stirred me almost to ecstasy."[12]

From the brief sketch above it seems that whatever flourishing is, it has a bio-psycho-social-spiritual character that is dynamic and evolving rather than static. Religion has a role in informing all of these features of flourishing, but there is also a significant and related research opportunity to clarify this terrain:

1. Models of human development are not often theoretically grounded in a broader theory about the nature of life, evolution, or change, so they are ignored or rejected without any sense of intellectual dissonance.
2. Many theories lack a broader vision of the good life against which to test their model with analytical rigor—we can't say what "better" is (e.g., more courageous) unless we have a prior

vision of the good in more general terms (e.g., courage as the preeminent virtue, making possible all others).

3. There is little consistency in the relevant variable and/or active ingredient when it comes to human beings getting "better."
4. The type of development in question varies—emotional, cognitive, volitional, moral, virtue, spiritual.
5. The competing theories have different ontological and epistemological assumptions, and therefore only partially commensurate evidence bases.
6. The unit of analysis varies; sometimes it's the ego, the person, the self, the mind, the soul.
7. Some theories are domain specific, applying for instance to leadership or teaching or relationships, and some are domain general.

As a result of these theoretical, empirical, and methodological challenges, the idea of "human growth" is theoretically and empirically neglected, which is unfortunate given that it plays such a central role in mediating the relationship between flourishing and religion.

Perhaps one way to revitalize religious traditions is for them to work together to provide the broader normative framework of meaning and purpose required to accommodate the fissiparous and protean idea of human growth. Moreover, this challenge is not merely theoretical or "a nice-to-have"; on the contrary, developing an intellectually grounded vision of flourishing is profoundly important and timely. Consider, for instance, the following statement in *Spirituality and Intellectual Honesty*, a self-published essay by philosopher Thomas Metzinger (2014), which speaks to the preeminent collective action problem of our time (but which is relevant to prospective societal breakdown more generally):

> Conceived of as an intellectual challenge for humankind, the increasing threat arising from self-induced global warming clearly seems to exceed the present cognitive and emotional abilities of our species. This is the first truly global crisis, experienced by all human beings at the same time and in a single media space, and as we watch it unfold, it will also gradually change our image of ourselves, the conception humankind has of itself as a whole. I predict that during the next decades, we will increasingly experience ourselves as failing beings.

"Failing beings" is close to being an exact opposite of human flourishing. The question of which is more likely to arise—flourishing or failing—seems to depend upon "the present cognitive and emotional abilities of our species." The contention this paper has begun to sketch is that those abilities are not fixed, and that religion has a central role to play in developing them for the better.

References

Batchelor, Stephen. 2016. *After Buddhism: Rethinking Dharma for a Secular Age*. New Haven: Yale University Press.

Bronner, Stephen Eric. 2011. *A Very Short Introduction to Critical Theory*. Oxford: Oxford University Press.

Dale, Edward J. 2014. *Completing Piaget's Project: Transnational Philosophy and the Future of Psychology*. St. Paul: Paragon House.

Foster, James D., and Glenn T. Moran. 1985. "Piaget and Parables: The Convergence of Secular and Scriptural Views of Learning." *Journal of Psychology and Theology* 13, no. 2: 97–103.

Kegan, Robert. 1983. *The Evolving Self*. Cambridge, Mass.: Harvard University Press.

Mascolo, Michael F., and Kurt W. Fischer. 2015. "The Dynamic Development of Thinking, Feeling, and Acting over the Lifespan." In *Handbook of Child Psychology and Developmental Science: Theory and Method*, edited by W. F. Overton et al., 113–61. Hoboken: John Wiley & Sons.

Mesle, C. Robert. 2008. *Process-Relational Philosophy: An Introduction to Alfred North Whitehead*. West Conshohocken, Pa.: Templeton Press.

Pieper, Joseph. 1977. *On Hope*. San Francisco: Ignatius Press.

Rowson, Jonathan. 2017. *Spiritualise: Cultivating Spiritual Sensibility to Address 21st Century Challenges*. RSA/Perspectiva.

———. 2019. "Bildung in the 21st Century: Why Sustainable Prosperity Depends upon Reimagining Education." Essay series for The Centre for the Understanding of Sustainable Prosperity. https://www.cusp.ac.uk/wp-content/uploads/09-Jonathan-Rowson-online.pdf.

Sachs, Jeffrey. 2017. "Economics and the Cultivation of Virtue." Lecture One. LSE. https://www.youtube.com/watch?v=ajrJbnXTwL8.

Williams, Rowan. 2014. *Faith and Human Flourishing: Religious Belief and Ideals of Maturity?* http://podcasts.ox.ac.uk/rowan-williams-lecture-faith-and-human-flourishing-religious-belief-and-ideals-maturity.

4

SPIRITUAL WELL-BEING AND HUMAN FLOURISHING

Conceptual, Causal, and Policy Relations

Tyler J. VanderWeele

Introduction

The present paper will discuss various conceptual and causal relations between temporal flourishing in this life and what might be understood as spiritual well-being from a theological perspective. The discussion of these relations is motivated by the question: Does religion contribute to human flourishing? To attempt to answer this question, different notions of flourishing or well-being should be distinguished. The paper will consider relevant distinctions and the different levels at which this question of the role of religion in human flourishing might be addressed. Discussion will be given to how competing notions of the good and the final end of the human person might come into play in considering this question, how these differing notions can also give rise to religious conflict, and how such conflicts might be navigated. The paper considers some policy implications of the discussion and, in light of the relevant distinctions, returns to the question: Does religion contribute to human flourishing?

Religion and Individual Flourishing

At the individual level, with regard to how participation in religion generally, and religious communities specifically, shapes numerous aspects of human flourishing, the data and research have become increasingly clear. Religious community contributes profoundly to numerous aspects of human flourishing. I have elsewhere discussed at greater length the evidence from rigorous longitudinal studies concerning the effects of religious service attendance on health and well-being.[1] The existing evidence suggests substantial effects on numerous health and well-being outcomes. In particular, large well-designed longitudinal research studies have indicated that religious service attendance is associated with greater longevity, less depression, less suicide, less smoking, less substance abuse, better cancer and cardiovascular disease survival, less divorce, greater social support, greater meaning and purpose in life, greater life satisfaction, more charitable giving, less crime, more volunteering, more prosocial behavior, and greater civic engagement.[2] While some of the early studies on this topic were methodologically weak, the study and research designs have become stronger and stronger, and for many of these outcomes, the associations are now considered well established. Religious service attendance powerfully affects health and well-being.

Participation in religious community contributes to this wide range of outcomes. But does this long list of outcomes constitute human flourishing? I have elsewhere provided some discussion of different domains of human flourishing around which I think there would be broad consensus as to their importance, consensus across different conceptions of flourishing. These domains include: happiness and life satisfaction, mental and physical health, meaning and purpose, character and virtue, and close social relationships.[3] The argument here is not that these domains fully constitute human flourishing, but rather that, however human flourishing might be conceived and in whatever else it might consist, there would be broad consensus that it includes these domains as well. Each of these domains arguably constitutes an end in and of itself and is nearly universally desired. The existing empirical evidence suggests that participation in religious community has important effects on each of these domains. The existing evidence is stronger for certain of these domains than others,[4] and at least some further rigorous empirical research might still be desired. There is also a need to better understand the extent to which the magnitude of these effects on these outcomes varies across cultural contexts, demographic factors, and religious traditions. Certainly, participation in religious community does not contribute positively to every individual in each of these domains. However, the evidence has become increasingly clear that, in the West at least, where the vast majority of this research has been conducted, the effects on average are positive, substantial, and profound. Religious community often contributes in important ways to human flourishing in this life.

Religion and Spiritual Well-Being

At another level, we might also consider how religion contributes to the final end of the human person, what might be thought of as the completion of human flourishing. Conceptions of the final end of the human person, or whether there is anything beyond death and extinction, are likely to be yet more diverse. Discussion of these matters is then more straightforward, and perhaps only possible, within the context of the understanding of a specific religious or philosophical tradition.

Within the understanding of any given religious tradition, religion itself will in general contribute to the fulfillment of human flourishing, at least as that religious tradition conceives of it; that is its orientation and purpose. Religion itself might be conceived of as the communal attempt to come to communion with the divine or transcendent. The stated end of many religious traditions is constituted by a communion with the divine or transcendent. This communion is seen as the final end of the human person. Certainly this is so with many of the central traditions within Christianity.[5] Many religious practices themselves are fundamentally oriented to the attainment of that end of communion with the divine or transcendent. Religion's focus is often on these transcendent ends.

In many ways, then, the effects of religious practice on temporal flourishing are, if not incidental, at least secondary, and it is perhaps remarkable, given the focus of religion on the transcendent, that participation in religious community affects so many human flourishing outcomes in this life as well. However, that the final end of the human person may not coincide simply with human flourishing in this life raises questions of the conceptual and causal relations between temporal flourishing in this life and such final well-being. Of course, these relations will likewise vary by religious tradition, and here I will briefly consider the question, and the potentially relevant concepts, within the context of the Christian tradition.

I have elsewhere suggested that *human flourishing* be understood as a state in which all aspects of a person's life are good.[6] *Eternal flourishing*, or *perfect well-being*, may be understood, within the Christian tradition, as final and complete communion with God. *Spiritual well-being* in this life might then be understood as a state in which one's life is oriented toward eternal flourishing, or as a state in which all aspects of a person's life are good with respect to his or her final end in God. *Temporal well-being* or *temporal flourishing* might be understood as those aspects of human flourishing that pertain to the goods in this life, thus inclusive of happiness and life satisfaction, mental and physical health, meaning and purpose, character and virtue, and close social relationships. A Christian would thus understand human flourishing as encompassing both spiritual and temporal well-being, with spiritual well-being being the component that is most central, that which brings a person to his or her final end in God.

Relations between Temporal Flourishing and Spiritual Well-Being

It has long been understood in the Christian tradition that temporal flourishing and spiritual well-being, while often mutually supportive, can come into conflict: "What does it profit a man to gain the whole world but lose his soul?" (Mark 8:36). The potential conflict is perhaps seen most clearly in Christian understandings of suffering. While suffering, as an experience of the loss of some temporal good, is to be understood as a deprivation, it can also be the source of transformation, of change and growth, of purification of desires, of reorientation to one's final end in God.[7] Saint Paul writes, "We even boast of our afflictions, knowing that affliction produces endurance, and endurance, proven character, and proven character, hope, and hope does not disappoint, because the love of God has been poured out into our hearts" (Rom 5:3-5). When temporal goods and the spiritual life come into conflict, the latter is to be given priority as it constitutes the person's orientation to his or her final end in God.

In understanding the relations between spiritual well-being and temporal flourishing, an analogy might be drawn with childhood development. When considering the flourishing of a child, this might be understood both with respect to the child's present state but also with respect to the child's development. Whether the child is happy and healthy and has good relationships is undoubtedly important, but for the child's growth and development into a responsible adult, some degree of instruction, formation, and discipline will be necessary, even if this makes the child temporarily unhappy and strains relationships.

Likewise, within a Christian understanding, a person's temporal flourishing, including their health and happiness, is not irrelevant—the created order was shaped by God to be good. However, for a person in the fallen order of the world to attain his or her final end in God, some giving up of aspects of temporal flourishing may be necessary for the sake of a greater spiritual well-being.

However, often spiritual well-being and temporal flourishing will be consonant. Health of the body and mind, a certain peace and rest and satisfaction, a set of supportive relationships, and a strength of character will facilitate the religious practices, prayer, communal life, service, and reflection that promote and constitute spiritual well-being. Likewise, these religious practices can contribute to temporal flourishing by developing community, facilitating mental health, shaping character, and giving one a sense of understanding, meaning, purpose, and satisfaction.

Furthermore, the center of spiritual life, charity (theologically understood as a love of or a friendship with God), includes also a profound love of neighbor, the seeking of the good of the other.[8] When practiced, this contributes not only to the good of the person loving[9] but also to those who are loved, and these good actions are furthermore likely to spread.[10] Again the spiritual life facilitates temporal flourishing. The focus on transcendence and on love for God and neighbor has perhaps often been the inspiration of religion's contributions to the development of hospitals, universities, economic systems, the arts, human rights, law, science, and the preservation of learning.[11] The reunification of temporal flourishing and spiritual well-being, both for an individual and for society, may be understood as part of the task of redemption. For the individual, a complete orientation to God in charity, a seeing of each circumstance, even those seemingly adverse, as an opportunity for faith and hope and love, can at least partially accomplish this reconciliation between spiritual well-being and at least certain aspects of temporal flourishing. Spiritual well-being does not eliminate, but rather relativizes, and ultimately transforms, the importance of temporal flourishing.

It is, however, in part, in the potential conflict between spiritual well-being and certain temporal goods or aspects of temporal flourishing that the perception can arise that religion suppresses human flourishing. Religious teachings can conflict with the desires for certain pleasures in certain contexts, can conflict with what are perceived to be as certain freedoms, and may be in tension with desires oriented principally toward the self rather than toward others and God. But, within a Christian understanding, when conflict arises, deference is to be given to spiritual well-being. Temporal goods and aspects of temporal flourishing may be suppressed.

Oppression of, or discrimination against, those who do not defer to a religious teaching can yet further detract from temporal flourishing. However, this way by which religion may detract from temporal flourishing is arguably not inherent to religious practice itself and is also arguably often contradicted by an ethic of charity and love. However, the conflict between spiritual well-being and temporal goods, discussed above, is intrinsic, in the world as it stands.

Religious Conflict and Human Flourishing

Further conflicts between spiritual well-being and temporal flourishing can arise also when considering not one, but several, religious traditions, and here there are of course tensions between different notions of spiritual well-being as well.[12] Such tensions will be present at the level of understanding and conception, but will also be present with respect to institutions and to competition. The presence of Christianity may be seen as inimical to the advancement of spiritual well-being from a Muslim perspective; and likewise, the presence of Islam adverse to the realization of spiritual well-being from a Christian perspective. Such conflicts have certainly played out, at times with devastating consequences, in human history. Religious wars and conflicts are often perceived as one of the central means by which religion detracts from human flourishing. While such wars have often had political motivations as well,[13] it seems clear that competing notions of spiritual well-being have likewise played a role. Can such conflicts be navigated?

When questions of final, ultimate, and supernatural ends and goods are at play, it seems clear that the potential for conflict, even violence, is substantial. It seems unlikely that it will be eliminated entirely. While religious teachings, properly framed, and exhortations to love and seek the good of the other may help reduce the potential for conflict, the potential is not eliminated. History has shown that the human actors in worldly affairs will often deviate from proper action and religious teachings, and perhaps especially so when the stakes seem so high. This will likely be so, even if religious teachings, properly interpreted, were capable, if followed, of preventing violence. Certainly the topic of interreligious dialogue and relations is a complex one, well beyond the scope of this already broad essay. However, several considerations should perhaps come into play and may be helpful in reflecting upon how to mitigate religious conflict from detracting from human flourishing.[14]

First, this problem of religious conflict detracting from human flourishing is a problem to be contended with; it is not one that can be avoided or ignored with the hope that religion will eventually decline. Eighty-four percent of the world's population identify with a religious tradition; the vast majority consider religion an important part of life. While religious affiliation is declining in certain pockets of the Western world, it is much less clear that this is the picture worldwide. Projections from the Pew Forum suggest even higher rates of religious affiliation worldwide by the year 2050. Religion will not be going away. The potential for conflict is one that is to be addressed, not neglected in the hope that religion itself will eventually pass. It will not. Second, interreligious dialogue holds at least some potential to help members of different religious groups understand what is held in common and what is distinctive about each tradition, potentially facilitating a greater understanding and mutual respect. A free exchange of ideas concerning theological beliefs and competing notions of spiritual well-being can allow religious adherents to make a case for their own particular religious understanding to others while, if carried out respectfully, hopefully also avoiding animosity and violence. Third, from certain Christian perspectives at least, spiritual well-being and communion with God require the free consent of the will.[15] The forcing of religion through violence cannot accomplish that; it cannot bring spiritual well-being. Policies that facilitate free practice of religion and also free exchange of ideas are more likely to bring about the spiritual well-being and the free conversion of the will that may be sought. Fourth, we must acknowledge that, for many who practice the various of the world's religions, some notion of spiritual well-being will likely be the central goal and priority. To neglect this is to misunderstand the nature of religious beliefs and their central place in notions of well-being for much of the world's population. This point will be developed somewhat further in the next section, and the possibility of the world's religions supporting their common ends will be discussed in the section following.

Measures of Tradition-Specific Spiritual Well-Being

Related to the importance of spiritual well-being to much of the world's population, in order to facilitate recognition of the spiritual ends of specific religious communities it may be good and helpful to begin to collect data on various tradition-specific notions of spiritual well-being. While certain generic measures of spiritual well-being have been put forward[16] and may be useful for some purposes, they are arguably not sufficiently generic to apply to nonmonotheistic or nontheistic religions, nor sufficiently specific to be of principal interest to most practicing religious communities. Other, even more generic, measures of spiritual well-being have been criticized on the grounds of assessing principally psychological well-being rather than spiritual well-being.[17] Tradition-specific measures would better allow for the assessment of more particular notions of spiritual well-being. For example, within the Christian tradition, measurement could be focused on various practices, beliefs, community life, service, prayer, character, and virtues, as being important in spiritual well-being in this life, and the means to the final end of communion with God. There, of course, must be acknowledgment of what can and cannot be measured; but simply because certain facets of spiritual well-being—the presence and operation of God's grace—cannot be measured, this does not mean that no progress can be made at all. A recent initial attempt at a measure of specifically Christian spiritual well-being is proposed elsewhere.[18] Measures could likewise potentially be developed across different religious traditions.

The development of new measures of tradition-specific spiritual well-being may facilitate an understanding and tracking of how various religious communities are faring and whether they perceive themselves as making progress toward attaining those ends they deem most important. The idea would not be to compare spiritual well-being across groups—indeed with different tradition-specific measures this would not be possible—nor to combine these measures with those of temporal flourishing. Rather, the hope of such measurement would be to acknowledge the importance of these ends of spiritual well-being to various religious communities, to provide a way to assess progress toward these ends or lack thereof, and to facilitate the capacity of bringing an empirically informed case for promoting these ends into policy discussions. Such advocacy would need to likewise acknowledge competing interests and ends of other communities, but this is the nature of political life. However, the use of such measures may help religious communities themselves in the discernment of how various government policies do, or do not, affect these communities' principal priorities. It may be the case that some forms of religiously motivated political efforts arise from the desire to shape political life in accord with religious beliefs, while not being able to bring the principal concerns of spiritual well-being into discussion because it is considered inadmissible or because no empirical data is available upon which to make a case.

Religion and Common Ends

While notions of spiritual well-being will vary across religious traditions, there are still many common ends concerning temporal flourishing upon which the various world religious traditions can arguably attain agreement. I have argued above and elsewhere[19] that among these ends are the following: happiness and life satisfaction, mental and physical health, meaning and purpose, character and virtue, and close social relationships. Policies can continue to aim to enhance these ends, even in the face of diverse religious traditions and competing notions of spiritual well-being. To the extent that these aspects of temporal flourishing contribute to spiritual well-being, as above, such policies will often also then promote spiritual well-being as well, and may do so across traditions. Policies aimed at facilitating and protecting the free practice of religious communities will, as noted at the beginning of this essay, also make substantial contributions to numerous aspects of temporal health and well-being. Even if there is lack of consensus on the nature of spiritual well-being, the protecting of the presence and practices of religious communities can itself contribute to temporal flourishing, as the now abundant evidence does indeed indicate.[20]

Conclusion

Does religion contribute to human flourishing? Within the understanding of specific religious traditions, undoubtedly religion contributes to the completion of human flourishing, to the attainment of final communion with God. Does religion contribute to temporal flourishing? The evidence strongly suggests that participation in religious communities promotes numerous aspects of individual flourishing, including happiness and life satisfaction, mental and physical health, meaning and purpose, character and virtue, and close social relationships. Does the presence of multiple religions and the potential conflict inherent therein necessarily inhibit human flourishing? Such conflict is arguably the greatest threat whereby religion may suppress human flourishing. These concerns must be acknowledged and addressed; they cannot be avoided. The goal would be a set of interreligious relations that would allow for a free exchange of understandings of competing notions of spiritual well-being, and for preventing conflicts to the extent possible, while allowing religious communities to pursue their own ends, to contribute to human flourishing in the numerous ways that they already do, and to seek, as best as possible, the final fulfillment of human flourishing, a communion with the transcendent and divine.

References

Aquinas, T. 1948. *Summa theologica*. Complete English translation in five volumes. Notre Dame, Ind.: Ave Maria Press.

Carroll, V., and D. Shiflett. 2001. *Christianity on Trial: Arguments against Anti-Religious Bigotry*. New York: Encounter Books.

Cavanaugh, W. T. 2009. *The Myth of Religious Violence*. New York: Oxford University Press.

Chancellor, J., S. Margolis, and S. Lyubomirsky. 2018. "The Propagation of Everyday Prosociality in the Workplace." *Journal of Positive Psychology* 13: 271–83.

Chen, Y., and T. J. VanderWeele. 2018. "Associations of Religious Upbringing with Subsequent Health and Well-Being from Adolescence to Young Adulthood: An Outcome-Wide Analysis." *American Journal of Epidemiology* 187, no.11: 2355–64.

Chida, Y., A. Steptoe, and L. H. Powell. 2009. "Religiosity/Spirituality and Mortality: A Systematic Quantitative Review." *Psychotherapy and Psychosomatics* 78, no. 2: 81–90.

Cohen, A. B., and K. A. Johnson. 2017. "The Relation between Religion and Well-Being." *Applied Research in Quality of Life* 12: 533–47.

Curry, O. S., L. A. Rowland, C. J. Van Lissa, S. Zlotowitz, J. McAlaney, and H. Whitehouse. 2018."Happy to Help? A Systematic Review and Meta-Analysis of the Effects of Performing Acts of Kindness on the Well-Being of the Actor." *Journal of Experimental Social Psychology* 76: 320–29.

Fowler, J. H., and N. A. Christakis. 2010. "Cooperative Behavior Cascades in Human Social Network." *Proceedings of the National Academy of Sciences* 107: 5334–38.

Fruehwirth, J., S. Iyer, and A. Zhang. 2018. "Religion and Depression in Adolescence." *Journal of Political Economy* 127, no. 3: 1178–209.

Goodman, L. E. 2014. *Religious Pluralism and Values in the Public Sphere*. Cambridge: Cambridge University Press.

Hummer, R. A., R. G. Rogers, C. B. Nam, and C. G. Ellison. 1999. "Religious Involvement and US Adult Mortality." *Demography* 36, no. 2: 273–85.

Iannaccone, L. R. 1998. "Introduction to the Economics of Religion." *Journal of Economic Literature* 36: 1465–96.

Idler, E. L. 2014. *Religion as a Social Determinant of Public Health*. New York: Oxford University Press.

John Paul II. 1984. *Salvifici Doloris*. Apostolic Letter. Vatican City: Libreria Editrice Vaticana.

Johnson, B. R. 2011. *More God, Less Crime: Why Faith Matters and How It Could Matter More.* West Conshohocken, Pa.: Templeton Press.

Johnson, B. R., S. J. Jang, D. B. Larson, and S. D. Li. 2001. "Does Adolescent Religious Commitment Matter? A Reexamination of the Effects of Religiosity on Delinquency." *Journal of Research in Crime and Delinquency* 38: 22–44.

Koenig, H. G. 2008. "Concerns about Measuring 'Spirituality' in Research." *Journal of Nervous and Mental Disease* 196: 349–55.

Koenig, H. G., D. E. King, and V. B. Carson. 2012. *Handbook of Religion and Health.* 2nd ed. Oxford: Oxford University Press.

Krause, N., and R. D. Hayward. 2012. "Religion, Meaning in Life, and Change in Physical Functioning during Late Adulthood." *Journal of Adult Development* 19: 158–69.

Li, S., O. I. Okereke, S. C. Chang, I. Kawachi, and T. J. VanderWeele. 2016a. "Religious Service Attendance and Lower Depression among Women: A Prospective Cohort Study." *Annals of Behavioral Medicine* 50: 876–84.

Li, S., M. Stamfer, D. R. Williams, and T. J. VanderWeele. 2016b. "Association between Religious Service Attendance and Mortality among Women." *JAMA Internal Medicine* 176, no. 6: 777–85.

Lim, C., and R. D. Putnam. 2010. "Religion, Social Networks, and Life Satisfaction." *American Sociological Review* 75: 914–33.

Paloutzian, R. F., and C. W. Ellison. 1982. "Loneliness, Spiritual Well-Being, and the Quality of Life." In *Loneliness: A Sourcebook of Current Theory, Research and Therapy*, edited by A. Peplau and D. Perlman, 224–37. New York: John Wiley & Sons.

Peterman, A. H., G. Fitchett, M. J. Brady, L. Hernandez, and D. Cella. 2002. "Measuring Spiritual Well-Being in People with Cancer: The Functional Assessment of Chronic Illness Therapy–Spiritual Well-Being Scale (FACIT–Sp)." *Annals of Behavioral Medicine* 24: 49–58.

Putnam, R. D., and D. E. Campbell. 2012. *American Grace.* New York: Simon & Schuster.

Schmidt, A. J. 2001. *Under the Influence: How Christianity Transformed Civilization.* Grand Rapids: Zondervan.

Schmidt, C. 1885. *The Social Results of Early Christianity.* London: Wm. Isbister Limited. Internet resource.

Shariff, A. F., A. K. Willard, T. Andersen, and A. Norenzayan. 2016. "Religious Priming: A Meta-Analysis with a Focus on Prosociality." *Personality and Social Psychology Review* 20, no. 1: 27–48.

Strawbridge, W. J., R. D. Cohen, S. J. Shema, and G. A. Kaplan. 1997. "Frequent Attendance at Religious Services and Mortality over 28 Years." *American Journal of Public Health* 87, no. 6: 957–61.

VanderWeele, T. J. 2017a. "Religious Communities and Human Flourishing." *Current Directions in Psychological Science* 26: 476–81.

———. 2017b. "Religion and Health: A Synthesis." In *Spirituality and Religion within the Culture of Medicine: From Evidence to Practice*, edited by J. R. Peteet and M. J. Balboni, 357–401. New York: Oxford University Press.

———. 2017c. "On the Promotion of Human Flourishing." *Proceedings of the National Academy of Sciences, U.S.A.* 31: 8148–56.

———. 2018. "Religious Communities, Health, and Well-Being—Address to the US Air Force Chaplain Corps Summit." *Military Medicine*, 5–6: 105–9.

VanderWeele, T. J., S. Li, A. Tsai, and I. Kawachi. 2016. "Association between Religious Service Attendance and Lower Suicide Rates among US Women." *JAMA Psychiatry* 73: 845–51.

VanderWeele, T. J., K. Long, and M. J. Balboni. In press. "On Tradition-Specific Measures of Spiritual Well-Being." In *Measuring Well-Being: Interdisciplinary Perspectives from the Social Sciences and the Humanities*, edited by M. Lee, L. D. Kubzansky, and T. J. VanderWeele. Oxford: Oxford University Press.

Vatican. 2000. *Catechism of the Catholic Church*. 2nd ed. Vatican City: Libreria Editrice Vaticana.

Volf, M. 2015. *Flourishing: Why We Need Religion in a Globalized World*. New Haven: Yale University Press.

Westminster. 2014. *Westminster Shorter Catechism*. Radford, Va.: SMK Books.

Wilcox, W. B., and N. H. Wolfinger. 2016. *Soul Mates: Religion, Sex, Love, and Marriage among African Americans and Latinos*. New York: Oxford University Press.

Woods, T. E., and A. Canizares. 2012. *How the Catholic Church Built Western Civilization*. Washington, D.C.: Regnery.

5

RELIGION AND HUMAN FLOURISHING IN THE EVOLUTION OF SOCIAL COMPLEXITY

HARVEY WHITEHOUSE

It has been argued that religion contributes to human flourishing in a wide range of ways, for example by making us healthier both physically and psychologically[1] or making us more moral.[2] There is also considerable evidence that religion fosters group bonding and commitment to community and that rituals play an important role in that process.[3] Rituals motivate prosociality via a number of different mechanisms, including cognitive dissonance,[4] costly signaling,[5] norm reinforcement,[6] and social synchrony.[7] Prosocial action has in turn been shown to make people measurably happier, not only for the recipients of acts of charity but also for those who act kindly and thus doubly contributing to human flourishing.[8] But in addition to any potential religion may have to promote happiness among individuals who perform or receive the benefits of virtuous acts, it has also contributed to human flourishing by helping to foster the rise and spread of ever more complex social formations. Religion has done so by increasing the commitment of individuals to group values and causes as well as facilitating trust and cooperation in forging and maintaining interpersonal transactions and institutionalized agreements. This chapter focuses primarily on the ways in which religion has contributed to the rise and spread of complex societies and the implications of this for human flourishing—past, present, and future.

Modes of Religiosity, Social Evolution, and Human Flourishing

Religious beliefs and practices readily serve as identity markers because they come in a great variety of locally distinctive variants. This is partly due to causal opacity—the fact that procedures have to be carried out a certain way and doctrines repeated, not because they are instrumentally useful but simply because that is the conventional (the "done" or the "proper") way to act, according to prevailing custom.[9] Deferring to local custom via imitation of causally opaque conventions is an affiliative process.[10] From an early age, children imitate causally opaque behaviors with even higher fidelity when primed with the threat of ostracism, apparently as a reinclusion behavior.[11]

Rituals that function as group identity markers come in two main varieties: rare but emotionally intense (low-frequency, high-arousal or "LFHA"), such as rites of passage and other transition rituals and routinized and dull (high-frequency, low-arousal or "HFLA"), such as the call to prayer or Sunday services.[12] These differences in the frequency and emotionality of rituals are thought to underpin two distinct "modes of religiosity": imagistic and doctrinal.[13]

The imagistic mode of religiosity is typified by rare and often traumatic ritual ordeals, such as painful initiations, scarification, and vision quests. Such experiences are recalled as distinct life experiences stored in episodic memory that shape participants' identities, both as individuals and as members of ritual communities, often by triggering long-term processes of reflection on what the rituals mean.[14] This produces very strong bonds among those who remember going through the experience together but cannot be expanded to include people who were not there at the relevant time. As such, this mode of ritual bonding produces relatively small face-to-face groups with rigid boundaries. These are commonly found in situations of high risk, for instance when facing outgroup threat or natural disasters. Imagistic rituals thus abound in military organizations (e.g., hazing, boot camps) or elites (e.g., fraternities and house-based rituals in historic universities and prestigious schools), as well as in small-scale warlike tribes, guerrilla forces, and terrorist cells. Such groups are well adapted to environments where individual survival depends on sticking together in the face of collective threats.

By contrast, the doctrinal mode of religiosity is typified by routinized (e.g., daily or weekly) collective rituals of the kind found in the temples, churches, mosques, and synagogues of the world religions.

Frequent repetition of the tradition's beliefs and practices ensures that deviations from the orthodoxy and orthopraxy are readily detected, facilitating standardization of the creed across large populations and stabilization over time. This style of religious transmission also allows complex bodies of teachings (e.g., doctrines and narratives) to become elaborated and codified in sermons and texts, which in turn encourages the establishment of expert orators and interpreters of the tradition. As religious hierarchies emerge, they provide also a mechanism for centralizing and policing the religious system, further consolidating the tendency toward homogenization of beliefs and practices. Such religions can spread far and wide, carried by relatively small groups of proselytizing leaders, missionaries, gurus, and prophets. One of the advantages of religions that spread efficiently and mobilize large followings is that they can use systems of taxation to convert small contributions into substantial centralized funds which in turn can be used to further impressive collective project and public works (ranging from religious architecture to professionalized priesthoods and standing armies).

There is now a substantial body of evidence that doctrinal and imagistic practices generate qualitatively different kinds of social glue.[15] LFHA rituals produce identity fusion,[16] a visceral sense of oneness with the group that motivates extreme self-sacrifice, such as a willingness to fight and die to protect one's fellows.[17] Emotionally intense rituals give rise to identity fusion by establishing lasting episodic memories that are both personally defining and essential to the identity of the group.[18] Social synchrony also increases identity fusion.[19] But while the effects of synchronous movement (e.g., dancing, marching, and parading) are short-lived and require repetition, the shared-experiences-pathway to fusion produces lifelong group alignments,[20] even if that process takes significant time to unfold.[21]

By contrast, HFLA rituals produce social identification, a more depersonalized form of group alignment which, although capable of motivating prosocial action and outgroup derogation, does not give rise to extreme self-sacrifice. Identification does not tap into personal agency to the same extent as fusion.[22] Since HFLA rituals are highly routinized, participants cannot remember each performance as a distinct episode and instead their knowledge of religious beliefs and practices take the form of semantic schemas and scripts.[23] Since this type of knowledge is socially learned from others, it does not form part of the essential personal self, in the same way as one's unique episodic memories do (and that undergird the fusion process).[24]

LFHA rituals have contributed to group bonding in human societies for tens of thousands of years and possibly much longer.[25] Such rituals served to bind together small bands of hunter-gatherers struggling to survive in the face of environmental challenges (us-versus-nature contests) and intergroup competition (us-versus-them contests).[26] Their contribution to human flourishing was essentially parochial. That is, imagistic practices facilitate the survival and reproductive success of group members in the face of environmental threats and often (e.g., in the case of chronic intergroup raiding and warfare) at the expense of rival groups. But the practices themselves probably did not contribute to net gains in individual happiness. On the contrary, since the effects of shared experience on personal transformation and group essence were most likely stronger for dysphoric rather than euphoric rituals, imagistic practices are generally more likely to evince negative emotions such as pain, fear, and disgust, rather than joy, love, jubilation, or other positive affective states. As such, the contribution of the imagistic mode of religiosity to human flourishing is, at best, mixed.

The doctrinal mode, characterized by HFLA rituals, is associated with the appearance of farming[27] and the rise of larger-scale settlements.[28] HFLA rituals, and the religious traditions they sustained, made possible identification with large groups sharing a relatively stable creed.[29] By routinizing the group's beliefs and practices, it became easier to detect and prevent unauthorized innovation and therefore to homogenize regional traditions.[30] The doctrinal mode of religiosity is therefore likely to have contributed early to the rise and spread of social complexity during and after the initial transition from foraging to farming.[31]

As doctrinal practices became ever more widespread, however, imagistic ones declined.[32] With the rise of increasingly large and hierarchical state formations, LFHA rituals have been suppressed as potentially seditious or pushed to the margins of society, e.g., surviving only among tribal groups over which control is difficult to exercise and which may therefore present a perennial threat to urban dynasties.[33] LFHA rituals have nevertheless often be encouraged or tolerated in special groups authorized by the state (e.g., professional militia, elite groups, and religious guilds) or have managed to assert themselves in unauthorized armed groups and terrorist organizations.[34]

Although a marked increase in the frequency of religious rituals may have been a necessary condition for the rise of social complexity, the contributions of the doctrinal mode of religiosity to human flourishing, at least for the majority of subject populations worldwide, have been somewhat mixed. On the one hand, early farming societies do not generally exhibit marked inequalities in status, power, or wealth.[35] During the early phases of animal domestication and plant cultivation associated with the rise of more frequent rituals and denser patterns of settlement, societies tended to grow larger but not markedly more centralized and hierarchical, and there is little evidence of systematic violence or coercion within or between groups. By contrast, the later appearance of so-called "archaic states" involved the monopolization of violence by powerful elites and the establishment of extreme forms of social inequality—for example, in the form of slavery and human sacrifice.[36] Nevertheless, social formations based on naked coercion have been progressively replaced by those adopting more consensual forms of governance,[37] a topic we investigate in the next section.

The Axial Age, Moralizing Gods, and Human Flourishing

The idea that top-down coercion in archaic states was replaced by more consensual forms of governance rooted in universalizing religious teachings and ethics has a long pedigree. It dates back at least as far as the work of Anquetil-Duperron (1771) and Stuart-Glennie (1873), for example. But this argument is perhaps most commonly associated nowadays with Jaspers and his notion of an "Axial Age"[38] associated with the spread of five ethical religions (Confucianism, Buddhism, Judaism, Zoroastrianism, and Greek philosophy). The defining features of Axiality can be distilled into a set of basic principles that emphasize shared moral norms, and legal codes, and the shared humanity of rulers and ruled, elites and commoners. Recent efforts to track the appearance of these defining features have utilized a new database of world history known as Seshat[39] which provides a stratified sample of the world's polities over the past ten thousand years and incorporates highly sophisticated measures of social complexity.[40] Analysis of the data in Seshat suggests that, contrary to Jaspers' original formulation, Axial features were not restricted to the first millennium BCE or to the five ethical religions mentioned above, and nor did they emerge as a single package in a linear fashion.[41] The new research suggests that some elements of Axiality occurred much earlier than Jaspers imagined, in regions not originally considered in the framework (e.g., North Africa and Anatolia), while in other regions only some of the features appear and not others (e.g., in East Asia and parts of the Mediterranean). More remarkably still, perhaps, the main concentration of Axial features as tracked in Seshat turns out to be not the first millennium BCE but the two thousand years that came afterwards. In other words, those features of religion and governance most congenial to human flourishing in complex societies became widespread more recently than many scholars, following Jaspers, had assumed.

Although more research is needed into the appearance of Axiality in world history before much can be said with confidence, there is now compelling evidence that some aspects of moralizing gods, one of the key Axial features, emerged after the sharpest rises in social complexity.[42] This finding runs somewhat against the grain of the well-known Big Gods Hypothesis, proposing that such gods are necessary to facilitate cooperation among relative strangers in complex societies.[43] The basic idea here is that as societies grew larger and anonymous transactions more commonplace, there would have been a growing risk that cooperation would break down because of the temptation to free ride and cheat with low risk of reputational damage. But if parties to such transactions believed in a punitive, all-seeing deity, they might be more likely to cooperate. Moreover, indications that prospective trading partners believe in a moralizing god might serve to increase trust. The hypothesis has some *prima facie* appeal. Moreover, the application of phylogenetic methods to infer the historical emergence of beliefs in supernatural punishment suggests that such beliefs preceded, and therefore may have facilitated, the rise of social complexity, at least in Austronesia.[44] A similar conclusion was reached following analysis of Viking archaeology.[45] On the other hand, there have also been studies suggesting that moralizing gods appear after and not before the rise of social complexity, at least in Western Eurasia.[46] Unfortunately, all such studies were limited by rather crude measures of social complexity and are region-specific rather than global. Here again, the application of data in Seshat has allowed a more ambitious approach based on the analysis for data on human history worldwide using much more sophisticated methods of tracking social complexity and moralizing gods.

Seshat researchers analyzed 47,613 records for 414 societies spanning the past 10,000 years from 30 regions around the world, based on 51 measures of social complexity and 4 measures of supernatural enforcement of morality, finding that moralizing gods first appear after and not before the steepest rises in social complexity worldwide.[47] If such gods arise at all, it would seem that they do so around the time that societies achieve a population of around one million individuals.

This "mega-society threshold" may correspond to a point beyond which the tensions between social classes, diverse ethnicities absorbed through trading and warfare, and other interest groups become so complex and interwoven that societies become fragile. One hypothesis currently being explored is that efforts to hold such societies together by means of top-down domination via coercive state apparatus weaken the social fabric to such a degree that the political system becomes vulnerable to internal rebellion, revolution, or invasion by more powerful neighbors. Empires that flourish and grow in these circumstances are, arguably, those that can achieve a modus vivendi based on sufficient consensus and trust between rulers and ruled and between diverse races and creeds. This, perhaps, is what the features of Axial Age religion provided.[48] On this view, human flourishing thus became a culturally evolved solution to collective action problems on an unprecedented scale. If this view is broadly correct, what does it imply for the future of human flourishing?

Harnessing Religion to Solve Global Collective Action Problems in the Future

If Axial Age religions, and specifically perhaps moralizing gods, were the key to the success of many societies that made it over the "mega-society threshold," then what are the implications of this for modern processes of secularization, for example in Europe? Declining belief in moralizing gods might imply a loss of vital tools for maintaining cooperation across competing coalitions based on class or race. Could this help to explain the divisive effects of emerging forms of populism and the declining fortunes of regional trade and governance networks such as the European Union? Will secular societies eventually succumb to more powerful political systems that mobilize belief in moralizing gods, provided by fast evolving varieties of fundamentalist Islam or evangelical Christianity? Not all such futures may be conducive to human flourishing, at least of the kind envisaged by champions of liberal values, protected minorities, and individual freedoms.

On the other hand, perhaps religion has a role to play in the future of human flourishing in other ways. Whatever trends toward secularization might imply for some Western countries, overall the world at large remains robustly religious (currently about 7 billion believers compared with just 500 million atheists). We know that religion has played a huge role in solving large-scale collective action problems in world history—from building pyramids and cathedrals to expanding empires. For good or ill, religion is a powerful binding force in human societies. Currently, the world faces unprecedented collective action problems such as human-caused global heating. Could religion's power to mobilize people behind ambitious projects provide part of the solution? All the major religions currently provide scriptural support for stewardship of the environment, and yet the implications of this for action on climate change have scarcely been recognized. To the extent that religion in general is capable of motivating prosocial action, perhaps now is the time to tap into the cohesive power of world religions to tackle the world's environmental crises. To do this requires an effective toolkit, building on what we know about relationship between ritual and social bonding, for example, and applying this in practical ways to produce positive outcomes.

Consider the following practical examples. Religious norms already influence consumer behavior in profound ways and on a global scale, for example, by imposing dietary restrictions. Such restrictions are not immutable, however, and could easily change. At present, Muslims in the UK consume 20 percent of all lamb and mutton despite forming less than 5 percent of the total population. And yet early Muslims were largely vegetarian, and Muhammad himself is thought to have mainly eaten only dates and barley. There are many textual sources in Islam railing against meat consumption, including the dictum "Do not make of your stomach a graveyard of animals." This kind of thinking has fueled the recent establishment of "Vegan-adan" as an alternative to Ramadan. Or consider an even more ambitious idea: imagine, for example, if most Catholics in South America decided to stop eating beef on religious grounds, based on biblical support for stewardship of the earth augmented perhaps by strong leadership from the Vatican.

Tapping into the cohesive power of religious rituals to address environmental issues could take many forms. For example, the recent EcoSikh movement recently launched the "Million Tree Project," which has set out to plant a million new trees to celebrate the 550th birthday of Sikhism's founder, Guru Nanak. Imagine if all religions of the world decided to celebrate major anniversaries in a similar fashion, perhaps in a peacefully competitive fashion that could help rapidly to replace the "lungs of the earth" so recently damaged by deforestation and yet so badly needed to absorb carbon emissions responsible for the climate crisis.

Harnessing religion to address global collective action problems is not the only way in which religion could contribute to human flourishing in the future. Another way is to expand the provenance and impact of beliefs in moralizing gods. Much previous work on the significance of moralizing "big" gods in cultural evolution has emphasized the role of such beliefs in facilitating cooperation in environments where detection risk is low, such as urban settings where crimes can more easily be committed anonymously. Such functions, however, are increasingly being taken over by increasingly sophisticated technologies of surveillance and data storage. But the notion of a supernatural "eye in the sky" is not simply about detecting and punishing transgressions; it could equally be about motivating cooperative acts across a variety of moral domains and in a great diversity of contexts. Recent comparative research on moral reasoning in a sample of sixty societies worldwide has shown that at least seven cooperative rules are judged morally good in all human societies, pointing to the existing of a universal moral compass.[49] These rules (take care of kin, be loyal to the group, reciprocate favors, be courageous, respect authority, share fairly, and never steal) are built into our evolved psychology, but what differs across human populations is the relative emphasis placed on each of these rules, and also the ways in which they are combined. This is true also of religions. For example, traditions of ancestor worship heavily emphasize obligations to kin and respect for elders, while warrior cults emphasize bravery in battle, and Abrahamic religions tend to emphasize the importance of reciprocity and honesty. While all the varied moral dimensions may find some kind of endorsement or scriptural support in every known religion, they are emphasized to different degrees and in different contexts, producing variation not only across traditions but also within them, especially when we consider how they change over time.

This suggests not only that religions in their current forms can motivate moral action to varying degrees across a range of contexts but also that each religious tradition has untapped potential to expand its capacity to engage our moral instincts in novel ways. For example, researchers have recently shown that conservationists tend to utilize only a small number of potential moral domains in mobilizing support for their efforts. Reciprocity looms large in conservation policy, emphasizing the moral obligation of users of resources to repay their debts to the environment.[50] Less extensively explored, however, are the many potential ways in which our moral commitments to conservation could be strengthened via other moral domains, by fostering feelings of kinship with other species, heroism in defending endangered species, awe for the majesty of the natural world, and respect for other owners of the planet besides ourselves. These are just a few examples, but they highlight not only underexploited moral intuitions in conservation policy but also in religion. While it may be possible to find theological grounds for each of the above moral stances on stewardship of the earth, they are not fully articulated and widely disseminated as divinely sanctioned injunctions. But they could be.

Conclusions

Debate about the role of religion in human flourishing will no doubt continue to rage, but to adjudicate on these big questions will require ongoing investment in large databases like Seshat as well as more systematic data collection in a diversity of societies worldwide, sampling particularly the sorts of populations typically neglected by the psychological and behavioral sciences. Understanding how and why rituals and moralizing gods may have helped societies to cooperate on ever grander scales is crucial not only to grasping religion's contribution to human flourishing in the past but also its potential to do so in the future. Tackling many of the threats faced by our species, and our planet as a whole, will depend on humankind's ability to cooperate on previously unimaginable scales, and especially on a global stage. Social glue and moral conviction, along with other human assets that have been linked to religion, may have an important role to play in ensuring the success of such endeavors.

References

Anquetil-Duperron, Abraham-Hyacinthe. 1771. *Zend-Avesta: Ouvrage de Zoroastre; Contenant les idées théologiques, physiques et morales de ce législateur.* 2 vols. Paris: Tilliard.

Aronson, E., and J. Mills. 1959. "The Effect of Severity of Initiation on liking for a group." *Journal of Abnormal and Social Psychology* 59, no. 2: 177–81. https://doi.org/10.1037/h0047195.

Atkinson, Q. D., and H. Whitehouse. 2011. "The Cultural Morphospace of Ritual Form: Examining Modes of Religiosity Cross-Culturally." *Evolution and Human Behavior* 32, no. 1: 50–62.

Barker, G. 2009. *The Agricultural Revolution in Prehistory: Why Did Foragers Become Farmers?* Oxford: Oxford University Press.

Baumard, N., A. Hyafil, I. Morris, and P. Boyer. 2015. "Increased Affluence Explains the Emergence of Ascetic Wisdoms and Moralizing Religions." *Current Biology* 25: 10–15.

Buhrmester, Michael, Dawn Burnham, Dominic Johnson, Oliver S. Curry, David Macdonald, and Harvey Whitehouse. 2018. "How Moments Become Movements: Shared Outrage, Group Cohesion, and the Lion

That Went Viral." *Frontiers in Ecology and Evolution* 6. doi: 10.3389/fevo.2018.00054.

Curry, O. S., Darragh Hare, Cameron Hepburn, Dominic D. P. Johnson, Michael Buhrmester, Harvey Whitehouse, and David W. Macdonald. 2019. "Cooperative Conservation: Seven Ways to Save the World." *Conservation Science and Practice*. https://doi.org/10.1111/csp2.123.

Curry, Oliver S., Daniel A. Mullins, and Harvey Whitehouse. 2019. "Is It Good to Cooperate? Testing the Theory of Morality-as-Cooperation in 60 Societies." *Current Anthropology* 60, no. 1. doi: 10.1086/701478.

Gantley, M., A. Bogaard, and H. Whitehouse. 2018. "Material Correlates Analysis (MCA): An Innovative way of Examining Questions in Archaeology Using Ethnographic Data." *Advances in Archaeological Practice* 6, no. 4: 384–84. doi: 10.1017/aap.2018.33.

Henrich, J. 2009. "The Evolution of Costly Displays, Cooperation and Religion: Credibility Enhancing Displays and Their Implications for Cultural Evolution." *Evolution and Human Behavior* 30, no. 4: 244–60. https://doi.org/10.1016/j.evolhumbehav.2009.03.005.

Henrich, J., S. J. Heine, and A. Norenzayan. 2010. "The Weirdest People in the World." *Behavioral and Brain Sciences* 33, nos. 2–3: 61–83.

Herrmann, P. A., C. H. Legare, P. L. Harris, and H. Whitehouse. 2013. "Stick to the Script: The Effect of Witnessing Multiple Actors on Children's Imitation." *Cognition* 129: 536–43.

Jackson, J. C., J. Jong, D. Bilkey, H. Whitehouse, S. Zollmann, C. McNaughton, and J. Halberstadt. 2018. "Synchrony and Physiological Arousal Increase Cohesion and Cooperation in Large Naturalistic Groups." *Nature: Scientific Reports* 8, no. 127. doi: 10.1038/s41598-017-18023-4.

Jaspers, K. 1953. *The Origin and Goal of History*. Translated by Michael Bullock. New Haven, Conn.: Yale University Press.

Jong, J., H. Whitehouse, C. Kavanagh, and J. Lane. 2015. "Shared Negative Experiences Lead to Identity Fusion via Personal Reflection." *PLoS ONE* 10, no. 12. doi: 10.1371/journal.pone.0145611.

Kavanagh, C. M., Jong, J., McKay, R., and Harvey Whitehouse. 2018. "Positive Experiences of High Arousal Martial Arts Rituals Are Linked to Identity Fusion and Costly Progroup Actions." *European Journal of Social Psychology*. doi.org/10.1002/ejsp.2514.

Legare, C. H., N. J. Wen, P. A. Herrmann, and H. Whitehouse. 2015. "Imitative Flexibility and the Development of Cultural Learning." *Cognition* 142: 351–61. doi: 10.1016/j.cognition.2015.05.020.

Malhotra, D. 2010. "(When) Are Religious People Nicer? Religious Salience and the 'Sunday Effect' on Prosocial Behaviour." *Judgment and Decision Making* 5: 138–43.

McKay, R., and H. Whitehouse. "Religion and Morality." 2015. *Psychological Bulletin* 141, no. 2: 447. http://dx.doi.org/10.1037/a0038455.

Mullins, D. A., D. Hoyer, C. Collins, T. Currie, K. Feeney, P. François, P. E. Savage, H. Whitehouse, and P. Turchin. 2018. "A Systematic Assessment of 'Axial Age' Proposals Using Global Comparative Historical Evidence." *American Sociological Review* 83, no. 3: 596–626.

Newson, Martha, M. D. Buhrmester, and H. Whitehouse. 2016. "Explaining Lifelong Loyalty: The Role of Identity Fusion and Self-Shaping Group Events." *PLoS ONE* 11, no. 8: e0160427. doi: 10.1371/journal.pone .0160427.

Norenzayan, A. 2013. *Big Gods: How Religion Transformed Cooperation and Conflict*. Princeton: Princeton University Press.

Paul-Labrador, M., D. Polk, J. H. Dwyer, I. Velasquez, S. Nidich, M. Rainforth, R. Schneider, and C. N. Merz. 2006. "Effects of a Randomized Controlled Trial of Transcendental Meditation on Components of the Metabolic Syndrome in Subjects with Coronary Heart Disease." *Archives of Internal Medicine* 166: 1218–24.

Raffield, B., N. Price, and M. Collard. 2017. "Religious Belief and Cooperation: A View from Viking-Age Scandinavia." *Religion, Brain, and Behavior* 9, no. 1: 1–21.

Rossano, M. J. 2012. "The Essential Role of Ritual in the Transmission and Reinforcement of Social Norms." *Psychological Bulletin* 138, no. 3: 529–49. doi: 10.1037/a0027038.

Sloan, R. P., and E. Bagiella. 2002. "Claims about Religious Involvement and Health Outcomes." *Annals of Behavioral Medicine* 24: 14–21.

Sosis, R. 2004. "The Adaptive Value of Religious Ritual." *American Scientist* 92: 166–72.

Stuart-Glennie, John Stuart. 1873. *In the Morningland or The Law of the Origin and Transformation of Christianity*. London: Longmans, Green, and Company.

Swann, W. B., A. Gómez, C. Huici, F. Morales, and J. G. Hixon. 2010. "Identity Fusion and Self-Sacrifice: Arousal as Catalyst of Pro-Group Fighting, Dying and Helping Behavior." *Journal of Personality and Social Psychology* 99: 824–41.

Swann, W. B., J. Jensen, Á. Gómez, H. Whitehouse, and B. Bastian. 2012. "When Group Membership Gets Personal: A Theory of Identity Fusion." *Psychological Review* 119, no. 3: 441–56.

Turchin, Peter, Rob Brennan, Thomas E. Currie, Kevin C. Feeney, Pieter François, Daniel Hoyer, J. G. Manning, Arkadiusz Marciniak, Daniel Mullins, Alessio Palmisano, Peter Peregrine, Edward A. L. Turner, and Harvey Whitehouse. 2015. "Seshat: The Global History Databank." *Cliodynamics: The Journal of Quantitative History and Cultural Evolution* 6, no. 1: 77–107.

Turchin, P., T. E. Currie, H. Whitehouse, et al. 2018a. "Quantitative Historical Analysis Uncovers a Single Dimension of Complexity That Structures

Global Variation in Human Social Organization." *Proceedings of the National Academy of Sciences of the United States of America (PNAS)* 115, no. 2: E144–E151.

Turchin, P., H. Whitehouse, A. H. Dupeyron, T. E. Currie, P. François, K. C. Feeney, D. Hoyer, D. Mullins, P. Peregrine, P. E. Savage, J. Baines, J. Bidmead, Á. D. Júlíusson, N. Kradin, O. Litwin, K. Reinhart, B. Ter Haar, and V. Wallace. Forthcoming. "The Rise and Fall of Human Sacrifice in the Evolution of Sociopolitical Complexity."

Turchin, P. H. Whitehouse, Pieter François, Daniel Hoyer, Selin Nugent, Jennifer Larson, R. Alan Covey, Mark Altaweel, Peter Peregrine, David Carballo, Gary Feinman, Vesna Wallace, Peter K. Bol, Andrey Korotayev, Nikolay Kradin, Eugene Anderson, Patrick E. Savage, Enrico Cioni, Jill Levine, Jenny Reddish, Eva Brandl, and Andrea Squitieri. 2018b. "Explaining the Rise of Moralizing Religions: A Test of Competing Hypotheses Using the Seshat Databank." SocArXiv. 10.31235/osf.io/2v59j.

Watson-Jones, R., C. H. Legare, H. Whitehouse, and J. Clegg. 2014. "Task-Specific Effects of Ostracism on Imitation of Social Convention in Early Childhood." *Evolution and Human Behavior* 35, no. 3: 204–10.

Watson-Jones, R. E., H. Whitehouse, and C. H. Legare. 2016. "In-Group Ostracism Increases High Fidelity Imitation in Early Childhood." *Psychological Science* 27, no. 1: 34–42. doi: 10.1177/0956797615607205.

Watts, J., S. J. Greenhill, Q. D. Atkinson, T. E. Currie, J. Bulbulia, and R. D. Gray. 2015. "Broad Supernatural Punishment but Not Moralizing High Gods Precede the Evolution of Political Complexity in Austronesia." *Proceedings of the Royal Society B Biological Sciences* 282: 1–7.

Watts, J., O. Sheehan, Q. D. Atkinson, J. Bulbulia, and R. D. Gray. 2016. "Ritual Human Sacrifice Promoted and Sustained the Evolution of Stratified Societies." *Nature* 532: 228–31. doi.org/10.1038/nature17159.

Whitehouse, H. 1992. "Memorable Religions: Transmission, Codification, and Change in Divergent Melanesian Contexts." *Man* (n.s.) 27, no. 3: 777–97.

———. 1995. *Inside the Cult: Religious Innovation and Transmission in Papua New Guinea*. Oxford: Oxford University Press.

———. 2000. *Arguments and Icons: Divergent Modes of Religiosity*. Oxford: Oxford University Press.

———. 2002. "Religious Reflexivity and Transmissive Frequency." *Social Anthropology* 10, no. 1: 91–103.

———. 2004. *Modes of Religiosity: A Cognitive Theory of Religious Transmission*. Walnut Creek, Calif.: AltaMira Press.

———. 2011. "The Coexistence Problem in Psychology, Anthropology, and Evolutionary Theory." *Human Development* 54: 191–99.

————. 2013. "Three Wishes for the World (with Comment)." *Cliodynamics: The Journal of Theoretical and Mathematical History* 4, no. 2.

————. 2018. "Dying for the Group: Towards a General Theory of Extreme Self-Sacrifice." *Behavioral and Brain Sciences* 41: e192. doi: 10.1017/S0140525X18000249.

Whitehouse, Harvey, Pieter François, Enrico Cioni, Jill Levine, Daniel Hoyer, Jenny Reddish, and Peter Turchin. 2019a. "Conclusion: Was There Ever an Axial Age?" In *The Seshat History of the Axial Age*, edited by Daniel Hoyer and Jenny Reddish. Chaplin, Conn.: Beresta Books.

Whitehouse, Harvey, Pieter François, Patrick E. Savage, Thomas E. Currie, Kevin C. Feeney, Enrico Cioni, Rosalind Purcell, Robert M. Ross, Jennifer Larson, John Baines, Barend ter Haar, Alan Covey, and Peter Turchin. 2019b. "Complex Societies Precede Moralizing Gods throughout World History." *Nature* 568: 226–29. doi.org/10.1038/s41586-019-1043-4.

Whitehouse, H., and I. Hodder. 2010. "Modes of Religiosity at Çatalhöyük." In *Religion in the Emergence of Civilization: Çatalhöyük as a Case Study*, edited by I. Hodder. Cambridge: Cambridge University Press.

Whitehouse, H., Jonathan Jong, M. D. Buhrmester, Á. Gómez, Brock Bastian, Christopher M. Kavanagh, Martha Newson, Miriam Matthews, Jonathan A. Lanman, Ryan McKay, and Sergey Gavrilets. 2017. "The Evolution of Extreme Cooperation via Intense Shared Experiences." *Nature: Scientific Reports* 7, no. 44292. doi: 10.1038/srep44292.

Whitehouse, H., and J. A. Lanman. 2014. "The Ties That Bind Us: Ritual, Fusion and Identification." *Current Anthropology* 55, no. 6: 674–95. https://doi.org/10.1086/678698.

Whitehouse, H., C. Mazzucato, I. Hodder, and Q. D. Atkinson. 2013. "Modes of Religiosity and the Evolution of Social Complexity at Çatalhöyük." In *Religion at Work in a Neolithic Society: Vital Matters*, edited by I. Hodder. Cambridge: Cambridge University Press.

Whitehouse, H., and B. McQuinn. 2012. "Ritual and Violence: Divergent Modes of Religiosity and Armed Struggle." In *Oxford Handbook of Religion and Violence*, edited by M. Juergensmeyer, M. Kitts, and M. Jerryson. Oxford: Oxford University Press.

Whitehouse, H., B. McQuinn, M. D. Buhrmester, and W. B. Swann. 2014. "Brothers in Arms: Libyan Revolutionaries Bond Like Family." *Proceedings of the National Academy of Sciences* 111, no. 50: 17783–85.

Wiltermuth, S. S., and C. Heath. 2009. "Synchrony and Cooperation." *Psychological Science* 20, no. 1: 1–5. doi: 10.1111/j.1467-9280.2008.02253.x.

6

THE NEXT GENERATION

Evolutionary Perspectives on Religion and Human Flourishing

DOMINIC D. P. JOHNSON

Introduction

Does religion contribute to human flourishing? I explore this question from the standpoint of evolutionary biology and natural selection. I argue that: (1) on the face of it, religious beliefs and behaviors pose an *evolutionary puzzle* because they are costly; (2) however, there are material benefits—adaptive advantages—that can exceed these costs, resulting in *net benefits* overall; (3) indeed, the costs in themselves can in fact serve to deliver the benefits, via *signaling*; (4) consequently, religion has (in the past) and may continue (today) to contribute to human "flourishing," as measured by *Darwinian fitness* (survival and reproductive success); and finally (5) while not all evolutionary theories of religion imply that it is *adaptive*, many do, suggesting a range of possible functions, mechanisms, and scales at which religion contributes to human flourishing.

The Costs of Religion: An Evolutionary Puzzle?

Religious beliefs and behaviors impose significant costs in the expenditure of time, effort, resources, and opportunity costs. Their widespread and pervasive practice therefore presents a puzzle for evolutionary scientists. How could they evolve? Since evolution "abhors waste,"[1] the pursuit of extravagant beliefs and behaviors that tax self-interest in the observance of nonexistent supernatural agents should have been stamped out by natural selection.[2]

Moreover, many argue that, beyond individuals merely wasting time and effort, religion actually exerts significant detrimental social effects of its own. Far from contributing to human flourishing, the "New Atheists" in particular—such as Richard Dawkins, Daniel Dennett, and Christopher Hitchens—argue that religion is bad for individuals, bad for education, bad for society, and bad for the world as a whole.[3] Whatever else it does, they lament, it fosters ignorance, hostility to science, sexual discrimination, violations of human rights, justifications for extremist projects or policies, racism, conflict, and war.

For them, evolution can explain religion, but only as an evolutionary "accident"—an unfortunate by-product of the sophisticated human brain—that serves no useful purpose and is taken to costly and nefarious extremes in its modern cultural manifestations. In this view, religion does *not* contribute to human flourishing. Indeed, it prevents it.

The Costs and Benefits of Religion: An Evolutionary Solution

However, you will have noticed that the arguments above focused exclusively on *negative* consequences of religion. Even if they are sometimes true, what about the *positive* consequences? In order to know whether any trait is adaptive or not, it is of course essential to weigh up both its negative *and* positive effects in the relevant environment. Positive effects are also often less noticeable than negative effects, because the latter's associated costs and failures draw special attention.

Net Effects: Obvious Costs and Non-Obvious Benefits

Many things in nature appear costly, but one important lesson that has emerged from biology is that we must focus not on the costs themselves, but on the *net* effects (that is, costs *plus* benefits, and the trade-offs made between them). Costs must be weighed against the beneficial consequences that incurring those costs may bring. This can be difficult because costs are often obvious (and thus an easy target for ridicule), while benefits are often non-obvious, indirect, or delayed in time (and thus are harder to see and demand more work to reveal). There are plenty of analogues in the natural world: Emperor penguins fast for months during the Antarctic winter, but only in the service of effectively incubating their eggs; peacocks carry around huge tails that make it hard to fly, but only in the service of successfully attracting mates; Arctic terns migrate halfway around the world every year, but only to enjoy everlasting summer.[4]

On the face of it, these are all astonishingly costly traits and behaviors, but they are not incurred for the fun of it. They are strategies that improve survival and reproductive success. The same logic applies to humans. We incur many costs in life, but those costs are often just the price of strategies that bring net benefits overall—including for example parental investment, altruism, sharing, and competition.[5] In the realm of religion, suppressing self-interest in the observance of religious morals, for example, can lead to short-term costs but reap long-term gains in enhanced reciprocity and mutual cooperation—for the individual as well as the group.[6]

The Benefits of Costs: Costly Signaling

Perhaps even more striking, sometimes it is *the costs in themselves* that provide the advantage. Precisely by incurring a large cost, one can send an important and unfakeable *signal* to others, demonstrating commitment, strength, or other desirable qualities.[7] If no such cost is incurred, a credible signal cannot easily be sent. Again, this is a widespread phenomenon in nature. The peacock mentioned above survives and thrives *despite* an enormous tail—though cumbersome, it is a signal of quality transmitted to potential mates.[8] This so-called "costly signaling" can thus explain costly traits not as maladaptive aberrations, but as adaptive features in themselves. Costly signaling has been explicitly applied to religious beliefs and behaviors and enjoys considerable empirical support.[9]

False Prophets? The Adaptive Advantages of "False" Beliefs

So evolution can explain religious practices—including when they are costly—as adaptive. But what about the fact that these costly behaviors hinge on beliefs in invisible agents or forces? If incurring costs is worthwhile or advantageous in itself, why not at least incur those costs about something tangible? In fact, it turns out that evolution can explain this as well. Natural selection has commonly eschewed truth-tracking in the evolution of effective judgment and decision-making because, while counterintuitive, accurate perceptions of the world are not always the best way of navigating effectively within it.[10] Instead, cognitive and motivational "biases" are commonplace adaptive heuristics that help to optimize behavior.[11] Under uncertainty, such biases can be a better or more efficient way to avoid making mistakes than pure economic rationality.[12] Cognitive and perceptual biases occur in a variety of domains, including self-perceptions, interpersonal perceptions, and perceptions of the physical world.[13] Indeed, even superstitious or "superstitious-like" beliefs have been argued to be biologically adaptive in animals as well as humans, because they serve to enhance the probability of detecting genuine dangers and thus help to avoid them.[14] Applied to religion, there is therefore an evolutionary argument that beliefs in supernatural agents contribute to adaptive behavior, *even if* (or precisely because) they are in some sense misleading or "false."[15]

Are Evolutionary Theories "Flourishing"?

Despite its costs, therefore, religion is not an evolutionary puzzle if it generates net benefits, credible signals, and adaptive beliefs. This opens up a huge range of hypotheses for what might constitute those benefits (e.g., cooperation, or collective action), signals (e.g., trustworthiness, group loyalty), and adaptive beliefs (e.g., optimism, supernatural punishment, or reward). The point of this chapter is not to review those many emerging evolutionary theories of religion, but to explore what any such theory implies for human "flourishing."[16]

I argue that, beyond its intrinsic explanatory power, evolutionary biology is useful precisely because it offers a concrete measure of flourishing in the yardstick of "Darwinian fitness" (that is, survival and reproductive success).[17] Darwin himself used the term "flourishing," especially when considering the kinds of qualities that would make human groups as a whole more successful. For example, in *The Descent of Man*, he wrote, "Those communities, which included the greatest number of the most sympathetic members, would flourish best and rear the greatest number of offspring."[18] Although Darwinian fitness is hardly the *only* conception of "flourishing" one might be interested in (among many others explored in this volume, such as economic, societal, psychological, spiritual flourishing, etc.), biological fitness offers one straightforward measure to complement others.[19]

Anything that increases Darwinian fitness is "adaptive" and will be *selected for* by natural selection over time. Anything that decreases

Darwinian fitness is "maladaptive" and will be *selected against* by natural selection over time. The costs of religious beliefs and behaviors may be prominent, and the benefits may be inconspicuous, but if they generate net fitness benefits over time, religion will evolve and spread and, in Darwin's book—and mine—that would constitute human flourishing.[20]

Evolutionary Theories of Religion: Adaptation and Mechanisms of Selection

It is important to remind ourselves, however, that not all evolutionary theories necessarily argue that religion is *adaptive* (see table 6.1). As in any other area of biology, evolutionary theory has to explain the existence of all traits, whether they are adaptive or not. Evolution explains *maladaptive* traits (which are detrimental to fitness) and *nonadaptive* traits (which are neutral to fitness) as the result of phylogenetic *legacies* or as *by-products* of other traits.[21] Note also that some traits may be classed as "adaptive" even if they are detrimental to their bearers, because the *trait itself* can be successful at evolving and spreading (as with Dawkins' notion of religion as a "cultural parasite").[22]

TABLE 6.1. CLASSES OF EVOLUTIONARY THEORIES OF RELIGION[23]

Adaptive Theories	Nonadaptive Theories
Group Adaptation	Legacy
Individual Adaptation	By-product
Cultural Parasite	

However, in general terms, most modern evolutionary theories of religion explain religious beliefs and behaviors as adaptive, arguing that they provide important functional advantages to their bearers.[24] The emerging consensus is thus that religion is generally helpful to individuals and groups, and this contributes to human flourishing. But *how* exactly do these different approaches argue that religious beliefs and behaviors contribute to human flourishing?

Group Selection: The Forbidden Fruit?

Some evolutionary theories of religion invoke "group selection" to explain how religion can be adaptive (table 6.1, top-left cell). They argue that, even if a given religious trait imposes costs on *individual* self-interest, if the *group as a whole* derives some benefit from that trait (say, greater moral behavior and suppression of self-interest), then all else equal, over time this group will outperform or outcompete other groups that lack it, and the trait will spread in the population.[25] Note here that, as a result of the trait, individuals themselves may be *worse* off, but if the same trait helps the group, the *trait* itself will spread as the group expands relative to other groups (this is analogous to a gene spreading because it confers heightened reproductive success, even if it increases the risk that any given individual bearer will die).

Group selection often appears especially relevant to religion because, as David Sloan Wilson put it, religion is "the groupiest thing around."[26] However, while group selection is possible, it is rare in nature and entails special conditions if selection at the level of the group is to overwhelm the typically more powerful forces of selection operating at the level of the individual.[27] Consequently, group selection has been, and for many still is, seen as flawed or misleading.[28] That's an argument for another day, but the point here is a simple one: whether we like group selection or not, we do not need to rely on it to explain the evolution of religion from an evolutionary perspective—selection at the individual level works too.

Individual Selection: The Forgotten Fruit?

Other evolutionary theories of religion have focused instead on "individual selection" to explain why religion is adaptive (table 6.1, row 2 left). This is the conventional starting point in biological explanations of behavior.[29] How does a given trait X increase the fitness of the individual? Applied to religion, this approach is powerful for several reasons, not least:

1. It can explain why biological natural selection might favor the *cognitive mechanisms underlying religious beliefs and behaviors* (invoking no group or cultural selection);
2. It can explain the evolutionary *origins of religion* in the small-scale foraging societies in which we evolved (during the Pleistocene environment of around two million to ten thousand years ago);
3. It can explain how specific religious beliefs and behaviors contribute to "flourishing" in terms of the concrete measure of *Darwinian fitness* accruing to individuals (as well as, not instead of, any other measure).

I have highlighted individual selection here, and in my other work, because I believe it has not been explored enough.[30] In biology, it should be the first question, not the last. Group selection has been a tempting alternative because the puzzle of religion described at the start appears to rule out individual benefits (at first glance), leaving group-level benefits as a fallback position. Moreover, different human groups often appear so distinctive and competition between them appears so high that it suggests conditions might be conducive to group selection, even if it is rare in other domains. But while group selection remains plausible in theory, individual selection remains probable and empirically stronger, and yet it is not studied in proportion to its promise.[31]

Cultural Evolution: Future Avenues

Finally, Darwinian selection may be operating not only on genes at the individual level (individual selection), or on genes at the group level (group selection), but on *cultural* traits—such as ideas, beliefs, practices, innovations, technologies, and artifacts.[32] As proponents argue, the same core features of Darwinian selection—variation, selection, and replication—apply equally well to changes over time in *cultural* traits as they do to changes in *genetic* traits, and perhaps especially in the case of religion (which is, after all, a cultural phenomenon in its social manifestations).[33] There are many consequences and implications, holding significant potential as well as leaving interesting outstanding questions.[34] The only one I want to emphasize here is the important *interaction* that can occur between biological and cultural evolution. Why is this important? Because it means that *Darwinian fitness* can still be an important measure of flourishing, even within the framework of *cultural* evolution.

Here's one example. Dispositions to religiosity are known to have a *genetic* component.[35] Meanwhile, the preference for large families is often a *cultural* trait (some cultures advocate it, others do not). Combining these genetic and cultural phenomena, modern religious populations are expanding faster than secular ones, sufficiently so that according to some models, the genes associated with religiosity "will eventually predominate" in the population.[36] We should therefore pay attention to evolution in action today as well as to the legacies of evolution in our past. By our biological measure of flourishing, religious communities are not only thriving, they are expanding at the expense of secular communities.[37]

To me, an evolutionary perspective offers compelling evidence that religion contributes to human flourishing (at least under certain conditions and given a certain definition of flourishing). After all, if it did not, then it is unlikely that we would observe religious beliefs and behaviors in every society ever known around the globe. Even Richard Dawkins, who generally argues that religion serves as a malicious force in human society, conceded that precisely "because Darwinian natural selection abhors waste, any ubiquitous feature of a species—such as religion—must have conferred some advantage or it wouldn't have survived."[38] Although he did not explore what those advantages might be, many other scholars since have been working on it, and have found an embarrassment of riches.

Material and Immaterial Flourishing

Before concluding, let me briefly explore forging some links between evolutionary and other perspectives on religion and human flourishing. It may strike some readers that an evolutionary perspective is too "simplistic," focusing on bland material interpretations of flourishing and leaving other conceptual or spiritual meanings unaddressed. My main response is simply to point out that this is deliberate. In a book offering a wide variety of approaches and definitions of flourishing, this chapter intentionally focuses on one specific chunk: it points out that an evolutionary perspective suggests religious beliefs and behaviors can promote flourishing, over and above any other causes and meanings of the term, as measured by Darwinian fitness. It can therefore be considered one part, at least, of a larger jigsaw puzzle.

But my second response takes up the challenge more directly, as one can at least ask whether evolution may help to identify or resolve links between philosophical and evolutionary approaches. Miroslav Volf's chapter with Matthew Croasmun and Ryan McAnnally-Linz on "Meanings and Dimensions of Flourishing" (this volume) suggests that thinking about flourishing has at least three different traditions. A "flourishing life" is one that is: (1) led well (invoking agency); (2) goes well (invoking circumstances); and (3) feels right (invoking emotions). An evolutionary perspective, while not denying unique insights from philosophy and theology, becomes interesting in this light because, as biologists may have noted, these different characteristics of flourishing have biological parallels with Nobel laureate Niko Tinbergen's famous "four causes of behavior."[39] Let us briefly review Tinbergen's insight and then apply it to flourishing.

Tinbergen realized that to understand any trait in nature it is vital to distinguish between its "proximate" cause (the physiological mechanisms that give rise to the trait) and its "ultimate" cause (the evolutionary problem that the trait evolved to solve), as well as its phylogenetic origins and developmental emergence.[40] Focusing only on one cause and ignoring the others generates great confusion in trying to understand behavior, in both humans and other animals. As an example, the *ultimate* explanation of birdsong is that it helps to assert territories and attract mates, but the *proximate* explanation is that as day length increases, hormones are released which stimulate the birds to sing.[41] Both explanations are correct, but each one only captures part of the story. If we want a complete understanding of behavior, for animals as well as for humans, then we have to consider both proximate and ultimate causes of that behavior.

Now we can apply the insight to flourishing. For a species to flourish, its behavior must be functionally adaptive (that is, in the terms of Volf et al., "led well") where the agency is natural selection itself (this is Tinbergen's *ultimate* explanation of behavior). Also, the behavior must be activated by physiological and neurological mechanisms (that is, in the terms of Volf et al., it must "feel right"), and of course senses and emotions are widely understood as important evolved mechanisms to motivate adaptive behavior, including moral sentiments (this is Tinbergen's *proximate* explanation of behavior).[42] Finally, all this must lead to material benefits (that is, in the terms of Volf et al., that things "go well"), which are the fitness benefits of the behavior for a given organism in a given ecological setting, and which lead to the trait being favored by natural selection. So in short, these three broad dimensions of flourishing have an analog, and perhaps even a driving mechanism, in evolutionary biology.

Volf and others are unlikely to be satisfied with a "reduction" of core philosophical and theological arguments to mechanistic biological ones, but the close analogy suggests there are at least avenues for further exploration. Evolution may extend our understanding—or at least our questioning—of perceptual, emotional, and spiritual aspects of flourishing, or indeed why, as evolved human beings (and evolved scholars!), we have come to deem those phenomena important for well-being. At the least, as Volf and others note, "Flourishing life is more than the meeting of the human animal's material needs, but it does not exclude these."[43] Tinbergen might have prompted us to ask an additional question, however: What evolved proximate mechanisms are being triggered to generate these seemingly spiritual motivations in the first place? They could just be evolution's way of making us behave adaptively, whatever we think they are.

Unfinished Symphony: Outstanding Gaps in Adaptive Theories of Religion

While evolutionary approaches have hugely advanced both our theoretical and empirical understanding of religion, there remain many open questions. Here are two big ones:

First and foremost, most studies look only at indirect measures of adaptive behavior, not true biological fitness. For example, many studies show that religious beliefs and behaviors increase cooperation.[44] But such studies do not necessarily tell us anything about whether that behavior had or has any impact on reproductive success. We merely *assume* that cooperation is good, fitness-enhancing behavior. If anything, it merely shows that religious beliefs and behaviors make people give money away, which itself is maladaptive, not adaptive. Where is the empirical evidence that religion promotes reproductive success? Given that this is a critical underlying assumption of evolutionary theories of religion, it is striking that so few researchers have sought any evidence for it.

Second, why have evolutionary theories of religion focused almost exclusively on behaviors that are positive? Natural selection favors behaviors that are *adaptive* for the organism, regardless of whether they are nasty or nice. For example, evolution is just as good at explaining predation, territoriality, and aggression as it is at explaining helping and cooperation. Yet scant attention is paid to adaptive theories of the role of religion in helping human individuals and communities to "flourish" when perhaps it matters most—in times of competition and conflict.[45] In politics and international relations, understanding the role of religion in intergroup competition and conflict—and thus also in conflict resolution—is one of the most active and important areas of contemporary research.[46] Yet evolutionary theories of religion have yet to venture far into this relatively uncharted territory.

While evolutionary approaches to religion have blossomed into a major field of research, many questions remain to be explored. If there is a consensus within the evolutionary literature, however, it is that religious beliefs and behaviors can contribute significantly to human flourishing in a variety of ways, whatever costs may also accompany them.

References

Andrews, P. W., S. W. Gangestad, and D. Matthews. 2002. "Adaptationism: How to Carry Out an Exaptationist Program." *Behavioral and Brain Sciences* 25: 489–553.

Atran, Scott, and Jeremy Ginges. 2012. "Religious and Sacred Imperatives in Human Conflict." *Science* 336, no. 6083: 855–57.

Barrett, Justin L. 2017. "Could We Advance the Science of Religion (Better) without the Concept 'Religion'?" *Religion, Brain and Behavior* 7, no. 4: 282–84.

Bering, J. M. 2010. *The Belief Instinct: The Psychology of Souls, Destiny, and the Meaning of Life.* New York: W. W. Norton.

Birkhead, Tim, Jo Wimpenny, and Bob Montgomerie. 2014. *Ten Thousand Birds: Ornithology since Darwin.* Princeton: Princeton University Press.

Brewer, J., M. Gelfand, J. C. Jackson, I. F. MacDonald, P. N. Peregrine, P. J. Richerson, P. Turchin, H. Whitehouse, and D. S. Wilson. 2017. "Grand Challenges for the Study of Cultural Evolution." *Nature Ecology and Evolution* 1, no. 3: 1–3.

Bulbulia, J. 2008. "Meme Infection or Religious Niche Construction? An Adaptationist Alternative to the Cultural Maladaptationist Hypothesis." *Method and Theory in the Study of Religion* 20: 67–107.

Bulbulia, J., R. Sosis, C. Genet, R. Genet, E. Harris, and K. Wyman. 2008. *The Evolution of Religion: Studies, Theories, and Critiques.* Santa Margarita, Calif.: Collins Foundation Press.

Cosmides, L., and J. Tooby. 1994. "Better than Rational: Evolutionary Psychology and the Invisible Hand." *American Economic Review* 84, no. 2: 327–32.

Creanza, Nicole, Oren Kolodny, and Marcus W. Feldman. 2017. "Cultural Evolutionary Theory: How Culture Evolves and Why It Matters." *Proceedings of the National Academy of Sciences (PNAS)* 114, no. 30: 7782–89.

Cronk, Lee. 2005. "The Application of Animal Signaling Theory to Human Phenomena: Some Thoughts and Clarifications." *Social Science Information* 44, no. 4: 603–20.

Curry, Oliver Scott, Daniel Austin Mullins, and Harvey Whitehouse. 2019. "Is It Good to Cooperate? Testing the Theory of Morality-as-Cooperation in 60 Societies." *Current Anthropology* 60, no. 1: 47–69.

Darwin, Charles. 1871. *The Descent of Man.* New York: Penguin Classics.

Davies, N. B., J. R. Krebs, and S. A. West. 2012. *An Introduction to Behavioural Ecology.* Chichester: Wiley Blackwell.

Dawkins, R. 1976. *The Selfish Gene.* Oxford: Oxford University Press.

———. 2006. *The God Delusion.* New York: Houghton Mifflin.

Dennett, Daniel C. 2006. *Breaking the Spell: Religion as a Natural Phenomenon.* New York: Viking.

Fiske, S. T., and S. E. Taylor. 2013. *Social Cognition: From Brains to Culture.* 2nd ed. New York: McGraw-Hill.

Foster, K. R., and H. Kokko. 2009. "The Evolution of Superstitious and Superstitious-Like Behaviour." *Proceedings of the Royal Society B: Biological Sciences* 276: 31–37.

Gigerenzer, Gerd. 2002. *Adaptive Thinking: Rationality in the Real World.* Oxford: Oxford University Press.

Gigerenzer, Gerd, and Henry Brighton. 2009. "*Homo Heuristicus*: Why Biased Minds Make Better Inferences." *Topics in Cognitive Science* 1:107–43.

Haselton, M. G., G. A. Bryant, A. Wilke, D. A. Frederick, A. Galperin, W. Frankenhuis, and T. Moore. 2009. "Adaptive Rationality: An Evolutionary Perspective on Cognitive Bias." *Social Cognition* 27: 733–63.

Haselton, Martie G., and Daniel Nettle. 2006. "The Paranoid Optimist: An Integrative Evolutionary Model of Cognitive Biases." *Personality and Social Psychology Review* 10, no. 1: 47–66. doi: 10.1207/s15327957pspr1001_3.

Hitchens, Christopher. 2007. *God Is Not Great: How Religion Poisons Everything.* New York: Twelve Books.

Johnson, D. D. P. 2009. "The Error of God: Error Management Theory, Religion, and the Evolution of Cooperation." In *Games, Groups, and the Global Good*, edited by S. A. Levin, 169–80. Berlin: Springer.

———. 2016. *God Is Watching You: How the Fear of God Makes Us Human.* New York: Oxford University Press.

Johnson, Dominic D. P., Daniel T. Blumstein, James H. Fowler, and Martie G. Haselton. 2013. "The Evolution of Error: Error Management, Cognitive Constraints, and Adaptive Decision-Making Biases." *Trends in Ecology and Evolution* 28, no. 8: 474–81. doi: 10.1016/j.tree.2013.05.014.

Johnson, D. D. P., and O. Kruger. 2004. "The Good of Wrath: Supernatural Punishment and the Evolution of Cooperation." *Political Theology* 5, no. 2: 159–76.

Johnson, D. D. P., H. Lenfesty, and J. P. Schloss. 2014. "The Elephant in the Room: Religious Truth Claims, Evolution and Human Nature." *Philosophy, Theology and the Sciences* 1, no. 2: 200–231.

Johnson, D. D. P., Michael E. Price, and Masanori Takezawa. 2008. "Renaissance of the Individual: Reciprocity, Positive Assortment, and the Puzzle of Human Cooperation." In *Foundations of Evolutionary Psychology: Ideas, Issues and Applications*, edited by C. Crawford and D. Krebs, 331–52. New York: Erlbaum.

Johnson, D. D. P., and Zoey Reeve. 2013. "The Virtues of Intolerance: Is Religion an Adaptation for War?" In *Religion, Intolerance and Conflict: A Scientific and Conceptual Investigation*, edited by S. Clarke, R. Powell, and J. Savulescu, 67–87. Oxford: Oxford University Press.

Johnstone, R. A. 1997. "The Evolution of Animal Signals." In *Behavioural Ecology: An Evolutionary Approach*, 4th ed., edited by J. R. Krebs and N. B. Davies, 155–78. Oxford: Blackwell Science.

Kenrick, Douglas T., and Vladas Griskevicius. 2013. *The Rational Animal: How Evolution Made Us Smarter than We Think*. New York: Basic Books.

Koenig, L. B., M. McGue, R. F. Krueger, and T. J. Bouchard. 2005. "Genetic and Environmental Influences on Religiousness: Findings for Retrospective and Current Religiousness Ratings." *Journal of Personality* 73, no. 2: 471–88.

Mayr, E. 1961. "Cause and Effect in Biology." *Science* 134: 1501–6.

McKay, Ryan T., and Daniel C. Dennett. 2009. "The Evolution of Misbelief." *Behavioral and Brain Sciences* 32: 493–561.

Mesoudi, A. 2011. *Cultural Evolution: How Darwinian Theory Can Explain Human Culture and Synthesize the Social Sciences*. Chicago: University of Chicago Press.

Norenzayan, A. 2013. *Big Gods: How Religion Transformed Cooperation and Conflict*. Princeton: Princeton University Press.

Norenzayan, A., and A. F. Shariff. 2008. "The Origin and Evolution of Religious Prosociality." *Science* 322: 58–62.

Norenzayan, A., A. F. Shariff, W. M. Gervais, A. K. Willard, R. McNamara, E. Slingerland, and J. Henrich. 2016. "The Cultural Evolution of Prosocial Religions." *Behavioral and Brain Sciences* 39: 1–65.

Norris, Pippa, and Ronald Inglehart. 2004. *Sacred and Secular: Religion and Politics Worldwide*. Cambridge: Cambridge University Press.

Pinker, Steven. 2012. "The False Allure of Group Selection." *Edge*, July 18. https://www.edge.org/conversation/steven_pinker-the-false-allure-of -group-selection.

Purzycki, Benjamin Grant, Coren Apicella, Quentin D. Atkinson, Emma Cohen, Rita Anne McNamara, Aiyana K. Willard, Dimitris Xygalatas, Ara Norenzayan, and Joseph Henrich. 2016. "Moralistic Gods, Supernatural Punishment and the Expansion of Human Sociality." *Nature* 530: 327–30.

Rowthorn, Robert. 2011. "Religion, Fertility and Genes: A Dual Inheritance Model." *Proceedings of the Royal Society B: Biological Sciences* 278, no. 1717: 2519–27.

Ruffle, B., and R. Sosis. 2007. "Does It Pay to Pray? Costly Ritual and Cooperation." *B.E. Journal of Economic Analysis and Policy* 7, Article 18: 1–35.

Schloss, J.P., and M. Murray, eds. 2009. *The Believing Primate: Scientific, Philosophical, and Theological Perspectives on the Origin of Religion*. Oxford: Oxford University Press.

Scott-Phillips, Thomas C., Thomas E. Dickins, and Stuart A. West. 2011. "Evolutionary Theory and the Ultimate-Proximate Distinction in the

Human Behavioral Sciences." *Perspectives on Psychological Science* 6, no. 1: 38–47.

Searcy, William A., and Stephen Nowicki. 2005. *The Evolution of Animal Communication: Reliability and Deception in Signaling Systems.* Princeton: Princeton University Press.

Shah, Timothy Samuel, and Monica Duffy Toft. 2006. "Why God Is Winning." *Foreign Policy* 155, July/August: 39–43.

Shariff, A. F., and A. Norenzayan. 2007. "God Is Watching You: Supernatural Agent Concepts Increase Prosocial Behavior in an Anonymous Economic Game." *Psychological Science* 18, no. 9: 803–9.

Shariff, A. F., A. Norenzayan, and J. Henrich. 2009. "The Birth of High Gods: How the Cultural Evolution of Supernatural Policing Agents Influenced the Emergence of Complex, Cooperative Human Societies, Paving the Way for Civilization." In *Evolution, Culture, and the Human Mind*, edited by M. Schaller, A. Norenzayan, S. Heine, T. Yamagishi, and T. Kameda, 119–36. New York: Psychology Press.

Shariff, Azim F., Aiyana K. Willard, Teresa Andersen, and Ara Norenzayan. 2016. "Religious Priming: A Meta-Analysis with a Focus on Prosociality." *Personality and Social Psychology Review* 20, no. 1: 27–48.

Sosis, Richard. 2003a. "Book Review of D. S. Wilson's *Darwin's Cathedral: Evolution, Religion, and the Nature of Society.*" *Evolution and Human Behavior* 24: 137–43.

———. 2003b. "Why Aren't We All Hutterites? Costly Signaling Theory and Religious Behavior." *Human Nature* 14: 91–127.

———. 2006. "Religious Behaviors, Badges, and Bans: Signaling Theory and the Evolution of Religion." In *Where God and Science Meet: How Brain and Evolutionary Studies Alter Our Understanding of Religion*, edited by Patrick McNamara, 61–86. Westport, Conn.: Praeger.

———. 2009. "The Adaptationist-Byproduct Debate on the Evolution of Religion: Five Misunderstandings of the Adaptationist Program." *Journal of Cognition and Culture* 9: 315–32.

———. 2011. "Why Sacred Lands Are Not Indivisible: The Cognitive Foundations of Sacralizing Land." *Journal of Terrorism Research* 2: 17–44.

Sosis, Richard, and Candace Alcorta. 2003. "Signaling, Solidarity, and the Sacred: The Evolution of Religious Behavior." *Evolutionary Anthropology* 12: 264–74.

Sosis, Richard, and W. Penn Handwerker. 2011. "Psalms and Coping with Uncertainty: Israeli Women's Responses to the 2006 Lebanon War." *American Anthropologist* 113: 40–55.

Standen, V., and R. Foley. 1989. *Comparative Socioecology: The Behavioural Ecology of Humans and Animals.* Oxford: Blackwell Scientific.

Tinbergen, N. 1963. "On Aims and Methods in Ethology." *Zeitschrift für Tierpsychologie* 20:410–33.

Trivers, Robert L. 1972. "Parental Investment and Sexual Selection." In *Sexual Selection and the Descent of Man*, edited by Bernard Campbell, 136–79. Chicago: Aldine.

———. 2011. *Deceit and Self-Deception: Fooling Yourself the Better to Fool Others.* London: Allen Lane.

VanderWeele, Tyler J. 2017. "On the Promotion of Human Flourishing." *Proceedings of the National Academy of Sciences (PNAS)* 31: 8148–56.

von Hippel, W., and R. Trivers. 2011. "The Evolution and Psychology of Self-Deception." *Behavioral and Brain Sciences* 34: 1–56.

Wade, Nicholas. 2009. *The Faith Instinct: How Religion Evolved and Why It Endures.* New York: Penguin.

West, S. A., C. El Mouden, and A. Gardner. 2011. "16 Common Misconceptions about the Evolution of Cooperation in Humans." *Evolution and Human Behavior* 32: 231–62.

Whitehouse, Harvey, and Jonathan A. Lanman. 2014. "The Ties That Bind Us: Ritual, Fusion, and Identification." *Current Anthropology* 55, no. 6: 674–95.

Whitehouse, Harvey, and Brian McQuinn. 2013. "Ritual and Violence: Divergent Modes of Religiosity and Armed Struggle." In *Oxford Handbook of Religion and Violence*, edited by M. Juergensmeyer, M. Kitts, and M. Jerryson, 597–619. Oxford: Oxford Univeristy Press.

Williams, G. C. 1966. *Adaptation and Natural Selection.* Princeton: Princeton University Press.

Wilson, David Sloan. 2002. *Darwin's Cathedral: Evolution, Religion, and the Nature of Society.* Chicago: University of Chicago Press.

———. 2005. "Testing Major Evolutionary Hypotheses about Religion with a Random Sample." *Human Nature* 16, no. 4: 419–46.

———. 2006. "Human Groups as Adaptive Units: Toward a Permanent Consensus." In *The Innate Mind: Culture and Cognition*, edited by P. Carruthers, S. Laurence, and S. Stich. Oxford: Oxford University Press.

Wilson, David Sloan, and Elliott Sober. 1994. "Reintroducing Group Selection to the Human Behavioural Sciences." *Behavioral and Brain Sciences* 17, no. 4: 585–654.

Wright, Robert. 1994. *The Moral Animal: Why We Are the Way We Are; The New Science of Evolutionary Psychology.* New York: Random House.

———. 2009. *The Evolution of God.* New York: Little, Brown.

Zahavi, A. 1975. "Mate Selection—A Selection for a Handicap." *Journal of Theoretical Biology* 53: 205–14.

7

RELIGIONS HELP US TRUST ONE ANOTHER

Adam B. Cohen

What Is Religion? What Is Flourishing?

In this volume, we are encouraged to think explicitly and critically about what we mean by religion and flourishing.

While many scholars who study religion focus on belief in supernatural agents, I agree with the prior chapters in this volume who argue that is a Western, and in some ways restrictive, view of religion. In this chapter, I am going to be talking about religious costly signals—like circumcising one's child, among many others. These can be motivated by very many things—including, certainly, belief in supernatural agents. Many Jews, for example, surely circumcise their sons because it is a divine commandment to do so. However, people often in engage in religious behaviors because of tradition, because they find rituals emotionally satisfying, because their communities expect them to, because it is simply a way of life. These are all fine by me, and fine by me regarding the intellectual points made in this chapter.

So how do these kinds of behaviors, and the variegated motivations for them, bear on how religion affects flourishing, in this chapter? Religious participation can certainly be emotionally satisfying, and this is surely one kind of flourishing. But it goes well beyond that. Participating in religious rituals, thinking of the panoply of motives I just discussed, as I will show below, can affect flourishing at an interpersonal level—it can help us trust each other, sometimes in surprising

85

ways (even across religious groups). Finally, religious rituals can embed us in larger communities, and continue centuries of tradition—enabling flourishing at a group level, both in the moment and across time.

Religious Costly Signals

On my son's eighth day of life, he was circumcised in a ceremony called a *brit milah*, or *bris*, continuing a tradition among Jews of literally thousands of years. Circumcision seems to have started in Genesis 17, in which Abraham was to circumcise himself and those in his household and cut off those that were not circumcised.

Positive emotions certainly abounded that day, as we were grateful for this beautiful and healthy addition to our family, surrounded by friends, and marked his entry into the Covenant, and prayed that he would lead a lifetime full of a love of learning, meaningful relationship, and good deeds (*Torah, chuppah*, and *maasim tovim*).

But it was also a difficult day, more difficult than I had imagined. And from there comes another source of flourishing. I had always imagined circumcision to be the most benign of surgeries. Indeed, the *mohel* we enlisted is a urological surgeon, who conducted the surgery as hygienically and humanely as possible, using anesthetic. Moreover, I never even considered the possibility of not ritually circumcising my son in accordance with Jewish tradition. Circumcision and the concomitant ceremony are an inviolable and formative part of Jewish identity and culture.

Nonetheless, I was distraught at the notion of my perfect and helpless son being harmed. To make matters worse, there was bleeding for quite some time, well after all of the guests had left, in what even the *mohel* urologist commented was "more blood than we like to see."

I expect these mixed feelings are common across a lot of religious traditions. Muslims also circumcise their sons, called *khitan* or *khatna*. One difference between Jewish and Muslim practices is that Jewish circumcision is to be done on the eighth day, while the age at which Muslims are circumcised varies by family and geography. Another important difference is that circumcision is not compulsory in Islam, as there is no direct verse in the Quran requiring it to be performed, but it is very strongly recommended and is known to be a *Sunnah* (custom/tradition of the prophet) because it was done by prophet Ibrahim (Abraham) and his son Ismail, and all the prophets after them observed it. Ibrahim circumcised himself at age eighty with an adze.

Religious Behaviors Can Be Puzzling

Circumcision is just one example of many religious behaviors that are hard to explain. Some religious behaviors (including circumcision) are physically risky and can endanger one's health, particularly before the advent of modern medicine. Some religious behaviors are financially onerous, like the practice of tithing. Others are vastly inconvenient. Muslims who eat only halal food must maintain constant vigilance living in a secular society like America to be sure that there are no pork products in their groceries.

It is indeed challenging to explain why people would choose to surgically alter their helpless and perfect newborn children. Indeed, many of the new atheists who are highly critical of religion consider such practices to be barbaric mutilations and disfigurements of children who are too young to consent to such procedures.

Religious behaviors like these present a puzzle as to their origins, functions, and meanings to the people who perform them, and hence, what link could there be to flourishing? The reasons why people might engage in these mystifying religious behaviors, which might be dangerous, inconvenient, or expensive, are many and varied, and different people may have different thoughts about this. But among the many reasons and functions is one interpretation that was imported from the field of biology.

The existence and functions of many animals' physical traits and behaviors are mystifying to biologists. The classic example is that a peacock has an elaborate tail, which is metabolically costly to produce and makes the animal easier to catch for predators. So why hasn't evolution stamped out this elaborate display? Evolution is supposed to be miserly and invest only in traits and behaviors that further survival and reproduction.

One explanation offered for these kinds of behaviors comes from costly signaling theory. The basic idea of costly signaling theory is that such behaviors are actually signals of the genetic quality of the organism—only a very genetically healthy and robust peacock can afford to build an elaborate tail and escape predators.

Strange as it may be to say, this logic has been imported into the psychology of religious behaviors. The idea is that circumcision, dietary laws, charity, and many other religious behaviors can be seen as signals of the commitment of the performer. Only a true believer or someone truly committed to their religious group, the thinking goes, would cut their harmless baby sons or avoid nutritious and delicious foods or give away their hard-earned money.

One immediate problem that comes up is that an imposter might want to enjoy the benefits of group living, without incurring the costs (economists and psychologists call this the free-rider problem). So, the theory goes, you want to impose restrictions that are diagnostic of the actor's sincerity, such as being too onerous to fake. Fasting for a whole month during Ramadan sure seems like that.

Following the logic of the peacock's tail, one might suppose that religious behaviors signal something—such as the commitment of the performer to his or her religious group. And the harder the signal is to fake, because it is costly or difficult to perform, the more you should pay attention to that signal.

Religion and Trust Research

Consider running into a profile on Facebook. It has a picture of a nice-enough-looking guy. His name is Ali. He is a biology major, his favorite color is green, and he says he likes pizza, hamburgers, and tacos but does not like ice cream. There's information about his religion, too. Ali is Muslim, believes in a God who forgives people, and does not donate money regularly to Muslim charities. In terms of hobbies, he likes movies, reading, and rock climbing.

Based on this admittedly impoverished information, do you find the person trustworthy? Would you lend him money or let him babysit your children? Or would you not feel comfortable making yourself vulnerable to him if you cannot control or monitor his actions? What about his profile makes you feel that way?

In our research, nearly four hundred ASU undergraduate Christian participants in our first study saw one of eight versions of this profile.[1] It was always the same picture of Ali, he was always a biology major, he always liked pizza, hamburgers, and tacos and rock climbing (I like rock climbing; as with parenting this would have been a lot easier if I had started decades ago), and he always didn't like ice cream. But other aspects of the profile varied. Half of the subjects saw Ali describe himself as a Christian and half Muslim. Half of the participants saw Ali say he believed in a punishing God versus a forgiving God, and half saw an Ali that gave to charity and half saw an Ali that did not give to charities associated with his religion. That is, there was every possible combination of being Christian or Muslim; believing in a forgiving or punishing God; and giving or not giving to charities.

After participants saw the profile, we asked them how much they trusted the person in the profile with 6 questions, which we combined into one trust scale: whether Ali (a) was benevolent, (b) had integrity, (c) had the ability to be trustworthy, and (d) was trustworthy, as well as (e) whether they would lend the target money and expect to get it back, and (f) whether they would trust the target with a sensitive secret.

Contrary to our predictions, the person in the Christian profile and the Muslim profile were trusted very much the same. Also contrary to our predictions, participants trusted targets who believed in a forgiving God as much as they trusted targets who believed in a punishing God.

Consistent with our predictions, when Ali donated to religious charities, he was trusted more than when he did not. But you will remember that our prediction was a little more subtle than that—that if Ali was Christian, donating to a Christian charity would make Christian subjects trust him more, but we also predicted that Christian subjects would trust Ali less if he were a Muslim donating to Muslim charities. However, we found no evidence for this prediction. Critically, donating to charity made subjects trust Ali more, regardless of whether he was Christian or Muslim.

In the experiment just described, Ali always looked the same, regardless of whether he was portrayed as Christian or Muslim, and whether he gave to charity or not. In a second experiment we made the difference in his religious affiliation more noticeable by using different pictures for Muslim and Christian profiles, with the Muslim ones (male and female) wearing traditional Muslim headgear, to make their ostensible religious affiliations more salient (a *hijab* or a *kefiyah*). In this experiment, even with this change, we found the very same pattern as we did in the experiment just described. Participants trusted targets who donated to religious charities more than those who did not, and again, donating to charity made the target person more trustworthy, regardless of whether he was portrayed as Christian or Muslim. This result, again, was suggesting that people trusted members of other religions as much as members of their own, and more commitment (even to another religion) meant more trust.

What if these results had little to do with religion, but were being driven by the fact that the person in the profiles was giving to charities (Christian charities and Muslim charities)? People could have been seeing charitableness as a good trait, and not been keying in too much on whether the charity was Christian or Muslim. This could have been why the participants trusted the charitable person in the profile more.

So, we changed our method further. In a third experiment, we asked participants to read different versions of a scenario about a man named Samir, who worked as a software engineer at a large company. This scenario had no picture of Samir and did not describe him as giving charity. Instead, in the scenario, he attended a work dinner at a steakhouse. Samir was very hungry because he had not eaten that day, but when he got to the restaurant, he realized that the food was not halal. The scenario goes on to explain that Samir either did or did not eat the food.

Some other participants saw a slightly different scenario in which the scenario was altered to make Sam a Catholic, who either did or did not eat meat at a steakhouse despite having given up meat for Lent. Another bunch of participants did not receive information about whether Sam or Samir ate the food, because we wanted to find out if adhering to religious dietary restrictions made people trust someone more, or if disregarding them would make people trust someone less, or both.

We measured trust as in the above experiments. When Sam or Samir did not eat the meat, he was most trusted. When Sam or Samir ate the meat anyway, he was least trusted. When no information was given about what he eats, trust was in the middle. Again, as in the prior experiments, these patterns were essentially identical, whether Catholic or Muslim.

In our next study we tried to assess people's views about links between religion and trustworthiness in a much more subtle way. We relied on a pervasive error people make in their judgments called the conjunction fallacy. When you make the conjunction fallacy, you think that two things happening together are more probable than one of those things happening by itself, because the combination of the two things just sounds more plausible than one of the things.

We used a scenario about a person, Mr. R., who either behaved in a very trustworthy or a very untrustworthy way. In the trustworthy story, Mr. R. backed into someone's car, and even though he could have just driven away, he left a note with his information. He found a wallet and returned it to its owner, even though he could have kept the money. In another version of the story, seen by a different set of participants, he behaved in a highly untrustworthy way, pretending to leave a note on the dented car, and keeping the money from the lost wallet.

We then asked our participants to pick the most likely option: (a) that Mr. R. was Catholic, (b) that he was Catholic and did obey all of his religion's rules and requirements, or (c) that he was Catholic and did not obey all of his religion's rules and requirements.

The logically and mathematically correct answer is (a), because the probability that he is Catholic *and* obeys his religion (or that he is Catholic *and doesn't* obey his religion) cannot be greater than the probability that he is just Catholic. Sometimes people do pick this correct answer, but people will very commonly pick a mathematically incorrect answer that just feels like it fits their vision of the person described better.

Regarding the untrustworthy scenario, the most common choice people picked was that Mr. R. was both Catholic and did not obey his religion. Virtually none of the participants in this condition thought a religious Mr. R. would have behaved in this untrustworthy way.

But these results were just about completely flipped when Mr. R. was highly trustworthy. People commonly thought he would be just Catholic or Catholic and obey his religion—almost no one thought this trustworthy man would be both Catholic and not obey his religion.

Now, what happens when Mr. R. is Muslim, as opposed to Catholic? The same thing. Again, if Mr. R. had been untrustworthy, the most common choice was that he was both Muslim and did not obey his religion's rules, and virtually no one picked that he would be both Muslim and obey his religion's rules.

In contrast, when Muslim Mr. R. was highly trustworthy, the most common choices were about evenly split for people to think he was either just Muslim or that he was Muslim and did obey his religion's rules. Critically, it was only a tiny minority of participants who thought he was Muslim and did not obey his religion's rules.

These results strongly suggest that people associate being trustworthy with being religious, regardless of whether the actor in the story is Christian or Muslim. Conversely, people associate being untrustworthy with being nonreligious, regardless of whether the actor in the story is Christian or Muslim.

Even Our Brains and Hearts Trust Religious People

Not being satisfied investigating a topic as important as religion and trust in our society by just using paper and pencil surveys, we have also investigated how people's brains and bodies help to make trust decisions.[2] Our participants played two trust-related games in the lab, ostensibly with a partner about which they read information. The partner was actually fictitious. In one of the games, the partner was supposedly relaying information about whether a coin toss landed on heads or tails, over and over again. The actual participant was to judge whether the fictitious partner was giving them true or false information (whether they trusted the partner), and the better judgments they made, the more money the participant stood to gain.

Actually the judgments were made randomly by a computer, but appeared to be made by a partner, presented as being either Christian or Muslim, and as either doing costly religious behaviors (like charity) or not. During this experiment, we measured people's brain activity via EEG. We paid particular attention to a certain pattern of brain activity (alpha desynchronization) along a certain set of sites (centro-parietal), measured via electrodes placed on the scalp. We saw more of this brain activity when a participant decided to trust the fictitious partner that costly signaled, and when the participant decided to distrust the fictitious partner that did not costly signal. Therefore, this relation between brain activity and trust decisions closely followed whether the fictitious partner was portrayed as being religious in a costly way but did not track at all whether the interaction partner was supposedly Christian versus Muslim.

These results show that our brains don't process information in a way that cares about whether our interaction partner is Christian or Muslim. Our brain processing does key in on whether the person is walking the walk and performing costly and inconvenient religious behaviors. When they are, our brain processing reflects an attitude of trust, and this pattern of brain activity prepares us to put our financial outcomes in their hands to a greater extent than when the person does not engage in religious behaviors.

This brainwave experiment indicated two important conclusions. First, it provided powerful evidence that people are not just placating the experimenters when they tell us they trust members of other groups or trust religious people more. Inasmuch as people can delude themselves or us, and paper and pencil survey measures can thus be inaccurate, people were surely not faking their brain activity. Second, this work provided important insights into how the brain processes information when it comes to trust decisions.

A second physiological experiment also supported similar conclusions, that our inclination is to trust people who engage in religious behaviors, whether they are of the same religion as ourselves, or not. In a somewhat similar lab experiment, we had participants playing the economic trust game, again with a fictional partner. The experimenter gave the participant a payment of $20, and the participant was told that they could hand over none or all or any amount of that payment to another participant. This fictitious partner was experimentally manipulated to have described themselves as being either Muslim or Christian, and as engaging in inconvenient and costly religious behaviors (like volunteering time to religious causes).

Once the participant decided to hand over some money to the partner, that money was tripled by the experiment (if the participant kept $5 and handed over $15, that $15 was tripled to $45). Then the participant was led to believe that the partner could decide to keep any amount of that $45 or hand any amount back to the participant. The more the actual participant trusts the fictitious participant, the more money they should hand over, because the fictitious partner might be generous and give back more money than the participant might have gotten by keeping all of the money for him or herself. While reading the profile of the other presumed participant and making the decision about how much (if any) money to hand over, the participant's peripheral autonomic physiology was measured, including their heart rate.

While believing they are interacting with a religious partner, participants showed faster heart rates and invested more money, perhaps indicating greater physiological engagement with the task and the ostensible interaction partner. Now oftentimes physiological data are hard to interpret. Changes in heart rate can indicate any number of emotional states, including being in love, being happy, or being angry or disgusted or nervous. You always have to make a little bit of a leap of faith when trying to link physiological activity to emotions. However, putting all of the results I have described in this paper together, it seems to be a fair interpretation to say that we trust religious people in our hearts, and our hearts don't seem to care whether someone shares our religion to be able to trust them.

Lots of Groups Trust Religious People

All the evidence in this paper so far, with a variety of experimental methods and even recordings from our brains and hearts, shows that being from different religions can facilitate trust. But the survey and physiological studies I have described so far have all been in ASU undergraduates. Do other people show the same effects of religion and trust?

It's not just ASU undergraduate Christians who show that religious behaviors increase trust, regardless of whether they are done by someone from the same group or a different religious group. We have replicated these findings with samples run on the internet, and by soliciting community participants from religious institutions like churches and mosques. The same relations I have been discussing between religion and trust occur whether participants are Catholics, Muslims, or even atheists.

Conclusion

The results described in this essay show how a kind of religious behavior—behaviors that can function as costly signals—can robustly promote one source of intrapersonal, interpersonal, group, and intertemporal flourishing.

References

Blais, Chris, Derek M. Ellis, Kimberly M. Wingert, Adam B. Cohen, and Gene A. Brewer Jr. In press. "Alpha Suppression over Parietal Electrode Sites Predicts Decisions to Trust." *Social Neuroscience.*

Hall, Deborah, Adam B. Cohen, Kaitlyn K. Meyer, Allison Varley, and Gene A. Brewer Jr. 2015. "Costly Signaling Increases Trust, Even across Religious Affiliations." *Psychological Science* 26: 1368–76.

8

RELIGION'S CONTRIBUTION TO PROSOCIALITY

Azim F. Shariff

What is the relationship between religion and prosociality? Opinions run hot while discussions of data run scant. Here, I'll review where the evidence stands on three much-debated questions, each addressing a different angle of the religion-prosociality relationship. In doing so, I'll draw not just on primary research that we've conducted in my lab, but also on two large meta-analyses we've conducted that bring together most of the empirical tests of religious prosociality from the last several decades.

Are the Religious More Prosocial? State of the Evidence

Though this question has enjoyed decades of empirical investigation, the literature has yet to offer up a firm and conclusive answer. Our meta-analysis does not provide one either, but it does summarize the 182 effects (across 99 samples involving nearly a quarter-million subjects) that fit our inclusion criteria.[1] Studies were included if they featured (a) some individual-level measure of religiosity, and (b) one or more dependent variables related to prosociality or antisociality. Overall, we found a small but consistent effect whereby the religious participants exhibited more prosociality and less antisociality than nonreligious participants, $r = .11$, $t(181) = 7.12$, $p < .001$.

However, this was a heterogeneous set of studies, from large representative surveys to small laboratory experiments conducted on undergraduates. We investigated how these and other factors (e.g., pro- versus antisociality measures, religious affiliation vs religious attendance, student versus nonstudent samples) moderated the overall effect we found. Few did, but one of the key differences between studies in this literature was that many studies used self-report measures of prosociality (e.g., answering questions about charitability or volunteerism), whereas many others used behavioral measures (e.g., economic games, like the dictator game). This distinction did appear to moderate the overall effect. Whereas religious people scored higher on self-report measures ($r = .16$, $t(180) = 9.31$, $p < .001$), this difference disappeared with behavioral measures, $r = .01$, $t(180) = 0.59$, $p = .55$ (fig. 8.1).

Now, there are two major explanations for this discrepancy—one focuses on the limitations of the self-report measures and another focuses on the limitations of the behavioral measures. The first and most obvious explanation is that the self-report measures are misaligned with reality, and the differences between religious and nonreligious reports of religiosity instead reflect differences in socially desirable responding. There is some evidence recommending this interpretation. Religious people routinely score higher on measures of self-enhancement—the tendency to see and report oneself in a positive light.[2] Is there something about religions that pressures their adherents to adopt or present rosier views of themselves?

Perhaps, but Sedikides and Gebauer actually argue for the opposite causal direction: religion doesn't make people more likely to self-enhance, instead, those high in self-enhancement are motivated to seek out different ways of satisfying that motive for seeing oneself as good. Religion can serve as such a tool—an idea proposed by Batson and Stocks (2004), among others. As Sedikides and Gebauer write, "It follows that people will be likely also to use religiosity, when readily available in the cultural context, to elevate the positivity of their self-views."[4] Thus, religious people report being more prosocial because self-enhancement is a third variable that makes them more religious *and* makes them want to appear or believe themselves to be more prosocial.

But this could be taken further. Given that being religious is also socially desirable and is also only measured by self-report, people's reports of their religiosity may *themselves* be inflated[5]—and, critically, by the same people inflating their reports of prosociality. We would expect that high self-enhancers would report higher religiosity and higher prosociality. On the other hand, those low in self-enhancement

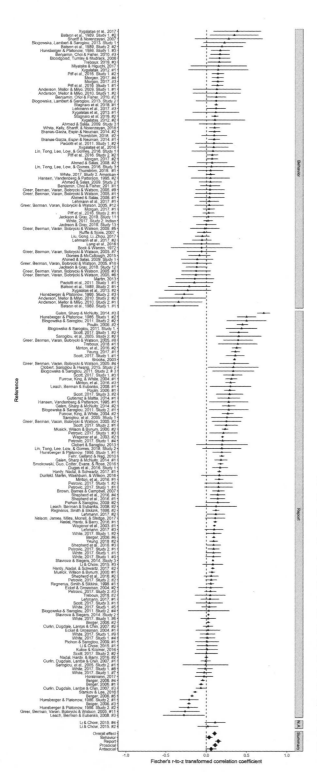

FIG. 8.1 FOREST
PLOT STUDIES THAT
CORRELATE RELIGIOSITY
WITH MEASURES OF
PROSOCIALITY AND
ANTISOCIALITY, BROKEN
DOWN BY WHETHER THE
DEPENDENT MEASURE
WAS BEHAVIORAL
(TOP HALF) OR SELF-
REPORT (BOTTOM
HALF). OVERALL, THE
RELIGIOUS WERE SHOWN
TO BE MORE PROSOCIAL
WHEN THIS WAS
MEASURED USING SELF-
REPORT, BUT NOT WHEN
THIS WAS MEASURED
BEHAVIORALLY.[3]

would be more honest in their reports, reporting lower religiosity and lower prosociality. Thus the relationship between reported religiosity and reported prosociality may not be correlating two independent constructs but instead simply be reflecting the differences between low and high self-enhancers. At the very least, we can expect that some of this relationship is due to this weakness of the self-report method.

However, we cannot wholly defer to the behavioral measures either. Psychologists have devised an ingenious array of tasks in hopes of capturing some real-world behavior within our labs. Isolating variables in those tightly controlled settings has many benefits, but the distance between the lab and the real world often strains how widely we can cast our conclusions. Does the fact that a religious person is no more generous that a nonreligious person in a dictator game played in the basement of a psychology department, or refuses to pick up "accidentally" dropped pencils, really indicate that she doesn't give more to charity when at home? It may contribute a small piece of evidence in support of such a claim, but it is far from conclusive.

The correlational research is also limited in terms of what it can tell us about whether religion is a causal force in prosociality. Asking whether the religious are more prosocial than the nonreligious is of course not the same as asking whether religion *causes* people to be more prosocial. The answers could be no and yes, respectively, if there were other, separate factors that encouraged the nonreligious to be prosocial. For example, there is some research showing that the nonreligious are more prosocially motivated by empathy,[6] whereas the religious are more motivated by divine commandment.[7] Both could be effective causal paths to prosociality. Thus, the next section reviews and evaluates the causal evidence for religion on prosociality.

Conclusion: A summary of the evidence produces mixed results, showing a religious advantage for self-report measures of prosociality and no advantage on behavioral measures of prosociality. Both measures have severe limitations, however.

Causal Evidence?

In the absence of randomly assigning newborn twins to be religious or atheistic, we are forced to use less conclusive methods to study the causal impact of religion on prosociality. One such method takes advantage of momentary experimental manipulations to investigate whether the religious situation has more of an effect on people's thoughts and behavior than does the religious disposition. For example, does having

FIG. 8.2 FOREST PLOT SHOWING THE RESULTS OF 25 STUDIES INVOLVING
RELIGIOUS PRIMING AND PROSOCIALITY DEPENDENT MEASURES. A POSITIVE
EFFECT EMERGED OVERALL AND WAS FOUND TO BE STRONGER AMONG RELIGIOUS
BELIEVERS.[9]

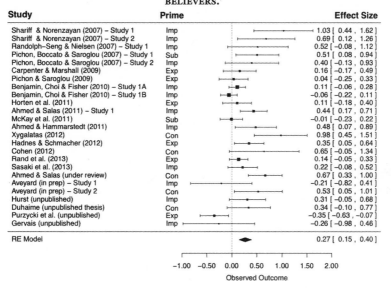

Study	Prime	Effect Size
Shariff & Norenzayan (2007) – Study 1	Imp	1.03 [0.44 , 1.62]
Shariff & Norenzayan (2007) – Study 2	Imp	0.69 [0.12 , 1.26]
Randolph–Seng & Nielsen (2007) – Study 1	Imp	0.52 [−0.08 , 1.12]
Pichon, Boccato & Saroglou (2007) – Study 1	Sub	0.51 [0.08 , 0.94]
Pichon, Boccato & Saroglou (2007) – Study 2	Imp	0.40 [−0.13 , 0.93]
Carpenter & Marshall (2009)	Exp	0.16 [−0.17 , 0.49]
Pichon & Saroglou (2009)	Exp	0.04 [−0.25 , 0.33]
Benjamin, Choi & Fisher (2010) – Study 1A	Imp	0.11 [−0.06 , 0.28]
Benjamin, Choi & Fisher (2010) – Study 1B	Imp	−0.06 [−0.22 , 0.11]
Horten et al. (2011)	Exp	0.11 [−0.18 , 0.40]
Ahmed & Salas (2011) – Study 1	Imp	0.44 [0.17 , 0.71]
McKay et al. (2011)	Sub	−0.01 [−0.23 , 0.22]
Ahmed & Hammarstedt (2011)	Imp	0.48 [0.07 , 0.89]
Xygalatas (2012)	Con	0.98 [0.45 , 1.51]
Hadnes & Schmacher (2012)	Exp	0.35 [0.05 , 0.64]
Cohen (2012)	Con	0.65 [−0.05 , 1.34]
Rand et al. (2013)	Exp	0.14 [−0.05 , 0.33]
Sasaki et al. (2013)	Imp	0.22 [−0.08 , 0.52]
Ahmed & Salas (under review)	Con	0.67 [0.33 , 1.00]
Aveyard (in prep) – Study 1	Imp	−0.21 [−0.82 , 0.41]
Aveyard (in prep) – Study 2	Con	0.53 [0.05 , 1.01]
Hurst (unpublished)	Imp	0.31 [−0.05 , 0.68]
Duhaime (unpublished thesis)	Con	0.34 [−0.10 , 0.77]
Purzycki et al. (unpublished)	Exp	−0.35 [−0.63 , −0.07]
Gervais (unpublished)	Imp	−0.26 [−0.98 , 0.46]
RE Model		0.27 [0.15 , 0.40]

−1.00 −0.50 0.00 0.50 1.00 1.50 2.00
Observed Outcome

participants read a religious passage or making them implicitly think
about God make them more generous? Dozens of studies have now
taken advantage of this method of religious "priming" to study its
effect on prosocial behavior. In a recent meta-analysis of all the studies
published to that point, we found consistent evidence that across the
various types of religious priming (e.g., subliminal priming in which
religious concepts are aroused below the threshold of consciousness,
or contextual priming including environmental factors such as the
presence of church buildings or prayer calls), there was consistent
evidence that such priming increased prosocial behavior (fig. 8.2).
The effect size was comparable to the mean effect size found in social
psychological studies.[8]

A subset of these studies allowed us to separately include the effects
for religious/high-religious and non-religious/low-religious participants. Meta-analyzing these studies shows there to be an even stronger
effect for the religious/non-religious participants ($g = 0.38$), and no
significant priming effect for the non-religious/low-religious participants ($g = 0.12$).

These studies, and indeed the meta-analysis thereof, have not been without criticism.[10] As psychologists have become more stringent in their experimental methods, they have begun employing techniques to reduce the likelihood of false positive results. Among these are larger sample sizes (which reduce flukes) and the preregistration of designs, hypotheses, and analyses (which reduces "researcher degrees of freedom," and thereby the ability of researchers to massage the data until they give up desired results). My collaborators and I have made use of both techniques in order to run more stringent versions of the religious priming studies. These eschew the embattled implicit priming technique in lieu of a more explicit and face-valid manipulation: simply asking participants to "think about God." In five preregistered studies, we have consistently found that doing so prompts religious believers—but, crucially, not nonbelievers—to give more to anonymous strangers in a dictator game.[11]

Taken altogether, the religious priming research indicates that prompting people to think about God does indeed cause them to be more prosocial. How do we reconcile this finding with the absence of a difference between how religious and nonreligious people behave—often on the same tasks—at baseline? If religious priming works, it is clearly not sufficient to encourage the religious to be *consistently* more prosocial. The conclusion I've arrived at in my reading of the literature is that the impact of religious primes is ephemeral—constantly being re-upped in order to return thoughts of God and religion to consciousness (which could explain the ubiquity of reminders of religion). The most compelling evidence for this is a study by Duhaime (2015), who investigated modified dictator game behavior among Moroccan shopkeepers during and in between the audible call to prayer. The participants were, at baseline, already very generous, but became even more so when the *azan* could be heard. However, this contextual religious priming effect was short-lived, disappearing after as little as twenty minutes. As a result, the current evidence suggests that a religious *disposition* is not sufficient to elicit more prosocial behavior. It needs to be repeatedly activated with a religious *situation*.

Conclusion: Tightly controlled religious priming research consistently shows that thinking about aspects of religion encourages believers, but not nonbelievers, to act more prosocially—at least temporarily.

Is Religious Prosociality Parochial?

When presented with evidence suggesting the religious are more charitable, or further that religion *causes* people to act more charitably, the next question is often about to whom they are being charitable. The selflessness of religious prosociality is diminished by implications that its selflessness is parochial—extended to kith and kin, but not beyond, and certainly not to religious outgroups.

Theoretically, in-group parochiality makes evolutionary sense. Societies that encouraged their members to be as generous to outgroup members as to ingroup ones left themselves vulnerable to exploitation. Outgroup members could freeride with impunity—accepting the generosity without any incentive to join or contribute to the group. This doesn't mean that it was culturally maladaptive to be generous to outgroup members *at all*.[12] However, mathematical modeling suggests that outgroup generosity needs to be less than that extended to the ingroup.

Empirically, we are nowhere close to resolving this question. Brooks (2006) observed that, while religious people do report giving more to religious charities than the nonreligious, they also report giving more to secular charities. But, as mentioned, correlational data based on self-reports come with caveats. Few studies have used priming methods to investigate the question. Preston and Ritter (2013) report that priming "religion" led to preferential generosity to ingroup members, whereas priming "God" increased prosociality to outgroup members. However, the combination of a convoluted method, (very) small sample sizes, and marginally significant effects mean that their conclusions should be interpreted with caution.

My team has been recently investigating this question with a straightforward research design that allows for larger sample sizes and thus more reliable results.[13] To do so, we have had online participants play a series of dictator games, some of which precede the injunction to "think about God," and some follow. Moreover, we give a (rigged) profile of the potential recipient of the participant's generosity. Each participant would play a dictator game with either ingroup targets or outgroup targets, one before receiving a prime, and one afterwards.

In one study, each participant (all of who were Christians) would be the dictators in a game with either Christians or Muslims as the recipients. Replicating our prior research, the results showed that participants were more generous following the invocation to think about God ($b = .014$, $p < .0001$). Thus, there was a main effect of prime. And as would be expected, collapsed across priming conditions, Christians gave more to Christians than to Muslims, albeit marginally. So there was a marginal main effect of target. However, the key question was whether the religious prime-motivated increase would be larger for Christians than for Muslims. That is, would there be a spreading interaction such that religiously inspired prosociality would preferentially be directed toward ingroup rather than outgroup members? As the left side of figure 8.3 indicates, this was not the case. There was no interaction; the prime nearly identically increased the degree to which Christians gave to both Christians and Muslims[14] ($b = .001$, $p = .83$). So, while it did not dissolve group differences by equalizing the total amount given to the ingroup and outgroup, nor did it exacerbate those differences by motivating Christians to primarily give more to other Christians.

However, despite the well-documented unpopularity of Muslims in America, they are still believers. It may be that religiously inspired prosociality is extended impartially to other People of the Book, or other religious believers, but not across the theist-atheist divide. As a result, we conducted another study with atheists as the outgroup target. Christians were again the ingroup target, and we added a third "unspecified" target group, for which we provided the other demographics information about the target, just not their religion. The pre- and post-prime conditions made for a 3×2 mixed design. Here, again, there were two main effects, but no interaction between the prime and the target. In other words, the God prime increased how much Christians shared in the dictator game, and the amount it did so did not differ whether the target was a Christian, an atheist, or unspecified (fig. 8.3, right side).

FIG. 8.3 WHILE THE PREDICTABLE MAIN EFFECTS EMERGE, DICTATOR GAME STUDIES SHOW NO INTERACTION BETWEEN THE RELIGIOUS PRIME AND THE INGROUP VERSUS OUTGROUP NATURE OF THE TARGETS. THIS SUGGESTS THAT RELIGIOUS PRIMING LEADS TO ROUGHLY EQUAL INCREASES IN GENEROSITY EXTENDED TO MEMBER OF THE INGROUP AND THE OUTGROUP.[15]

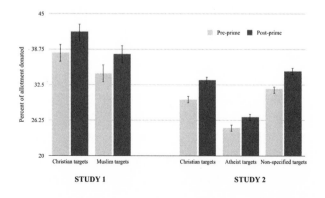

These data support the idea of religious prosociality being equally extended to outgroups (even atheists), rather than being preferentially extended to the ingroup. Similar effects have been found in Fiji, Israel, and Palestine, with Hindu, Jewish, and Muslim samples.[16] We can't freely generalize to all religions and all places at all times, but from this diverse sample, we are finding consistent results that prosociality inspired by religion is less parochial than many would have suspected.

Conclusion: Though it may be intuitive, there is little evidence that religiously inspired prosociality is parochial. Instead there is emerging evidence that it is universally extended.

The findings reviewed here will not be the final word on the connection between religion and prosociality. However, the empirical approach they have taken—however imperfect—has provided a better foothold toward understanding whether and how religion contributes to prosociality than the prior centuries of empirically weak and unconstrained debate.

References

Batson, C. D., and E. L. Stocks. 2004. "Religion: Its Core Psychological Functions." In *Handbook of Experimental Existential Psychology: An Emerging Synthesis*, edited by T. Pyszczynski, S. L. Koole, and J. Greenberg, 141–55. New York: Guilford.

Billingsley, J., C. Gomes, and M. McCullough. 2018. "Implicit and Explicit Influences of Religious Cognition on Dictator Game Transfers." *Royal Society Open Science* 5. doi: 10.1098/rsos.170238.

Brooks, A. C. 2006. *Who Really Cares: The Surprising Truth about Compassionate Conservatism*. New York: Basic Books.

Cox, D., R. P. Jones, and J. Navarro-Rivera. 2014. *I Know What You Did Last Sunday: Measuring Social Desirability Bias in Self-Reported Religious Behavior, Belief, and Identity*. Washington, DC: Public Religion Research Institute. http://publicreligion.org/site/wp-content/uploads/2014/05/AAPOR-2014-Final.pdf.

Duhaime, E. P. 2015. "Is the Call to Prayer a Call to Cooperate? A Field Experiment on the Impact of Religious Salience on Prosocial Behavior." *Judgment and Decision Making* 10, no. 6: 593.

Gervais, W. M., and M. B. Najle. 2018. "How Many Atheists Are There?" *Social Psychological and Personality Science* 9, no. 1: 3–11. https://doi.org/10.1177/1948550617707015.

Ginges, J., M. Pasek, J. M. Kelly, C. Shackelford, C. White, A. Norenzayan, and A. F. Shariff. 2020. *No Evidence That Religious Prosociality Is Parochial*. Unpublished manuscript. The New School for Social Research.

Hadaway, C. K., P. L. Marler, and M. Chaves. 1998. "Overreporting Church Attendance in America: Evidence That Demands the Same Verdict." *American Sociological Review* 63, no. 1: 122–30.

Kelly, J. M., S. R. Kramer, and A. F. Shariff. 2018. *Self-Report Measures, but Not Behavioral Measures, Suggest a Religious Advantage in Prosociality: A Meta-Analysis.* Unpublished manuscript. Irvine: University of California.

Piazza, J., and J. F. Landy. 2013. "'Lean Not on Your Own Understanding': Belief That Morality Is Founded on Divine Authority and Non-Utilitarian Moral Thinking." *Judgment and Decision Making* 8, no. 6: 639–61.

Preston, J. L., and R. S. Ritter. 2013. "Different Effects of Religion and God on Prosociality with the Ingroup and Outgroup." *Personality and Social Psychology Bulletin* 39, no. 11: 1471–83.

Richard, F. D., C. F. Bond Jr., and J. J. Stokes-Zoota. 2003. "One Hundred Years of Social Psychology Quantitatively Described." *Review of General Psychology* 7: 331–63.

Saslow, L. R., R. Willer, M. Feinberg, P. K. Piff, K. Clark, D. Keltner, and S. R. Saturn. 2013. "My Brother's Keeper? Compassion Predicts Generosity More among Less Religious Individuals." *Social Psychological and Personality Science* 4, no. 1: 31–38.

Sedikides, C., and J. E. Gebauer. 2010. "Religiosity as Self-Enhancement: A Meta-Analysis of the Relation between Socially Desirable Responding and Religiosity." *Personality and Social Psychology Review* 14: 17–36.

Shariff, A. F., A. K. Willard, T. Andersen, and A. Norenzayan. 2016. "Religious Priming: A Meta-Analysis with a Focus on Prosociality." *Personality and Social Psychology Review* 20, no. 1: 27–48.

Stark, R. 1996. *The Rise of Christianity: How the Obscure, Marginal, Jesus Movement Became the Dominant Religious Force.* New York: HarperOne.

van Elk, M., D. Matzke, Q. F. Gronau, M. Guan, J. Vandekerckhove, and E.-J. Wagenmakers. 2015. "Meta-Analyses Are No Substitute for Registered Replications: A Skeptical Perspective on Religious Priming." *Frontiers in Psychology* 6: 1365. doi: 10.3389/fpsyg.2015.01365.

Watson, J. B. 1930. *Behaviorism.* Rev. ed. Chicago: University of Chicago Press.

White, C. J. M., J. M. Kelly, A. F. Shariff, and A. Norenzayan. 2019. "Supernatural Norm Enforcement: Thinking about Karma and God Reduces Selfishness among Believers." *Journal of Experimental Social Psychology* 84, 103797. https://doi.org/10.1016/j.jesp.2019.03.008.

9

RELIGION'S CONTRIBUTION TO POPULATION HEALTH

Key Theoretical and Methodological Considerations

Christopher G. Ellison

Introduction

The essays in this volume cast fresh light on the important issue of whether, and how, religion may promote human flourishing. This chapter focuses on an important component of well-being: the domain of population health. Scholarly interest in the religion-health connection has a long history in medicine, theology, and other fields, indeed, perhaps longer than many current researchers in this area have fully recognized.[1] Over the past twenty-five to thirty years, however, a vibrant body of increasingly rigorous empirical work has investigated the links between multiple facets of religion and a wide array of mental and physical health outcomes, including mortality. Contributors to this flourishing line of research have come from multiple disciplines, including sociology, psychology, public health, psychiatry, epidemiology, medicine, nursing, and others.

Although the findings of this literature are complex and defy easy summary, they have been exhaustively cataloged in dozens of systematic

105

reviews and meta-analyses.[2] An important source of information about this voluminous literature has been the encyclopedic *Handbook of Religion and Health*, organized by Harold Koenig and his various colleagues; two editions are in print and yet a third edition is currently in active preparation.[3] These vital sources and many others outline a wealth of evidence that aspects of religion bear largely (but not exclusively) salutary associations with a range of mental and physical health outcomes, including mortality (or longevity).

Here I have three main objectives: (1) to provide a brief review of some key elements of the literature on religion and population health; (2) to outline some of the key explanatory pathways or mechanisms via which multiple dimensions of religion may influence health and well-being; and (3) to identify several important directions for further exploration that will help to clarify whether, and to what extent, religion actually influences health and well-being.

At least two caveats should be entered at this point. First, this discussion is primarily focused on theory and research regarding community-dwelling populations, i.e., persons who—even if suffering from health problems—are well enough to live on their own or with family members. Although there is a large, parallel body of work on religion and health outcomes based on clinical samples (samples drawn from institutionalized settings, clinics and hospitals, etc.), and although this line of research is extremely important, it is beyond the scope of this discussion. Second, this paper addresses research issues pertaining to studies conducted in the United States and other developed Western societies. In a related vein, this discussion is centered primarily on persons who are—or were once—Christian (religiously or culturally). Specific insights may also be germane to other monotheistic religions (i.e., Judaism and Islam), although the literatures on religion as it is related to health in these traditions and societies are less developed and are growing slowly.[4] The remainder of the discussion proceeds with these caveats in mind.

Religion, Health, and Mortality: What the Research Tells Us

Mortality. As noted above, the religion-health field has flourished over the past few decades, with increasingly sophisticated studies exploring the complex links between religion and a range of health outcomes. One particularly impressive body of work centers on mortality.[5] To be sure, a long tradition of work explores religion and mortality (or longevity), but much of the early work was of two types. One line of research employed group-based comparisons, in which the longevity patterns of special populations—such as religious groups with distinctive health lifestyles (e.g., Seventh-day Adventists, Latter-day Saints) and religious professionals or virtuosi, including clergy and members of cloistered religious communities—have been compared with patterns in the general population.[6] Another strand of work has involved ecological studies, in which the religious composition of areal units (cities, counties, or countries) has been associated with rates of all-cause or cause-specific mortality (reminiscent of Durkheim's)[7] classic study of differential suicide rates in Catholic versus Protestant regions of Western Europe).[8]

Although there is much to be learned from these two types of studies, most recent studies of religion and mortality have capitalized on large-scale individual-level databases, at both community and national levels. To date, there are dozens of studies of this type, the bulk of which have tended to focus on the association between religious involvement and mortality risk.[9] This pertains primarily to overall mortality, although there is limited evidence that the protective effects of religious factors may vary by cause of death as well.[10] Most of the religion-mortality studies thus far have been conducted in the United States; within the U.S., there are studies focusing on specific subgroups, such as older adults, African American adults, Hispanic elders, and others.[11] There are also scattered studies on this topic from other industrialized nations (e.g., Denmark, Israel), along with a smaller emerging body of research in developing nations as well (e.g., Mexico).[12] By far the most common religious indicator in the religion-mortality literature has been the self-reported frequency of attendance or participation in religious activities, an indicator that is known to be over-reported in the United States and other societies, and may well serve as a reasonable proxy for overall religiosity.[13] Fewer studies have investigated the possible role of private religious devotional activities (e.g., frequency of prayer), receipt and provision of church-based social support, and other indicators.[14] The comparatively small number of studies incorporating these measures reflects significant data limitations. Therefore, these results have been limited and largely noncumulative in scope.

Physical Health. A vast literature examines associations between various facets of religious involvement and a broad array of health outcomes (Koenig et al. 2001, 2012). This body of work is enormous, the outcomes are diverse, and not surprisingly, the findings are complex. Many, though not all, of the population-based studies of religion and physical health have focused on older adults. One particular area of longstanding interest has been overall health, as gauged by self-rated health (i.e., health optimism or pessimism), and other subjective indications of health status and health trajectories. (To be sure, such measures have been criticized, and their validity and reliability have been called into question [Zajacova and Dowd 2011].) Overall physical health has also been measured in terms of symptom counts, number of chronic conditions, and other broad indicators. Although the evidence is not unequivocal, a number of studies have found that more religious individuals—especially those who attend services more often—tend to have better physical health at baseline, and in longitudinal studies they have more favorable trajectories over subsequent data collection points (Koenig et al. 2012; Oman 2018).

In addition to the many studies that examine overall and/or subjective measures of health status, the religion-health field has also extended to research linking religious factors with a vast array of specific diseases, disorders, and conditions (Koenig et al. 2001, 2012). For example, studies of older adults have documented salutary associations between religious involvement—again, often gauged in terms of religious attendance, although some other religious factors have also been considered—with slower rates of mobility decline (using both self-reports and performance-based measures of mobility) and trajectories of other activities of daily living (ADLs), as well as slower rates of cognitive decline.[15] Also on the list of chronic diseases that have been linked with religion are cardiovascular and circulatory issues (especially blood pressure, hypertension, and stroke), certain site-specific cancers (especially those that are often linked with behavioral factors such as smoking and heavy alcohol consumption), and numerous others.[16] In recent years, large-scale (usually nationwide) epidemiologic and survey data-collection efforts have increasingly moved away from reliance on self-reported health data toward biological indicators such as ambulatory blood pressure, waist-to-hip ratios, saliva tests to gauge cortisol and other stress hormones, blood assays to measure immune functioning, and much more. A small but growing body of work now associates religious factors—primarily but not exclusively religious attendance—with such outcomes.[17]

Mental Health. A voluminous literature has also explored links between multiple dimensions of religious involvement and mental health.[18] Although a vast array of specific mental health outcomes has been examined, several specific outcomes have received the lion's share of attention from scholars. Most of this work—hundreds of studies—has centered on symptoms of depression, anxiety, and nonspecific psychological distress.[19] The examination of these outcomes has been made easier by the widespread availability and easy use of standard, validated measures of such psychological outcomes (e.g., the CES-D depression measure, the RAND Mental Health Inventory, and many others). A much smaller number of population-based studies have explored links between religious involvement and the risk of affective disorders, such as major depressive disorder, generalized anxiety disorder, and other anxiety-related disorders.[20] To date, few studies have explored whether religion affects remission of depression or other psychiatric outcomes, especially in general population samples. In addition to this research showing that religious factors are inversely associated with negative psychological states and disorders, a large literature spanning several decades has linked religious factors with subjective well-being. Many specific domains have been considered in this work; however, there is a long tradition of distinguishing between affective well-being (e.g., personal happiness) and cognitive well-being (e.g., life satisfaction).[21]

Although findings in this line of inquiry are not unequivocal, the weight of the evidence suggests that at least some aspects of religious involvement may have favorable implications for mental health. Findings are perhaps most consistent with respect to subjective well-being. There is little evidence of consensus regarding which aspects of religion are most important for mental health. Indeed, compared with the literature on religion and physical health, work on mental health has tended to consider a wider array of religious domains. To be sure, much of this work reports apparently salutary effects of religious attendance and other facets of organizational religious involvement. However, researchers also commonly consider non-organizational facets of religion, such as private practices (e.g., prayer, meditation, scriptural study), religious orientations (e.g., intrinsic versus extrinsic), general (or generic) measures of religiosity (e.g., salience), and religious certainty, along with more specific measures of religious functions (e.g., coping, support) that are geared specifically to the study of health and well-being.[22]

Key Explanatory Pathways

Viewed broadly, theorists and researchers have identified a number of pathways or mechanisms via which religious factors may contribute to—or undermine—mental and physical health and well-being. Although a number of overarching perspectives have been discussed, perhaps the most widely used framework has been the "stress process" (or stress-and-coping) model.[23] Working within the common framework also brings religion-health scholars into conversation with a wider community of social and behavioral science researchers who study social influences on health and health disparities, mainly in the United States and other developed societies. Briefly, this perspective understands group differences in health and well-being in terms of (a) differential exposure to chronic and acute stressors (i.e., major life events, chronic conditions, daily hassles) and (b) differential vulnerability to these stressors.[24] Social stressors tend to erode health and well-being, whereas social resources (social integration and support) and psychological resources (positive self-concept and sense of control, among others) tend to bolster health in general, and they may also play a particularly important role in moderating (buffering) the deleterious effects of stress on health and well-being. Scholars working in this tradition have identified a number of ways in which aspects of religion may affect (a) the various components in the model (e.g., number or severity of stressors, levels of social support) and (b) the relationships among these various components.[25] Among the most important links are the following:

Health Behaviors. It is well established that religious involvement tends to deter a number of negative health behaviors (e.g., tobacco use, excessive alcohol consumption, illicit drug use, risky sexual practices).[26] These patterns are especially pronounced among adherents of specific religious traditions with particular behavioral and lifestyle codes (e.g., Seventh-day Adventists, Latter-day Saints, etc.).[27] In addition, religious involvement (e.g., attendance) is also associated with certain positive health practices (e.g., preventive service utilization) although the precise theoretical mechanisms underlying these patterns are not always clear.[28] For a handful of health behaviors (e.g., diet and exercise, and BMI), however, any effects of religious involvement may be modest and may even be negative.

Differential Exposure to Stressors. In addition to influencing health practices, religious groups and traditions tend to shape broader lifestyle choices through moral teaching, spiritual modeling, and many other mechanisms. Thus, religious involvement may be inversely associated with marital and relationship problems, interpersonal conflicts, legal hassles, and other stressful events and conditions.[29] This may be another pathway through which religion influences health and well-being.

Social Resources. Religious congregations are network-driven entities, and they offer a fertile environment for the cultivation of friendships and social activities. Regular churchgoers enjoy larger and denser social networks than other persons.[30] (To some extent this pattern may also reflect selectivity; extraverts and "joiners" may gravitate toward religious organizations as they do to other social opportunities.) Congregations also serve as conduits for various types of social support: tangible or instrumental (i.e., goods, services, information), socio-emotional, and spiritual. Support is conveyed through formal programs (i.e., special-purpose ministries, pastoral counseling) and informal means (i.e., exchanges among church members).[31] A number of studies have shown that giving support (informally, to fellow members, and formally, through volunteering) may be more beneficial for health and well-being than receiving support.[32]

Psychological Resources. Contrary to early critical discussions (e.g., the work of Albert Ellis),[33] it is now well recognized that religious communities and cognitions may contribute to positive self-concept, including: (a) self-esteem, or the global sense of moral self-worth; (b) sense of control, or the perceived ability to manage one's own affairs and achieve desired goals; and (c) sense of mattering, or inferred significance.[34] These elements of the self-concept may be influenced by reflected appraisals and opportunities to build competencies and confidence within congregations, as well as by perceptions of positive regard by a divine other. Within the stress process tradition, it has been established that these components of self-concept are conducive to health and well-being in general and that they are especially helpful in mitigating the otherwise damaging health effects of stressful events and conditions. Of course, other psychological resources (e.g., optimism, meaning, and purpose) may also have roots within religious groups as well as religious cognitions.[35]

Character Strengths and Virtues. A growing body of recent research has highlighted the implications of various character strengths and virtues for health and well-being. This is vast terrain, but these are among the most widely researched character strengths: forgiveness, hope, meaning and purpose, gratitude and humility. Several very broad empirical patterns are noteworthy. In many studies these character strengths are directly associated with outcomes gauging mental and physical health and well-being.[36] In addition, they may help to explain how more generic measures of religious engagement (e.g., attendance and organizational participation) "work" to influence health and well-being. Finally, some character strengths may buffer the effects of stressful events and conditions on health outcomes.[37]

Religious Coping Styles and Practices. An important line of work pioneered by Pargament and many students and colleagues has identified numerous specific styles of religious coping, i.e., constructive or problematic ways in which individuals draw upon religious beliefs, communities, and practices to deal with stressful events or conditions.[38] This line of work illustrates the diverse ways in which religion may be relevant to the stressor-appraisal process—i.e., in primary appraisals, when individuals interpret and assign meaning to a given event or conditions and assess the ways in which this may tax existing capacities or may challenge self-understanding or assumptive worldviews, and in secondary appraisals, when individuals review their inventory of resources available to deal with stressors. Although some individuals use religion in passive fashion (e.g., relying on God to deal with their problems), far more people perceive that they are forming collaborative problem-solving partnerships, in which God is an active participant and a "force multiplier" in their own coping attempts.[39]

Going Forward: Some Key Issues and Questions

Conceptualizing and Measuring Religion. How should we conceptualize and measure health-relevant religious domains? One recurrent issue in this area involves how best to conceptualize and measure religion for health research. Early studies in this field focused heavily on generic measures of religion, such as the frequency of attendance at religious services, the frequency of private practices (e.g., prayer), overall religious salience, and intrinsic religious motivation (i.e., the inclination to carry faith commitments into other areas of life), among others.[40] In research on mortality and certain physical health outcomes (especially those using biomarkers), such generic measures (especially attendance) have remained dominant, because they are the only items available in large-scale secondary epidemiologic databases. Such measures are suboptimal; they are affected by various response biases,[41] and their meaning for health is often ambiguous, leaving researchers to wonder whether apparent attendance effects are really due to congregational worship (or other) experiences, or whether attendance is a proxy for other unmeasured facets of religion.[42]

Thus, over the past two decades, investigators have developed more fine-grained, theoretically grounded, and direct measures of health-relevant religious domains (e.g., gauging congregational support practices, religious coping practices, character strengths, and many other areas). To date, unfortunately, relatively few major epidemiologic data collection efforts have incorporated these more sophisticated religious measures, which has significantly hindered growth and clarity in this field. This has also occasioned debate among researchers over modeling strategies, and specifically over the best ways to specify the role of hypothesized "mediators" or mechanisms.

Two areas of conceptualization and measurement clearly deserve further work and refinement. One of these involves the study of religious cognitions. Although early researchers in the religion-health field were expressly discouraged from pursuing the potential role of religious beliefs—out of concern that this might taint religion-health research as unduly sectarian or partisan—an emerging body of research has linked a number of specific religious beliefs with salutary health (particularly mental health) outcomes. Examples of such beliefs include the following: (a) God images (especially belief in a loving, forgiving deity), (b) the sense of divine control, (c) attachment to God (especially a secure versus insecure versus anxious attachment style), and (d) belief in (perceptions of) an afterlife.[43] There is now at least some evidence that each of these religious cognitions bears direct associations with aspects of personal well-being and also moderates the links between stressful events and conditions and health-related outcomes.[44] But this research remains in its early stages, and considerably more work is needed (a) to clarify how cognitions "work" with respect to health and (b) to specify which health-related outcomes are (and are not) linked with these (and perhaps other) religious cognitions.

Another important area that deserves continued attention involves the "dark side" of religion, or what have been called "spiritual struggles." Although much of the literature on the religion-health connection reports (what appear to be) salutary associations between multiple dimensions of religion and diverse health outcomes, it is also important to acknowledge the pernicious side of religious beliefs, experiences, practices, and communities for health and well-being. This aligns well with an early tradition of anti-religious critiques and analysis (e.g., the work of Albert Ellis,[45] among many others). Most attention has been focused on three types of spiritual struggles: (a) divine struggles, or troubled (perceived) relationships with God (e.g., feelings of anger and estrangement vis-à-vis God); (b) intrapsychic struggles, or chronic and unresolved religious doubting, which deprives individuals of the benefits of a coherent religious meaning system (or "plausibility structure," in Berger's famous terms)[46] and also distances them from clergy and coreligionists who might help them work through their ambivalence over matters of faith, dogma or doctrine, and so on; and (c) inter-personal struggles, or conflicts with coreligionists, or disputes about religious matters, or negative interactions within religious settings or contexts (e.g., about matters of church administration, politics, etc.).[47] However, there are other aspects to the "dark side" of religion, including unwholesome correlates or effects of certain constellations of belief (e.g., preoccupation with themes of sinfulness, divine judgment and punishment, etc.).[48] A focus on the two faces of religion for health and well-being—or as Pargament has characterized it, on "the bitter and the sweet"[49]—is essential for a fuller grasp of the complex, nuanced ways in which religion may link with these outcomes, and also to maintain scientific credibility within the broader scholarly community.

   The Contingent Nature of the Religion-Health Connection. For whom, and under what circumstances, is religion most (and least) beneficial for health and well-being? A wealth of theory and evidence suggests that the association between religion and health (perhaps especially mental health) may be stronger for persons experiencing stressful events and conditions as compared with others. But viewed more broadly, how do the links between religious domains and health or well-being vary across population subgroups?

   Religion (as a resource or set of resources) may also differ in its value depending on the location of individuals or groups within the stratification system(s) (i.e., socioeconomic, racial/ethnic, gender, etc.) of the wider population. Such a viewpoint is highly consistent with sociological theories about religion as a "compensatory" resource, which date to the early (classical) days of sociological scholarship (e.g., Weber, Marx and Engels). Scholars in this tradition have long argued that religion is an important balm and source of comfort and aid for persons from marginalized social backgrounds.[50] This also aligns with the broader resource compensation perspective proposed by scholars in the stress process tradition in sociology, psychology, and allied fields. This perspective holds that any resource will be proportionately more valuable for health and well-being of persons and groups that lack viable alternatives.[51]

   Consistent with this perspective, a growing body of literature has reported that many aspects of religion are more closely linked with (salutary) health outcomes for persons from lower SES backgrounds (e.g., those with low levels of education), those from racial/ethnic minority populations (e.g., African Americans versus non-Hispanic Whites), and others from marginalized statuses.[52] Within the stress process tradition, there is a broader literature that aligns with this, showing that religious practices, beliefs, and cognitions play a particularly valuable role in shaping health and well-being for individuals facing stressful events and conditions that are most common among persons from lower SES and racial minority backgrounds, such as chronic poverty, discrimination, poor neighborhood quality, and others.[53] One important consideration of analyses of this type involves the distinction between (a) *levels* of religion (or religiosity) and (b) *effects* of each increment in religion (or religiosity), and these are issues that warrant further consideration by scholars in multiple disciplines going forward. In any event, however, this line of work integrates theories and findings from work on religion, stress process, and SES and racial health disparities in important ways that may remain productive and generative for some time.

Yet another approach to this question of "who benefits" has to do with broader contextual issues. Several recent studies using data from multiple nations and societies have shown that the link between religion and rudimentary measures of health and well-being (e.g., life satisfaction and happiness, self-rated health) varies across national religious contexts;[54] persons in relatively religious settings seem to derive greater health benefit from their own religious involvement than those in contexts where religion is less common, not normative, and (in extreme cases) regulated and even persecuted by governments.[55] Additional research is needed to sort out the implications of these findings, and to gauge their relevance for a broader array of health-related outcomes.

Religious contexts may moderate the associations between individual religious involvement and health outcomes in other ways as well. For example, it will be important to view the potential moderating role of religious context at the city or county level within a single country, such as the United States, e.g., whether one is a member of the religious majority or minority.[56] It may also be useful to consider the role of congregational contexts. For example, the cultivation of social support networks and other religious resources may be accelerated or hindered, depending on the characteristics (i.e., the composition) of congregations in which individuals are situated.[57] And local congregations (even within the same denomination) may vary significantly in their approach (i.e., programming, services, and discourse) concerning health and well-being. A final contextual factor may be family religious composition. We know that the role of religion in shaping marital or intimate (and intergenerational) relationships depends heavily on the religious "fit" or compatibility among family members;[58] it may be worth exploring whether same-faith couples (gauged in terms of similar affiliations, levels of commitment, doctrinal beliefs, etc.) are more efficient in (re-)producing religiously defined health habits and lifestyles, forging congregational social bonds and support networks, and promoting coherent religious meaning systems as compared with other couples. This is a significant but largely neglected research direction that would rethink the nature of the religion-health connection by defining "religion" as an embedded characteristic of couples and families, rather than merely as an individual attribute like age or education.

What else might modify the links between religious engagement and health or well-being? One issue that researchers must confront is the shifting terrain and climate for religion within the United States and other societies. Briefly, the proportion of U.S. adults (and this is even more dramatic among young adults) with no religious preference or affiliation (and these mean slightly different things!) is rapidly rising. For the overall U.S. adult population, this figure is approaching 25 percent.[59] Around 40 percent of U.S. adults report attending services "about once or twice a year" or less. (And the real figures may be higher.) Studies reveal large cohort-based declines in organizational and nonorganizational religious practices (but less dramatic shifts in beliefs).[60] The field of religion-health studies could benefit greatly from the accumulation and analysis of more systematic data that allow the disaggregation of age, period, and cohort effects on the associations between religious factors and a range of health-related outcomes. In addition, we should continue to broaden the terrain of religion-health research—to new countries/societies of course, but also to disaggregate the internally heterogeneous category of nonreligious adults within the United States (and other western societies), to distinguish between religiously nonaffiliated persons, agnostics, committed atheists, and others, and to ferret out the role of religious and other factors in shaping mental and physical health within this emerging, but clearly growing, population.[61]

Religion and Biological Functioning. One final area that warrants further development (among many other possibilities) is the connection between religion and biology. This can take many forms, but two of those seem particularly important. First, research on religion and health have largely neglected the potential complicating role of genetics.[62] This is a significant oversight because (a) genetic differences contribute to individual variation on virtually all aspects of mental and physical health and biological functioning; and (b) there is mounting evidence regarding the heritability of religion, although the degree of probable genetic influence depends heavily on the dimension of religion under consideration. There are several possible ways in which genetic and religious factors may work together to shape health and well-being. One of these involves gene-environment correlations, which may be passive, evocative, or active in nature. Thus, it is possible that individuals share genes with people who also contribute to (or are part of) their environments (e.g., family members), an example of passive correlation. A second possibility is evocative correlation. This occurs when one's genetic makeup may elicit responses from others in our environment (e.g., negative reactions such as avoidance or positive ones such as empathy and friendliness). Yet a third possibility involves active correlation, in which individuals may actively seek or construct environments (e.g., congregational settings) that fit with their genetic tendencies or motivations. Any of these forms of gene-environment correlation would suggest that omitting the possible role of genetics would be a mistake and could confuse the interpretation of common findings regarding the associations between aspects of religion and health. In addition to gene-environment correlation, another possibility is gene-environment interaction. For example, this would occur if religious practices, experiences, or cognitions delayed or suppressed genetic influences on health, or if genetic factors moderated the link between religious involvement and aspects of health or well-being. In any event, closer attention to the interplay of genetics and religion in shaping health outcomes seems important to advance this field.

A relatively recent area of research has explored connections between religious involvement (often measured in rudimentary fashion, in terms of religious attendance) and direct measures of biological functioning, as opposed to self-reports of health status, which may be imprecise and may be biased by health optimism or other factors. To date, much of this work has clustered under the rubric of allostatic load, which refers to the chronic dysregulation of multiple physiological systems—e.g., autonomic nervous system, HPA axis, cardiovascular system, immune function, metabolic system, and others—as a result of recurrent or ongoing exposure to high levels of stress.[63] This chronic over-activation of multiple systems takes a toll on overall physical health and has been linked with a wide array of chronic and acute diseases. Several studies have explored the associations between religious involvement—often gauged in terms of religious attendance—and various indicators of biological functioning, using multiple specifications, that reflect over-activation of one or a number of these interrelated systems. In most instances, distinct advantages accrue to individuals who attend services regularly, as compared with their less-religious counterparts.[64] Moreover, in at least one study, variations in allostatic load by frequency of religious attendance helped to explain a nontrivial portion of the association between attendance and mortality risk in a large sample of U.S. adults.[65] Research in this area remains in its early stages, and exploring links between multiple religious dimensions and biological functioning holds great promise in clarifying the ways in which religious factors may "get under the skin" and influence health.

Conclusion

Does religion influence health? It certainly seems to be the case, but we need to know more about which empirical associations are truly causal as opposed to correlational, which implies the value of a host of innovations and improvements in statistical estimation and modeling that are beyond the scope of this paper. This also underscores the need for better understanding of the diverse mechanisms that link specific aspects of religion with particular health outcomes, as well as the need to explore heterogeneity and subgroup variation in the nature of religious effects on health. Closer attention to the issues raised here will help to clarify whether and how religion really contributes to this vital area of human flourishing.

References

Ano, Gene G., and Erin B. Vasconcelles. 2005. "Religious Coping and Psychological Adjustment to Stress: A Meta-Analysis." *Journal of Clinical Psychology* 61: 461–80.

Baker, Joseph O., Samuel Stroope, and M. H. Walker. 2018. "Secularity, Religiosity, and Health: Physical and Mental Health Differences between Atheists, Agnostics, and Non-Affiliated Theists Compared to Religiously Affiliated Individuals." *Social Science Research* 75: 44–57.

Benjamins, Maureen R., and Carolyn Brown. 2004. "Religion and Preventative Health Care Utilization among the Elderly." *Social Science and Medicine* 58: 109–18.

Berger, Peter L. 1967. *The Sacred Canopy*. Garden City, N.Y.: Doubleday.

Billingsley, Andrew. 1999. *Mighty Like a River: The Black Church and Social Reform*. New York: Oxford University Press.

Bradshaw, Matt, and Christopher G. Ellison. 2010. "Financial Hardship and Psychological Distress: Exploring the Buffering Role of Religion." *Social Science and Medicine* 71: 196–204.

Brenner, Philip. 2011. "Identity Importance and the Overreporting of Reli-
   gious Service Attendance: Multiple Imputation of Religious Attendance
   Using the American Time Use Study and the General Social Survey."
   Journal for the Scientific Study of Religion 50: 103–15.
Bruce, Marino A., et al. 2017. "Church Attendance, Allostatic Load, and
   Mortality in Middle-Aged Adults." *PLoS ONE* 12, no. 5: e0177618.
   https://doi.org/10.1371/journal.pone.0177618.
Cozier, Yvette C., et al. 2018. "Religious and Spiritual Coping and the Risk
   of Incident Hypertension in the Black Women's Health Study." *Annals
   of Behavioral Medicine* 52: 989–98.
Durkheim, Emile. 1951 (1897). *Suicide.* New York: Free Press.
Ellis, Albert L. 1962. *Reason and Emotion in Psychotherapy.* Secaucus, N.J.:
   Lyle Stuart.
Ellison, Christopher G. 1991. "Religious Involvement and Subjective Well-
   being." *Journal of Health and Social Behavior* 32: 80–99.
Ellison, Christopher G., Matt Bradshaw, Sunshine Rote, Jennifer Storch,
   and Marcie Trevino. 2008. "Religion and Alcohol Use among College
   Students: Exploring the Role of Domain-Specific Religious Salience."
   Journal of Drug Issues 38: 821–46.
Ellison, Christopher G., and Amy M. Burdette. 2012. "Religion and the
   Sense of Control among U.S. Adults." *Sociology of Religion* 73: 1–22.
Ellison, Christopher G., Jeffrey A. Burr, and Patricia L. McCall. 1997. "Reli-
   gious Homogeneity and Metropolitan Suicide Rates." *Social Forces* 76:
   273–99.
Ellison, Christopher G., Reed T. DeAngelis, Terrence D. Hill, and Paul
   Froese. 2019. "Sleep Quality and the Stress-Buffering Role of Religion:
   A Mediated Moderation Analysis." *Journal for the Scientific Study of
   Religion* 58: 251–68.
Ellison, Christopher G., and Kevin J. Flannelly. 2009. "Religious Involve-
   ment and Risk of Major Depression in a Prospective Nationwide Study
   of African American Adults." *Journal of Nervous and Mental Disease*
   197: 568–73.
Ellison, Christopher G., and Linda K. George. 1994. "Religious Involve-
   ment, Social Ties, and Social Support in a Southeastern Community."
   Journal for the Scientific Study of Religion 33: 46–61.
Ellison, Christopher G., and Andrea K. Henderson. 2011. "Religion and
   Mental Health: Through the Lens of the Stress Process." In *Toward a
   Sociological Theory of Religion and Health*, edited by A. Blasi, 11–44.
   Boston: Brill.
Ellison, Christopher G., Robert A. Hummer, Shannon Cormier, and Richard
   G. Rogers. 2000. "Religious Involvement and Mortality Risk among
   African American Adults." *Research on Aging* 22: 630–67.

Ellison, Christopher G., Neal M. Krause, Bryan C. Shepherd, and Mark Chaves. 2009. "Size, Conflict, and Opportunities for Interaction: Congregational Effects on Members' Anticipated Support and Negative Interaction." *Journal for the Scientific Study of Religion* 48: 1–15.

Ellison, Christopher G., Scott Schieman, and Matt Bradshaw. 2014. "The Association between Religiousness and Psychological Well-Being in Late Life: Is There an Educational Gradient?" In *Religion and Inequality in America: Research and Theory on Religion's Role in Stratification*, edited by L. Keister and D. Sherkat, 263–88. New York: Cambridge University Press.

Ellison, Christopher G., and Xiaohe Xu. 2014. "Religion and Families." In *Wiley-Blackwell Companion to the Sociology of Families*, edited by J. Scott, J. Treas, and M. Richard, 277–99. New York: Wiley.

Enstrom, James E., and Lester Breslow. 2008. "Lifestyle and Reduced Mortality among Active California Mormons, 1980–2004." *Preventive Medicine* 46: 133–36.

Exline, Julie J., Kenneth I. Pargament, Joshua B. Grubbs, and Ann Marie Yali. 2014. "The Religious and Spiritual Struggles Scale: Development and Initial Validation." *Psychology of Religion and Spirituality* 6: 208–22.

Exline, Julie J., Crystal L. Park, J. M. Smyth, and Michael P. Carey. 2011. "Anger toward God: Social-Cognitive Predictors, Prevalence, and Links with Adjustment to Bereavement and Cancer." *Journal of Personality and Social Psychology* 100: 129–48.

Flannelly, Kevin J. 2017. *Religious Beliefs, Evolutionary Psychiatry, and Mental Health in* America. New York: Springer.

Flannelly, Kevin J., Andrew J. Weaver, David B. Larson, and Harold G. Koenig. 2002. "A Review of Mortality Research on Clergy and Other Religious Professionals." *Journal of Religion and Health* 41: 57–68.

Gillum, R. Frank. 2005. "Frequency of Attendance at Religious Services and Cigarette Smoking in American Women and Men: The Third Health and Nutrition Examination Study." *Preventive Medicine* 41: 607–13.

Gillum, R. Frank, and Cheryl L. Holt. 2010. "Associations between Religious Involvement and Behavioral Risk Factors for HIV/AIDS in American Women and Men in a National Health Survey." *Annals of Behavioral Medicine* 40: 284–93.

Gillum, R. Frank, and Deborah D. Ingram. 2006. "Frequency of Attendance at Religious Services, Hypertension, and Blood Pressure: The Third National Health and Nutrition Examination Study." *Psychosomatic Medicine* 68: 382–85.

Gillum, R. Frank, Dana E. King, T. O. Obisesan, and Harold G. Koenig. 2008. "Frequency of Attendance at Religious Services and Mortality in a U.S. National Cohort." *Annals of Epidemiology* 18: 124–29.

Hayward, R. David, and Marta Elliott. 2014. "Cross-National Analysis of the Influence of Cultural Norms and Government Restrictions on the Relationship between Religion and Well-Being." *Review of Religious Research* 56: 23–43.

Hill, Peter C., and Kenneth I. Pargament. 2003. "Advances in the Conceptualization and Measurement of Religion and Spirituality: Implications for Physical and Mental Health Research." *American Psychologist* 58: 64–74.

Hill, Terrence D., Jacqueline L. Angel, Christopher G. Ellison, and Ronald J. Angel. 2005. "Religious Attendance and Mortality: An 8-Year Follow-Up of Older Mexican Americans." *Journals of Gerontology: Series B* 60: S102–9.

Hill, Terrence D., Matt Bradshaw, and Amy M. Burdette. 2016. "Health and Biological Functioning." In *Handbook of the Sociology of Religion*, edited by D. Yamane, 11–28. New York: Springer.

Hill, Terrence D., Amy M. Burdette, Jacqueline L. Angel, and Ronald J. Angel. 2006. "Religious Attendance and Cognitive Functioning among Older Mexican Americans." *Journals of Gerontology: Series B* 61: P3–9.

Hill, Terrence D., Amy M. Burdette, John Taylor, and Jacqueline L. Angel. 2016. "Religious Attendance and the Mobility Trajectories of Older Mexican Americans: An Application of the Growth Mixture Model." *Journal of Health and Social Behavior* 57: 118–34.

Hill, Terrence D., Sunshine M. Rote, Christopher G. Ellison, and Amy M. Burdette. 2014. "Religious Involvement and Biological Functioning in Late Life." *Journal of Aging and Health* 26: 766–85.

Hill, Terrence D., Joseph Saenz, and Sunshine Rote. 2020. "Religious Participation and Mortality in Mexico." *Journals of Gerontology: Series B.*

Hout, Michael, and Claude Fischer. 2014. "Explaining Why More Americans Have No Religious Preference: Political Backlash and Generational Succession, 1987–2012." *Sociological Science* 1: 423–47.

Hummer, Robert A., Christopher G. Ellison, Richard G. Rogers, Benjamin E. Moulton, and Ron R. Romero. 2004. "Religious Involvement and Mortality in the United States: Review and Perspective." *Southern Medical Journal* 97: 1223–30.

Hummer, Robert A., Richard G. Rogers, Charles B. Nam, and Christopher G. Ellison. 1999. "Religious Involvement and U.S. Adult Mortality." *Demography* 36: 273–85.

Idler, Ellen L. 2011. "Religion and Adult Mortality." In *International Handbook of Adult Mortality*, edited by R. Rogers and E. Crimmins, 345–77. New York: Springer.

Idler, Ellen L., Daviad A. Boulifard, Erich Labouvie, Yung Y. Chen, Tyrone J. Krause, and Richard J. Contrada. 2009. "Looking Inside the Black Box of 'Attendance at Religious Services': New Measures for Exploring an Old Dimension of Religion and Health Research." *International Journal for the Psychology of Religion* 19: 1–20.

Idler, Ellen, J. Blevins, M. Kiser, and C. Hogue. 2017. "Religion, a Social Determinant of Mortality? A 10-Year Follow-Up of the Health and Retirement Study." *PLoS ONE* 12, no. 12.

Idler, Ellen L., and Stanislav V. Kasl. 1997. "Religion among Disabled and Non-Disabled Persons II: Attendance at Religious Services as a Predictor of the Course of Disability." *Journals of Gerontology Series B* 52: S306–16.

Idler, Ellen L., et al. 2003. "Measuring Multiple Dimensions of Religion and Spirituality for Health Research: Conceptual Background and Findings from the 1998 General Social Survey." *Research on Aging* 25: 329–66.

Koenig, Harold G., Dana King, and Verna B. Carson. 2012. *Handbook of Religion and Health.* 2nd ed. New York: Oxford University Press.

Koenig, Harold G., Michael E. McCullough, and David B. Larson. 2001. *Handbook of Religion and Health.* New York: Oxford University Press.

Koenig, Harold G., and Saad Al Shohaib. 2014. *Health and Well-Being in Islamic Societies.* New York: Springer.

Krause, Neal. 2003. "Religious Meaning and Subjective Well-Being in Late Life." *Journals of Gerontology: Series B* 58: S160–70.

———. 2006a. "Church-Based Social Support and Mortality." *Journals of Gerontology: Series B* 61: S140–46.

———. 2006b. "Gratitude toward God, Stress, and Health in Late Life." *Research on Aging* 28: 163–83.

———. 2008a. "Aging in the Church: How Social Relationships Affect Health." West Conshohocken, Pa.: Templeton Press.

———. 2008b. "The Social Foundation of Religious Meaning in Life." *Research on Aging* 30: 395–427.

Levin, Jeff. 2016. "'For They Knew Not What It Was': Rethinking the Tacit Narrative History of Religion and Health Research." *Journal of Religion and Health* 56: 28–46.

Levin, Jeff, and Michele F. Prince, eds. 2013. *Judaism and Health: A Handbook of Practical, Professional, and Scholarly Resources.* New York: Jewish Lights.

Lim, Chaeyoon, and Robert D. Putnam. 2010. "Religion, Social Networks, and Life Satisfaction." *American Sociological Review* 75: 914–33.

Lin, Nan, and Walter W. Ensel. 1989. "Life Stress and Health: Stressors and Resources." *American Sociological Review* 54: 382–99.

Lu, Yun, and Xiaozhao Y. Yang. 2020. "The Two Faces of Diversity: The Relationships between Religious Polarization, Religious Fractionalization, and Self-Rated Health." *Journal of Health and Social Behavior* 61: 79–95.

McConnell, Kelly M., Kenneth I. Pargament, Christopher G. Ellison, and Kevin J. Flannelly. 2006. "Examining the Links between Spiritual Struggles and Symptoms of Psychopathology in a National Sample." *Journal of Clinical Psychology* 62: 1469–84.

McEwen, Bruce S. 1998. "Stress, Adaptation, and Disease: Allostasis and Allostatic Load." *Annals of the New York Academy of Sciences* 840: 33–44.

Miller, Lisa, Priya Wickramaratne, Marc J. Gameroff, Mia Sage, Craig E. Tenke, and Myrna M. Weissman. 2012. "Religiosity and Major Depression in Adults at High Risk: A 10-Year Prospective Study." *American Journal of Psychiatry* 169: 89–94.

Oman, Doug, ed. 2018. *Why Religion and Spirituality Matter for Public Health.* New York: Springer.

Pargament, Kenneth I. 1997. *The Psychology of Religion and Coping.* New York: Guilford.

———. 2002. "The Bitter and the Sweet: An Evaluation of the Costs and Benefits of Religiousness." *Psychological Inquiry* 13: 168–81.

Pargament, Kenneth I., Joseph Kennell, William Hathaway, Nancy Grevengoed, Jon Newman, and Wendy Jones. 1988. "Religion and the Problem-Solving Process: Three Styles of Religious Coping." *Journal for the Scientific Study of Religion* 27: 90–104.

Pargament, Kenneth I., Harold G. Koenig, and Lisa M. Perez. 2000. "The Many Methods of Religious Coping: Development and Validation of the RCOPE." *Journal of Clinical Psychology* 56: 519–43.

Park, Crystal L. 2017. "Religious Cognitions and Well-Being: A Meaning Perspective." In *The Happy Mind: Cognitive Contributions to Well-Being*, edited by M. D. Robinson and M. Eid, 443–58. New York: Springer.

Pearlin, Leonard I., Elizabeth Menaghan, Morton Lieberman, and J. T. Mullan. 1981. "The Stress Process." *Journal of Health and Social Behavior* 22: 337–56.

Pescosolido, Bernice A., and Sharon Georgianna. 1989. "Durkheim, Suicide, and Religion: Toward a Network Theory of Suicide." *American Sociological Review* 54: 33–48.

Phillips, Roland L. 1975. "Role of Lifestyle and Dietary Habits in Risk of Cancer among Seventh-day Adventists." *Cancer Research* 35: 3513–22.

Rogers, Richard G., Patrick Krueger, and Robert A. Hummer. 2010. "Religious Attendance and Cause-Specific Mortality in the United States." In *Religion, Families, and Health: Population-Based Research in the United States*, edited by C. Ellison and R. Hummer, 292–320. New Brunswick, N.J.: Rutgers University Press.

Ross, Catherine, and John Mirowsky. 2006. "Sex Differences in the Effect of Education on Depression: Resource Multiplication or Resource Substitution?" *Social Science and Medicine* 63: 1400–13.

Schieman, Scott, Alex Bierman, and Christopher G. Ellison. 2010. "Religious Involvement, Beliefs about God, and the Sense of Mattering among Older Adults." *Journal for the Scientific Study of Religion* 49: 517–35.

———. 2013. "Religion and Mental Health." In *Handbook of the Sociology of Mental Health*, 2nd ed., edited by C. Aneshensel, J. Phelan, and A. Bierman, 457–78. New York: Springer.

Schieman, Scott, Alex Bierman, Laura Upenieks, and Christopher G. Ellison. 2017. "Love Thy Self? How Belief in a Supportive God Shapes Self-Esteem." *Review of Religious Research* 59: 293–318.

Schieman, Scott, Tetyana Pudrovska, and Melissa A. Milkie. 2005. "The Sense of Divine Control and Self-Concept: A Study of Race Differences in Late Life." *Research on Aging* 27: 165–96.

Schieman, Scott, Tetyana Pudrovska, Leonard I. Pearlin, and Christopher G. Ellison. 2006. "The Sense of Divine Control and Psychological Distress: Variations across Race and Socioeconomic Status." *Journal for the Scientific Study of Religion* 45: 529–49.

Schwadel, Philip. 2011. "Age, Period, and Cohort Effects on Religious Activities and Beliefs." *Social Science Research* 40: 181–92.

Sethi, Sheena, and Martin E. P. Seligman. 1993. "Optimism and Fundamentalism." *Psychological Science* 4: 256–59.

Smith, Timothy B., Michael E. McCullough, and Justin Poll. 2003. "Religiousness and Depression: Evidence for a Main Effect and the Moderating Influence of Stressful Life Events." *Psychological Bulletin* 129: 614–36.

Stroope, Samuel, and Joseph O. Baker. 2018. "Whose Moral Community? Religiosity, Secularity, and Self-Rated Health across Communal Religious Contexts." *Journal of Health and Social Behavior* 59: 185–99.

Taylor, Robert J., Linda M. Chatters, Karen Lincoln, and Amanda Toler Woodward. 2017. "Church-Based Exchanges of Informal Social Support among African Americans." *Race and Social Problems* 9: 53–62.

Taylor, Robert J., Christopher G. Ellison, Linda M. Chatters, Jeffrey S. Levin, and Karen D. Lincoln. 2000. "Mental Health Services within Faith Communities: The Role of Clergy in Black Churches." *Social Work* 45: 73–87.

Troyer, Henry. 1988. "Review of Cancer among Four Religious Sects: Evidence That Lifestyles Are Distinctive Sets of Risk Factors." *Social Science and Medicine* 26: 1007–17.

Uecker, Jeremy E., Christopher G. Ellison, Kevin J. Flannelly, and Amy M. Burdette. 2016. "Belief in Human Sinfulness, Belief in Experiencing

Divine Forgiveness, and Psychiatric Symptoms." *Review of Religious Research* 58: 1–26.

Upenieks, Laura, Steven L. Foy, and Andrew Miles. 2018. "Beyond America: Cross-National Context and the Impact of Religious versus Secular Organizational Membership on Self-Rated Health." *Socius* 4: 1–19.

Zajacova, Anna, and Jennifer L. Dowd. 2011. "Reliability of Self-Rated Health in U.S. Adults." *American Journal of Epidemiology* 174: 977–83.

10

OFFENDER-LED RELIGIOUS MOVEMENTS

*Identity Transformation, Rehabilitation, and
Justice System Reform*

BYRON R. JOHNSON

Background

Recent scholarship from a host of disciplines falls within the broad categories of "social well-being" or "human flourishing." This research improves our understanding of how people experience happiness, find purpose, meaning, or hope, to mention just a few. Life experiences that lead to contentment, optimism, resiliency, and thriving in the midst of difficult circumstances are additional markers of human flourishing. In fact, one can make the case that the field of positive psychology is simply an example of the scientific study of human thriving.

As a mounting body of evidence on human flourishing continues to develop, scholars are also examining the ways in which religion may be consequential for flourishing and well-being.[1] Research like this is helpful because it shows that the influence of religion is far more complicated than one might assume. When people think of religion in the United States, they may think of the prevalence of houses of worship (300,000 to 500,000) in cities and communities from coast to coast.[2]

People may also recall hearing about public opinion polls indicating that a very high percentage of Americans believe in God, and frequently pray.[3] But the influence of religion is far more complicated and consequential than attendance at religious services or the acknowledgment that many regularly pray. Indeed, a great deal of empirical evidence documents the ways in which religious involvement is linked to many different types of physical and mental health outcomes.[4]

A growing subset of this research demonstrates how religious involvement may help to decrease crime,[5] as well as protect individuals residing in disadvantaged communities from engaging in illegal behavior.[6] In addition, there is a developing literature indicating religion can help to foster sobriety,[7] or even promote prosocial behavior among offenders.[8] Published studies have even confirmed the effectiveness of certain faith-based programs in reducing recidivism among former prisoners as well as the economic benefit to society of crime desistance.[9]

Relatedly, scholars have also examined how religious congregations enhance social capital and provide networks of social support that may foster human flourishing.[10] Although the evidence is still quite preliminary, there is a growing research literature confirming that faith-based interventions can be significant in addressing other contemporary social problems (e.g., drug treatment, prisoner rehabilitation, homelessness, etc.).[11] In sum, there is empirical evidence documenting that measures of religiosity (i.e., levels of participation or commitment) may help change an offender's identity, and be linked to other important prosocial outcomes (e.g., generosity, service to others, or civic engagement).[12]

Religion behind Bars: From Bible Studies to Faith-Based Prisons

It is easy to understand how and why people may view prisons as the antithesis of human flourishing. Prisons are known for many things, but far less understood is the fact that correctional facilities tend to be intensely religious places. Recent scholarship suggests religion can engender human flourishing even within a prison.[13] Moreover, a mounting body of research documents the beneficial impact of religion on crime, delinquency, and prisoner reentry. In fact, there is an emerging "positive criminology" literature that provides preliminary evidence that may inform how scholars, professionals, and volunteers think about contemporary approaches to offender treatment and justice system reform more generally.[14]

A series of multivariate studies examining the effectiveness of Prison Fellowship (PF) programs tend to support the notion that PF participants fare significantly better. In the first study, Young and his coauthors investigated long-term recidivism among a group of federal inmates trained as volunteer prison ministers and found that the PF group had a significantly lower rate of recidivism than the matched group.[15] In the second study, Johnson and colleagues examined the impact of PF religious programs on institutional adjustment and recidivism rates in two matched groups of inmates from four adult male prisons in New York State. After controlling for level of involvement in PF-sponsored programs, inmates who were most active in Bible studies were significantly less likely to be rearrested during the yearlong follow-up period.[16] In a follow-up to this study, Johnson extended the New York research on former inmates by increasing the length of study from one to eight years and found that frequent Bible study participants were less likely to be rearrested two and three years after their release.[17]

In one of the more anticipated studies of a faith-based intervention, Johnson published a six-year evaluation of Prison Fellowship's (PF) expressly Christian, faith-based prerelease prison program known as the InnerChange Freedom Initiative (IFI).[18] Johnson and Larson evaluated the InnerChange Freedom Initiative, an eighteen- to twenty-four-month-long faith-based prison program launched in 1997 in Houston, Texas, and operated by Prison Fellowship (a Christian prison ministry). They found program participants were significantly less likely to be arrested than a matched group of prisoners not receiving this religious intervention (eight to twenty, respectively) during a two-year postrelease period.[19] Johnson and Larson also found that the presence of a faith-motivated mentor was critical in helping ex-prisoners remain crime-free following release from prison.[20]

A separate outcome evaluation reported similar results from Minnesota's InnerChange Freedom Initiative, a faith-based prisoner reentry program that has operated within Minnesota's prison system since 2002 (modeled after the InnerChange Freedom Initiative in Texas). Duwe and King (2013) examined recidivism outcomes among a total of 732 offenders released from Minnesota prisons between 2003 and 2009. A series of regression analyses document that participation in IFI significantly reduced the likelihood of rearrest (26 percent), reconviction (35 percent), and re-incarceration (40 percent) of former prisoners. [21] A new study extends the research on IFI by conducting a cost-benefit analysis of the program. Because IFI relies heavily on volunteers and program costs that are privately funded, the program involves no additional expense for the State of Minnesota. This study focused on estimating the program's benefits by examining recidivism and postrelease employment. The findings showed that during its first six years of operation in Minnesota, IFI produced an estimated benefit of $3 million, which amounts to approximately $8,300 per participant.[22]

In yet another study of Prison Fellowship, Kerley and associates explored the relationship between participation in Operation Starting Line (OSL), a faith-based prison event, and the subsequent experience of negative emotions and incidence of negative behaviors.[23] OSL participants were less likely to experience negative emotions and to engage in fights and arguments with other inmates or prison staff. The results from this study are consistent with previous research and were supported in a second study where Kerley surveyed prisoners in order to determine whether levels of reported religiosity were associated with reduced levels of arguing and fighting. The study found religiosity directly reduces the likelihood of arguing and indirectly reduces the likelihood of fighting.[24]

These positive criminology approaches can draw upon secular as well as faith-based models. In the Minnesota Department of Corrections, mentors who visit offenders in prison are associated not only with faith-based programs such as the InnerChange but also with community service agencies that are not necessarily faith-based. For example, in the Twin Cities (Minneapolis and St. Paul) metropolitan area, organizations like Amicus—which recently merged with Volunteers of America–Minnesota—have provided volunteers with opportunities to mentor offenders in prison since the 1960s.[25] Programs like InnerChange, Amicus, and the Salvation Army are doing important "positive criminology"–style work, some of which is faith-based and some of which is not. Decision-makers interested in cost-effective approaches to crime desistance among offender populations should pay attention to these promising approaches.

America's Bloodiest Prison Establishes a Seminary

The Louisiana State Penitentiary (aka Angola) is located in Angola, Louisiana, and is America's largest maximum-security prison, housing over 6,300 inmates in five separate complexes spread over 18,000 acres of a working prison farm. Cellblock and dormitory units are still called "camps" at Angola, a remnant of the traditional assignment of slaves to "work camps" across various locations of the property, a former slave plantation.[26] The property first became known as "Angola" because it

FIG. 10.1 THE NEW ORLEANS THEOLOGICAL BAPTIST SEMINARY AT ANGOLA.[30]

was this region of Africa that supplied its slaves. Roughly 75 percent of inmates currently serving time at Angola are serving life sentences.[27] A "life sentence" in Louisiana means "natural life," expiring only upon the inmate's death.[28] The average sentence for "non-lifers" at Angola in 2012 was 92.7 years.

For many decades, most guards at Angola were convicts themselves. Armed with rifles and shotguns, these "trusties" guarded the periphery of the camps, under orders to shoot anyone attempting to escape. While the use of convict guards saved money, it also contributed in large measure to the brutality and low morale of prisoners at Angola over the years. By the 1960s, rampant violence surfaced in headlines featuring a sinister partnership between inmates and state corrections staff operating prostitution rings and illicit drug markets at the prison. Such commonplace corruption and violence led to Angola's reputation for being the "bloodiest prison in America."[29]

In 1995, Burl Cain was appointed the new warden at Angola. Knowing the dismal history and challenge of this under-resourced and notorious prison, Cain knew it was necessary to do something dramatically different to put Angola on a more humane and prosocial trajectory. His idea was a novel one: establish a Bible college as a means of providing educational programs for prisoners and to give them another chance to make something positive out of their life. Cain was optimistic a prison-based seminary could successfully train prisoners to become ministers who over time would become effective change agents in the prison, ultimately replacing a culture of violence and corruption with a culture that was redemptive, hopeful, and personally transformative.

Later that year, Warden Cain was able to convince leaders of the New Orleans Baptist Theological Seminary to open a satellite campus within the walls of the Louisiana State Penitentiary. The building housing the Angola seminary was paid for with private donations. While legal doctrine has long rejected the notion that inmates have anything positive to contribute to the management of prisons, the Angola prison seminary and its unique inmate minister program operation challenge this notion.

The Role of Religion in Identity Transformation and Offender Rehabilitation

In 2012, I led a research team in launching a major five-year study of prisoners at Angola, especially those participating in the Bible college. Previous research on religion within prisons had focused largely on faith-based programs administered by faith-motivated volunteers and generally confirms that these programs can increase prosocial behavior inside of prison and even reduce recidivism following release from prison.[31] However, very little was known about what happens when inmates form and lead their own religious groups, interpret theology from inside of prison, and practice their faith communally inside the cellblocks. Our research culminated in a book entitled *The Angola Prison Seminary: Effects of Faith-Based Ministry on Identity Transformation, Desistance, and Rehabilitation* (Hallett et al. 2016).

Over a period of five years, our research team analyzed survey data from 2,200 inmates at the Louisiana State Penitentiary (aka Angola), and conducted more than one hundred life-history interviews of inmates and staff at this maximum security prison formerly known as one of the most violent and corrupt prisons in America. We examined the role of religious education and involvement in inmate-led religious congregations that was central to transforming prisoners and the housing units where they reside.

Utilizing a mixed-methods approach, a series of studies were produced that document the process of identity transformation and the catalytic role that religion plays in this process. We also found significant linkages between participation in the prison seminary and

FIG. 10.2 BIBLE COLLEGE STUDENTS IN THE SEMINARY LIBRARY.
(PHOTO BY AUTHOR)

FIG. 10.3 AN INMATE MINISTER PREACHING AT ONE OF ANGOLA'S TWENTY-NINE
INMATE-LED AND AUTONOMOUS CONGREGATIONS. (PHOTO BY AUTHOR)

inmate-led churches on crime desistance, rehabilitation, and prosocial behavior within the prison environment. Most importantly, the research points to the central role of inmate-led efforts to bring about these salutary findings.[32] Inmate ministers lead most of Angola's roughly two dozen autonomous churches, but their ministry transcends these formal gatherings. Their unique status also grants them a relative freedom of movement to minister among their peers on a daily basis. As one inmate minister described it, we have "the opportunity to actually practice what we preach. It gives us the opportunity to actually *be* the church instead of just *having* church." This sense of service is the hallmark of an authentic faith that is common among inmate ministers we observed.

Ethnographic accounts of inmate graduates of Angola's unique prison seminary program suggest that inmate ministers assume a number of pastoral service roles throughout the prison. Inmate ministers establish their own churches and serve in lay-ministry capacities in hospice, cellblock visitation, tier ministry, officiating inmate funerals, and through tithing with "care packages" for indigent prisoners. Despite the fact they are serving life sentences without the possibility of parole, inmate ministers are able to find meaning and purpose for their lives. The inmate ministers assist others in finding that meaning, thereby providing them with the human grace and dignity they may have thought they lost or perhaps never had.

By embracing religion and being afforded the opportunity to choose a better self, inmates transform their lives, come to care about others, and display their humanity on a daily basis. Several themes of positive criminology emerge from inmate narratives: (a) the importance of respectful treatment of inmates by correctional administrations, (b) the value of building trusting relationships for prosocial modeling and improved self-perception, (c) repairing harm through faith-based intervention, and (d) spiritual practice as a blueprint for positive self-identity and social integration among prisoners.[33]

Though research on how incarcerated offenders can help other prisoners change is rare, the Field Ministry program within the Texas Department of Criminal Justice is a current example. The program enlists inmates who have graduated from a prison-based seminary to work as "field ministers," serving other inmates in various capacities.[34] Scholars have recently examined whether inmate exposure to field ministers is inversely related to antisocial factors and positively to prosocial ones at three maximum-security prisons where the Field Ministry program operates. Preliminary results indicate inmates exposed

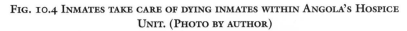

FIG. 10.4 INMATES TAKE CARE OF DYING INMATES WITHIN ANGOLA'S HOSPICE
UNIT. (PHOTO BY AUTHOR)

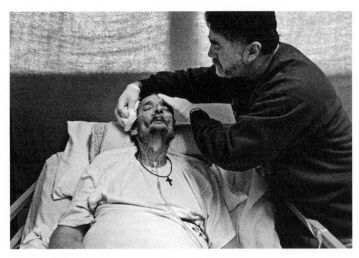

to field ministers more frequently and for a longer period tended to report lower levels of criminological risk factors (e.g., legal cynicism) and aggressiveness, and higher levels of virtues (e.g., humility), predictors of human agency (e.g., a sense of meaning and purpose in life), religiosity, and spirituality. We find that prisoners who are the beneficiaries of the inmate-led field ministry help other prisoners make positive and prosocial changes. We conclude that inmate ministers play an important role in fostering virtuous behavior[35] and achieving the goal of offender rehabilitation.[36] Moreover, we find that some offenders in prison should be viewed as potential assets waiting to be reformed with the help of other offenders.[37]

A 2017 book and documentary film, both titled *If I Give My Soul: Faith behind Bars in Rio de Janeiro*, argue that inmate-led Pentecostalism thrives inside of prison because it offers prisoners—mostly poor, darker-skinned young men—a platform to live moral and dignified lives in a social context that treats them as less than human, or "killable."[38] And a recent study conducted in El Salvador by scholars at Florida International University concludes that the only realistic hope for incarcerated MS-13 gang members to desist from a life of crime and violence is by means of a conversion to Christianity and subsequent involvement in Evangelical or Pentecostal churches.[39] This initial study is intriguing, but more rigorous and systematic research is necessary

FIG. 10.5 PHOTOGRAPH FROM ARTICLE APPEARING IN THE APRIL/MAY 2018
ISSUE OF *THE ECONOMIST.*[40]

to understand how, if at all, inmate-led religious interventions may be linked to positive and consequential outcomes.

Research on Offender-Led Religious Movements

In the book *The Wounded Healer* (1979), Henri Nouwen states, "the great illusion of leadership is to think that man can be led out of the desert by someone who has never been there."[41] This line of reasoning would seem to suggest that prisoners may well be the most appropriate people to aid other inmates in the process of being reformed. Who is more equipped to challenge, affirm, or relate to a prisoner than another prisoner? Similarly, offenders participating in twelve-step programs are essentially working from a similar "wounded healer" paradigm—where addicts help other addicts stay sober through various social support and acts of service. Perhaps there is an authenticity unique to offenders that enables them to be connected to other offenders in ways that free-world people cannot.

A new line of research is necessary that will focus specifically on religious groups indigenous to the cellblocks—what I am calling Offender-Led Religious Movements (ORMs). ORMs have the capacity to provide participants a strong identity, an alternative moral framework, and a set of embodied practices that emphasize virtue and character development. Though there are significant roadblocks to the proliferation of ORMs, this innovative approach to rehabilitation and reform holds significant potential to transform the character of not only individual prisoners, but particular cellblocks or housing units, and possibly entire correctional facilities. Though nearly invisible to scholars and coreligionists on the outside, studying ORMs may provide rich insight on how virtue and character is developed inside of correctional facilities through inmate-led religious groups. This kind of research will help scholars and practitioners understand if ORMs can provide a path for prisoners to experience an identity transformation that is consistent with the need to rehabilitate offenders. Moreover, this line of research will shed light on how, if at all, ORMs emphasize or facilitate prosocial behavior, spiritual awakening, service to others, prayer, perseverance, and forgiveness. It will address questions such as: How and why do ORMs emerge? What character traits and virtues are promoted by ORMs? How are these values and behaviors developed by prisoners participating in ORMs? And what impact do ORMs have on the broader prison environment? How can social scientists measure the impact of ORMs on individual offenders, housing units, and the prison environment more generally?

Implications for Justice System Reform

Today there is widespread consensus on the need for criminal justice reform. Preliminary research into offender-led religious movements suggest that these movements may be a key factor in rethinking some of our approaches to correctional programs and rehabilitation. Obviously, we need empirical research to confirm the nature, prevalence, and consequences of these movements. Are ORMs isolated or quite common? Are these inmate-led interventions effective? If so, can ORMs be replicated in different jurisdictions and correctional environments?

The question regarding potential replication of ORMs, however, presents policy makers with a dilemma. ORMs, like those led by inmate pastors at Angola, pose a legal challenge to correctional agencies. The well-documented trusty system, dating back to the early 1900s, allowed inmates to wield authority over prisoners. Angola was one of many prisons where correctional staff designated select inmates to control and administer physical punishment to other inmates based on a hierarchy of power. The legal case of *Gates v. Collier*[42] ended the flagrant abuse of inmates under the trusty system at the Mississippi State Penitentiary (Parchman) that had existed for many decades. Other states using the trusty system were also forced to give it up under this ruling. Following the *Gates v. Collier* decision, states adopted policies preventing prisoners to hold positions of authority over other prisoners.

This legal decision and subsequent policy change has made it virtually impossible to organize and establish inmate-led congregations. In spite of this, at least twenty states have launched prison seminaries. Nonetheless, Louisiana remains the only state so far to allow inmates to form and lead their own religious congregations. Thus, Angola is the only prison we know of that allows inmate-led churches to exist.

Interviewing inmate pastors at Angola, as well as correctional officers and other prison administrators, it is apparent that inmate ministers do not have "authority" over other inmates. A more accurate description is that ministers simply serve other prisoners. Indeed, the varied acts of service that our research uncovered at Angola suggest that inmate pastors represent anything but abusive authority. As one inmate minister expressed to us, "[M]y status as Inmate Minister makes me even more of a servant to others, to give my time to the advancement of God's mission, which is the comforting of his people: 'Feed my sheep.'"[43]

In an age of evidenced-based government, empirical research can provide policy makers and practitioners in government and the private sector with findings and data that can be used to produce better interventions and outcomes. The current push for criminal justice reform has brought together leaders from both sides of the political aisle. However, solutions to criminal justice reform often remain difficult to find because of budgetary constraints. Research in the subfield of positive criminology suggests that positive and restorative approaches—including those that cultivate social connectedness and support, service to others, spiritual experience, personal integrity, and identity change—may be more effective than traditional approaches to punishment.[44]

Consistent with restorative justice practices, these approaches seek to develop active responsibility on the part of individuals who have grown accustomed to a lifestyle of irresponsibility.[45] From this perspective, correctional practices should be devised to promote virtue. Consequently, the goal of justice or punishment should not be to inflict pain or exact revenge but rather to reconstruct and reform individuals.[46]

If offender-led religious movements are found to foster rehabilitation and identify transformation and to be associated with recidivism reduction, one can argue for the potential of ORMs to make for safer prisons and communities, and to do so as a cost-effective alternative. Thus, it would seem to make sense to pay more attention to these kinds of faith-based approaches and to promote them as potential aids to the common good. Policy makers and practitioners should have access to rigorous research which evaluates the value of ORMs in addressing topics like rehabilitation, drug treatment, educational and vocational programs, prisoner reentry, and criminal justice reform more broadly.

References

Braithwaite, John. 2005. "Between Proportionality and Impunity: Confrontation, Truth, Prevention." *Criminology* 43: 283–305.

Brooks, Arthur C. 2007. *Who Really Cares: The Surprising Truth about Compassionate Conservatism.* New York: Basic Books.

Carleton, Mark T. 1971. *Politics and Punishment: The History of the Louisiana State Penal System.* Baton Rouge: Louisiana State University Press.

Cnaan, Ram A., and Stephanie C. Boddie. 2001. "Philadelphia Census of Congregations and Their Involvement in Social Service Delivery." *Social Service Review* 75, no. 4: 559–80.

Cruz, Jose M., Jonathan D. Rosen, Luis E. Amaya, and Yulia Vorobyeva. 2018. *The New Face of Street Gangs: The Gang Phenomenon in El Salvador.* Miami: Florida International University.

Duwe, Grant, Michael Hallett, Joshua Hays, Sung Joon Jang, and Byron R. Johnson. 2015. "Bible College Participation and Prison Misconduct: A Preliminary Analysis." *Journal of Offender Rehabilitation* 54: 371–90.

Duwe, Grant, and Byron R. Johnson. 2013. "Estimating the Benefits of a Faith-Based Correctional Program." *International Journal of Criminology and Sociology* 2: 227–39.

Duwe, Grant, and Byron R. Johnson. 2016. "The Effects of Prison Visits from Community Volunteers on Offender Recidivism." *Prison Journal* 96: 279–303.

Duwe, Grant, and Michelle King. 2013. "Can Faith-Based Correctional Programs Work? An Outcome Evaluation of the InnerChange Freedom Initiative in Minnesota." *International Journal of Offender Therapy and Comparative Criminology* 57: 813–41.

Ellison, Christopher G., Jennifer A. Trinitapoli, Kristin L. Anderson, and Byron R. Johnson. 2007. "Religion and Domestic Violence: An Examination of Variations by Race and Ethnicity." *Violence against Women* 13, no. 11: 1094–1112.

Gates v. Collier, 501 F.2d 1291 (5th Cir. 1974).

Glewwe, Paul, Phillip H. Ross, and Bruce Wydick. 2018. "Developing Hope among Impoverished Children: Using Child Self-Portraits to Measure Poverty Program Impacts." *Journal of Human Resources* 53, no. 2: 330–55. 10.3368/jhr.53.2.0816-8112R1.

Grammich, Clifford, C. Kirk Hadaway, Richard Houseal, Dale E. Jones, Alexei Krindatach, Richey Stanley, and Richard H. Taylor. 2012. *2010 U.S. Religion Census: Religious Congregations and Membership Survey.*

Association of Statisticians of American Religious Bodies. Fairfield, Ohio: Glenmary Research Center.

Hallett, Michael, Joshua Hays, Byron R. Johnson, Sung Joon Jang, and Grant Duwe. 2016. *The Angola Prison Seminary: Effects of Faith-Based Ministry on Identity Transformation, Desistance and Rehabilitation.* West Conshohocken, Pa.: Templeton Press.

———. 2017. "First Stop Dying: Angola's Christian Seminary as Positive Criminology." *International Journal of Offender Therapy and Comparative Criminology* 61, no. 4: 445–63.

Hays, Joshua, Michael Hallett, Byron R. Johnson, Sung Joon Jang, and Grant Duwe. 2018. "Inmate Ministry as Contextual Missiology: Best Practices for America's Emerging Prison Seminary Movement." *Perspectives in Religious Studies* 45, no. 1: 69–79.

Jang, Sung Joon, and Byron R. Johnson. 2001. "Neighborhood Disorder, Individual Religiosity, and Adolescent Drug Use: A Test of Multilevel Hypotheses." *Criminology* 39: 501–35.

———. 2011. "The Effects of Childhood Exposure to Drug Users and Religion on Drug Use in Adolescence and Young Adulthood." *Youth and Society* 43: 1220–45.

———. 2017. "Religion, Spirituality, and Desistance from Crime: Toward a Theory of Existential Identity Transformation." In *International Handbook of Criminal Careers and Life-Course Criminology*, edited by Arjan Blokland and Victor van der Geest, 74–86. New York: Routledge.

Jang, Sung Joon, Byron R. Johnson, Joshua Hays, Michael Hallett, and Grant Duwe. 2017. "Religion and Misconduct in "Angola" Prison: Conversion, Congregational Participation, Religiosity, and Self-Identities." *Justice Quarterly* 35, no. 3: 412–42.

———. 2018. "Existential and Virtuous Effects of Religiosity on Mental Health and Aggressiveness among Offenders." *Religions* 9: 182. doi: 10.3390/rel9060182.

Johnson, Andrew. 2017. *If I Give My Soul: Faith behind Bars in Rio de Janeiro.* New York: Oxford University Press.

Johnson, Byron R. 2004. "Religious Programs and Recidivism among Former Inmates in Prison Fellowship Programs: A Long-Term Follow-Up Study." *Justice Quarterly* 21, no. 2: 329–54.

———. 2006. *The InnerChange Freedom Initiative: A Preliminary Evaluation of a Faith-Based Prison Program.* Institute for Studies of Religion (ISR Research Report). Waco: Baylor University. http://www.BAYLORISR .org/publications/reports/.

———. 2011. *More God, Less Crime: Why Faith Matters and How It Could Matter More.* West Conshohocken, Pa.: Templeton Press.

———. 2012. "Can a Faith-Based Prison Reduce Recidivism?" *Corrections Today* 73: 60–62.

———. 2018a. "The Role of Religion in Advancing the Field of Criminology." In *Religion and the Social Sciences: Basic and Applied Research Perspectives*, edited by Jeff Levin, 181–207. West Conshohocken, Pa.: Templeton Press.

———. 2018b. "Why Religious Freedom Is Good for Inmates, Prisons, and Society." In *The Wiley Handbook of Christianity and Education*, edited by William Jeynes, 119–40. New York: Wiley-Blackwell.

Johnson, Byron R., Grant Duwe, Michael Hallett, Joshua Hays, Sung Joon Jang, Matthew T. Lee, Maria E. Pagano, and Stephen G. Post. 2017. "Faith and Service: Pathways to Identity Transformation and Correctional Reform." In *Finding Freedom in Confinement: The Role of Religion in Prison Life*, edited by Kent Kerley, 3–23. Santa Barbara: Praeger.

Johnson, Byron R., and Sung Joon Jang. 2012. "Religion and Crime: Assessing the Role of the Faith Factor." In *Contemporary Issues in Criminological Theory and Research: The Role of Social Institutions*, edited by Richard Rosenfeld, Kenna Quinet, and Crystal Garcia, 117–50. Collected Papers from the American Society of Criminology 2010 Conference. Belmont, Calif.: Wadsworth.

Johnson, Byron R., Sung Joon Jang, David B. Larson, and Spencer D. Li. 2001. "Does Adolescent Religious Commitment Matter? A Reexamination of the Effects of Religiosity on Delinquency." *Journal of Research in Crime and Delinquency* 38: 22–44.

Johnson, Byron R., David B. Larson, Sung Joon Jang, and Spencer D. Li. 2000a. "The "Invisible Institution" and Black Youth Crime: The Church as an Agency of Local Social Control." *Journal of Youth and Adolescence* 29: 479–98.

———. 2000b. "Who Escapes the Crime of Inner-Cities: Church Attendance and Religious Salience among Disadvantaged Youth." *Justice Quarterly* 17: 701–15.

Johnson, Byron R., with David B. Larson and Timothy G. Pitts. 1997. "Religious Programming, Institutional Adjustment and Recidivism among Former Inmates in Prison Fellowship Programs." *Justice Quarterly* 14, no. 1: 145–66.

Johnson, Byron R., Matthew T. Lee, Maria E. Pagano, and Stephen G. Post. 2015. "Alone on the Inside: The Impact of Social Isolation and Helping Others on AOD Use and Criminal Activity." *Youth and Society* 50, no. 4: 529–50. doi: 10.1177/0044118X15617400.

———. 2016. "Positive Criminology and Rethinking the Response to Adolescent Addiction: Evidence on the Role of Social Support, Religiosity, and Service to Others." *International Journal of Criminology and Sociology* 5: 75–85.

Johnson, Byron R., Brett Thompkins, and David Webb. 2006. *Objective Hope—Assessing the Effectiveness of Religion and Faith-Based Organizations: A Systematic Review of the Literature*. Institute for

Studies of Religion (Research Report). Waco: Baylor University. www.BAYLORISR.org/publications/reports/.

Johnson, Byron R., and William Wubbenhorst. 2017. "Assessing the Faith-Based Response to Homelessness in America: Findings from Eleven Cities." Program on Prosocial Behavior. Waco: Baylor University.

Kerley, Kent R., Todd L. Matthews, and Troy C. Blanchard. 2005. "Religiosity, Religious Participation, and Negative Prison Behaviors." *Journal for the Scientific Study of Religion* 44: 443–57.

Kerley, Kent R., Todd L. Matthews, and Jeffrey T. Schulz. 2005. "Participation in Operation Starting Line, Experience of Negative Emotions, and Incidence of Negative Behavior." *International Journal of Offender Therapy and Comparative Criminology* 49: 410–26.

Koenig, Harold G., Dana E. King, and Verna B. Carson. 2012. *Handbook of Religion and Health.* 2nd ed. New York: Oxford University Press.

Krause, Neal, and R. David Hayward. 2013. "Measuring Communities of Faith: A Preliminary Investigation." *Journal of Religion, Spirituality, and Aging* 25, no. 3: 258–76.

———. 2014a. "Religious Involvement, Practical Wisdom, and Self-Rated Health." *Journal of Aging and Health* 26, no. 4: 540–58.

———. 2014b. "Work at Church and Church-Based Social Support among Older Whites, Blacks, and Mexican Americans." *Journal of Religion, Spirituality, and Aging* 26, no. 1: 22–40.

Krause, Neal, R. David Hayward, Deborah Bruce, and Cynthia Woolever. 2014. "Gratitude to God, Self-Rated Health, and Depressive Symptoms." *Journal for the Scientific Study of Religion* 53, no. 2: 341–55.

Lee, Matthew T., Maria E. Pagano, Byron R. Johnson, and Stephen G. Post. 2016. "Love and Service in Adolescent Addiction Recovery." *Alcohol Treatment Quarterly* 34, no. 2: 197–222.

Lee, Matthew T., Maria E. Pagano, Byron R. Johnson, Stephen G. Post, and George S. Leibowitz. 2017. "From Defiance to Reliance: Spiritual Virtue as a Pathway towards Desistence, Humility, and Recovery among Juvenile Offenders." *Spirituality in Clinical Practice* 4, no. 3: 161–75.

Louisiana Department of Corrections. 2015. Briefing book. Baton Rouge: Louisiana Dept or Corrections. http://www.doc.la.gov/wp-content/uploads/2009/10/Jan2015bb.pdf.

Maslin, Sarah E. 2018. "Can Religion Solve El Salvador's Gang Problem?" *The Economist: 1843.* https://www.1843magazine.com/features/can-religion-solve-el-salvadors-gang-problem.

Melton, J. Gordon, and Todd Ferguson. 2016. *The Churches of McLennan County, Texas: A 2015 Snapshot.* Institute for Studies of Religion. Waco: Baylor University.

Nellis, Ashley. 2010. *Throwing away the Key: The Expansion of Life without Parole Sentences in the United States.* Washington, D.C.: The Federal

Sentencing Reporter. http://sentencingproject.org/doc/publications/inc_federalsentencingreporter.pdf.

Nouwen, Henri J. M. 1979. *The Wounded Healer.* New York: Random House.

Pagano, Maria E., Alexandra R. Wang, Brieana M. Rowles, T. Lee, and Byron R. Johnson. 2015. "Social Anxiety and Peer-Helping in Adolescent Addiction Treatment." *Alcoholism: Clinical and Experimental Research* 39, no. 5: 887–95.

Putnam, Robert D., and David Campbell. 2012. *American Grace: How Religion Divides and Unites Us.* New York: Simon & Schuster.

Rideau, Wilbert. 1985. *The Angolite.* Louisiana State Penitentiary.

Ronel, Natti, and Ety Elisha. 2011. "A Different Perspective: Introducing Positive Criminology." *International Journal of Offender Therapy and Comparative Criminology* 55, no. 2: 30525.

Ronel, Natti, and Dana Segev, eds. 2015. *Positive Criminology.* New York: Routledge.

Stark, Rodney. 2008. *What Americans Really Believe.* Waco: Baylor University Press.

———. 2015. *The Triumph of Faith: Why the World Is More Religious than Ever.* New York: Intercollegiate Studies Institute.

Ulmer, Jeffrey T., Scott Desmond, Sung Joon Jang, and Byron R. Johnson. 2010. "Teenage Religiosity and Changes in Marijuana Use during the Transition to Adulthood." *Interdisciplinary Journal of Research on Religion* 6: 1–19.

———. 2012. "Religiosity and Dynamics of Marijuana Use: Initiation, Persistence, and Desistence." *Deviant Behavior* 33: 448–68.

VanderWeele, Tyler J. 2017a. "Religious Communities and Human Flourishing." *Current Directions in Psychological Science* 26: 476–81.

———. 2017b. "On the Promotion of Human Flourishing." *Proceedings of the National Academy of Sciences* 31: 8148–56.

———. 2018. "Is Forgiveness a Public Health Issue?" *American Journal of Public Health* 108: 189–90.

Wydick, Bruce, Paul Glewwe, and Laine Rutledge. 2013. "Does International Child Sponsorship Work? A Six-County Study of Impacts on Adult Life Outcomes." *Journal of Political Economy* 121: 393–436.

———. 2017. "Does Child Sponsorship Pay Off in Adulthood? An International Study of Impacts on Income and Wealth." *World Bank Economic Review* 31: 434–58.

Young, Mark John Gartner, Thomas O'Conner, David B. Larson, and Kevin Wright. 1995. "Long-Term Recidivism among Federal Inmates Trained as Volunteer Prison Ministers." *Journal of Offender Rehabilitation* 22: 97–118.

11

SOME BIG-DATA LESSONS ABOUT RELIGION AND HUMAN FLOURISHING[1]

David G. Myers

Throughout human history, religion has been associated both with great evils (from yesterday's Crusades to today's gay-bashing) and with great good (the founding of hospitals, universities, hospices, and antislavery movements). It is a "stunning historical paradox," Stephen Jay Gould observed, "that organized religion has fostered, throughout Western history, both the most unspeakable horrors and the most heartrending examples of human goodness."[2]

But history aside, is today's religious life, on balance, more heartless or humanitarian? More vile or virtuous? More guilt-laden or glad-hearted? Without assessing religion's truth claims, I will first summarize positive associations between religious engagement and happiness, health, and helping. But then the plot will thicken, as we consider a curious "religious engagement paradox"—showing that these positive associations across *individuals* are reversed when comparing more versus less religious *places*. In short, individual and aggregate data tell different stories.

Comparing Religious and Irreligious Individuals

Happiness

Across time, actively religious people have reported greater happiness. In Gallup surveys, those scoring highest in "spiritual commitment"

FIG. 11.1 AVERAGE NUMBER OF DAILY POSITIVE AND NEGATIVE EMOTIONS, BY
CHURCH ATTENDANCE. (JANUARY 2–DECEMBER 31, 2011; GALLUP-HEALTHWAYS
WELL-BEING INDEX)[4]

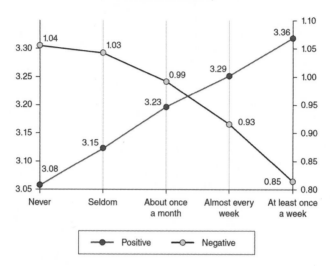

(agreeing, for example, that "My religious faith is the most important influence in my life") were doubly likely, compared to those least
spiritually committed, to report being "very happy."[3] In 2009–2010
surveys of 676,080 Americans, "very religious" adults have had "higher
overall wellbeing" and been "less likely to have ever been diagnosed
with depression."[5] And in the 2011 Gallup daily survey, more frequent
religious attendance predicted more positive emotions and fewer negative emotions (fig. 11.1).

Such "mere correlations" do not, of course, indicate which direction
the traffic runs between happiness and religiosity (or whether both are
manifestations of some underlying factor). But a German panel study
that followed 12,000 lives across twenty years found that those who
became more religious gained in life satisfaction, while those whose
religiosity waned became less satisfied. "Religious beliefs and activities
can make a substantial difference to life satisfaction," the researchers
concluded.[6]

Various subcomponents of "the religious factor" help explain its
association with well-being. For many people, religious engagement
entails

- *social support*—including from the 350,000 faith communities
  in the United States.[7]

- *enhanced meaning and purpose*—a sense that their lives mean something in a universe that has coherence.
- *impulse control*—thanks to greater self-monitoring and self-regulation.
- *self-acceptance*—for those who assume and embrace God's love and grace.
- *terror-management*—via an ultimate hope when confronting even death.

People sometimes argue that the religion variable is "nothing but" these components. Thus, controlling for them would surely "squeeze the juice" out of the religion factor. Indeed, yes, much like a hurricane actually has little effect once one controls for the rain, wind, and storm surge. Religion, like a hurricane, is a package variable.

Health

In Medline, the word root "religio" appeared in 6,788 abstracts in the last thirty-five years of the twentieth century and in 21,622 in the first seventeen-plus years of the twenty-first century. That's 3.2 times the research in half as many years. As other conference contributors will note, these include epidemiological demonstrations of greater longevity among those religiously engaged. Moreover, this is true for both men and women (and thus does not merely reflect women being both longer-lived and more religious). As figure 11.2 suggests, the religious engagement effect may be mediated by healthier behavior, greater social support, and more positive emotions.[8]

FIG. 11.2 MEDIATING INFLUENCES ON THE RELIGIOUS ENGAGEMENT EFFECT.

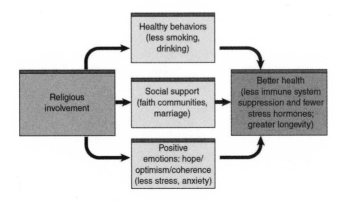

Helpfulness

Christopher Hitchens claimed religion is "violent, irrational, intolerant, allied to racism and tribalism and bigotry, invested in ignorance and hostile to free inquiry, contemptuous of women and coercive toward children."[9] Evolutionists (including David Sloan Wilson[10] and E. O. Wilson[11]) and their interpreters presume that religion is widespread because it is socially adaptive—by fostering morality, social cohesion, and group survival. Who is more often right?

International surveys reveal that actively religious Jews in Israel, Catholics in Spain, Greek Orthodox in Greece, Calvinists in the Netherlands, and Lutherans in Germany express less hedonism and self-orientation.[12] And the U.S. General Social Survey (tinyurl.com/ generalsocialsurvey) reveals that "volunteering" has been considered an "important obligation" by 16 percent of religious nonattenders and by 38 percent of those who attend services at least weekly.

But do they walk the prosocial talk? Repeated surveys report that volunteerism and charitable giving are substantially greater among Americans who are actively religious (e.g., Putnam and Campbell).[13] And, as figures 11.3 and 11.4 illustrate, global data from the Gallup World Poll extend the association between religiosity and generosity (with time and money).[14]

To further explore helping behavior, we could ask who is most likely to

- adopt children and provide foster care,
- mentor at-risk children, ex-prisoners, and immigrants,
- provide disaster relief via volunteerism and contributions,
- seek careers as helping professionals or teachers, and
- include a substantial charitable component in their will?

The Religious Engagement Paradox

Religion has been a mixed blessing. On the one hand, it has been a source of needless guilt, the suppression of women and people of color, and anti-gay brutality. Moreover, by presuming that God is on one's side, religion has been used to justify ingroup bias, tribalism, and war. On the other hand, religious engagement, especially in relatively religious Western countries such as the U.S., is, as we have seen, associated with happiness, health, and helping.

FIG. 11.3 GALLUP WORLD POLL, 2000+ PER COUNTRY × 140 COUNTRIES, 2006–2008.

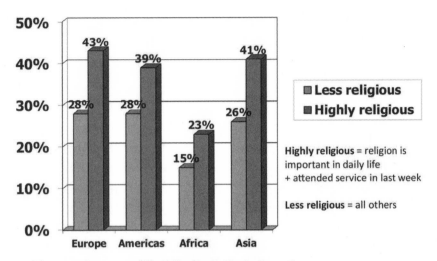

Have you done any of the following in the last month:
Donate to charity

FIG. 11.4 GALLUP WORLD POLL.

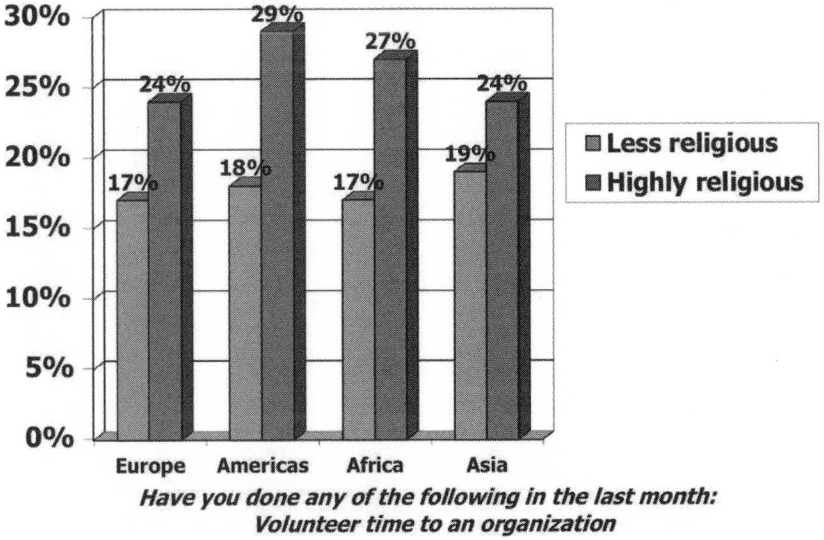

Have you done any of the following in the last month:
Volunteer time to an organization

But there is more to the story, for these positive correlations between individuals' religious engagement and their flourishing *reverse* when we compare more versus less religious *places.* To restate this curious, unexpected, and repeated finding, religious engagement correlates *positively* with human flourishing across *individuals* (as we have seen) and *negatively* across *places.* Said simply, religious individuals and irreligious places tend to be flourishing. Consider the evidence.

Emotional Well-Being

I first stumbled across these paradoxical results when exploring Gallup World Poll data from 152 countries. In contrast to the positive religion/ well-being correlations mentioned above, I discovered a striking *negative* correlation across countries' percent of their people declaring that religion is "important in your daily life" and their average life satisfaction score (fig. 11.5). Ergo, despite religion's individual-level associations with the good life, at the aggregate (country) level it was associated with the bad life.

FIG. 11.5 GALLUP WORLD POLL, 2006–2008.

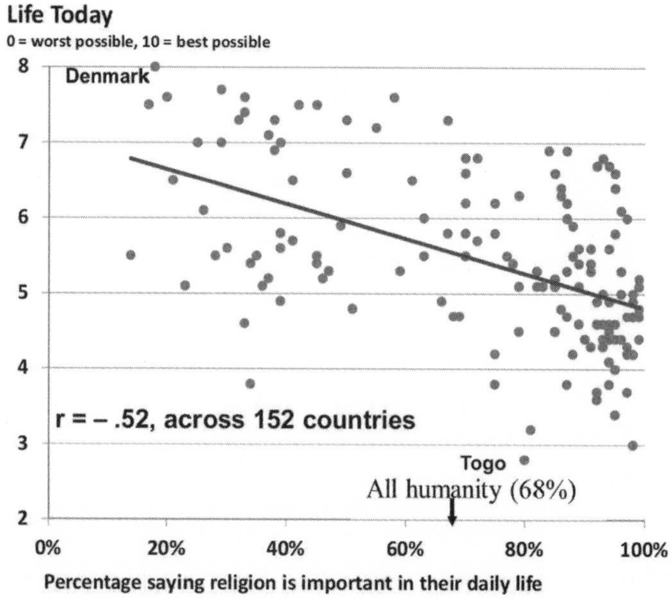

Life Today
0 = worst possible, 10 = best possible

r = − .52, across 152 countries

Togo

All humanity (68%)

Percentage saying religion is important in their daily life

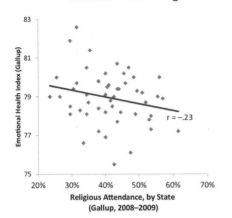

Emotional Well-Being   FIG. 11.6

r = −.23

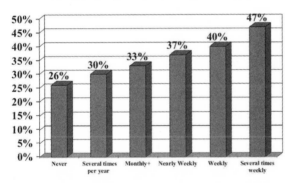

% Very Happy and Religious
Attendance (n = 57,226, NORC, 1972–2016)

FIG. 11.7 NATIONAL
OPINION RESEARCH
CENTER GENERAL
SOCIAL SURVEY.

Similarly, *across U.S. states*, religious engagement predicts modestly *lower* emotional well-being, as assessed by Gallup's "emotional health index" (which asked people, for example, if, "yesterday," they felt treated with respect all day, smiled and laughed a lot, learned or did something interesting, and experienced each of the following feelings: enjoyment, worry, sadness, stress, anger, happiness, and depression) (fig. 11.6).

Yet, to further document a point made earlier, *across individuals, religious engagement predicts greater self-reported happiness.* In National Opinion Research Center General Social Surveys, actively religious individuals more often report being "very happy" (fig. 11.7). This association between religiosity and well-being is evident within many other countries in the Gallup World Poll and also in World Values Survey data, Australian national surveys,[15] and in various other surveys.[16]

Life Expectancy

Across states, religious engagement predicts shorter life expectancy. Religious attendance rates correlate negatively with state average life expectancy (fig. 11.8).[17] Yet *across individuals, religious engagement predicts longer life expectancy* (fig. 11.9). In epidemiological studies, including a meta-analysis of sixty-nine studies, religious *individuals* live longer.[18]

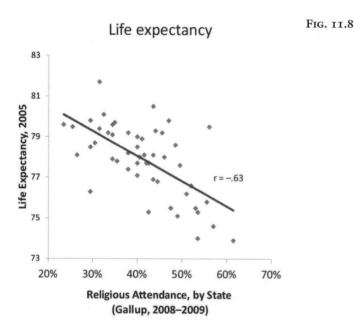

Life expectancy

FIG. 11.8

$r = -.63$

Religious Attendance, by State
(Gallup, 2008–2009)

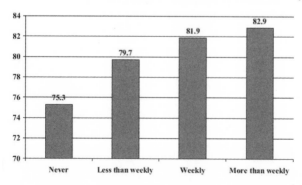

FIG. 11.9

Life Expectancy at Age 20, by Worship Attendance

(21,204 Americans in National Health Interview Survey)

Smoking

The life expectancy variations are attributable partly to smoking rate differences. *Across states, religious engagement predicts higher smoking rates.* With the dramatic exception of Utah, more religious states (such as in the American South) report more smoking (fig. 11.10). Yet *across individuals, religious engagement predicts lower smoking rates* (fig. 11.11). (In National Opinion Research Center General Social Surveys, actively religious individuals have reported smoking much less.)

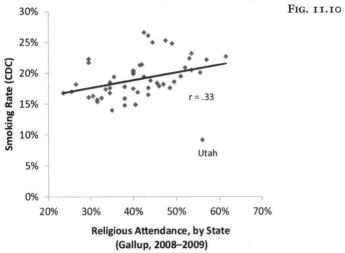

FIG. 11.10

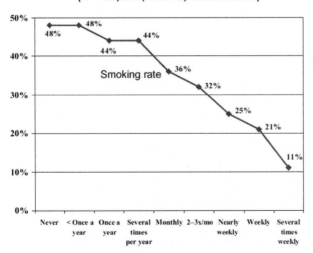

FIG. 11.11

Crime Rates

Across states, religious engagement predicts higher crime rates (fig. 11.12). Total crime is the sum of property + violent crime as reported in the FBI Uniform Crime Report. Yet *across individuals, religious engagement predicts lower crime rates* (fig. 11.13). In National Opinion Research Center General Social Surveys, actively religious individuals are much less likely to report having been arrested.

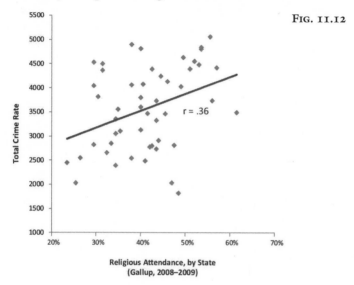

FIG. 11.12

r = .36

Total Crime Rate

Religious Attendance, by State
(Gallup, 2008–2009)

Religious Attendance and Arrest Rate   FIG. 11.13

(n=10,535, General Social Survey, 1972-2008)

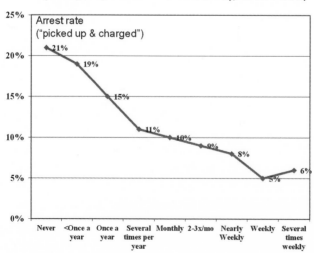

Arrest rate
("picked up & charged")

21%
19%
15%
11%
10%
9%
8%
5%
6%

Never | <Once a year | Once a year | Several times per year | Monthly | 2-3x/mo | Nearly Weekly | Weekly | Several times weekly

Divorce

Across states, religious engagement is virtually uncorrelated with divorce rates. 2008 divorce rates, reported as share of marriages, correlate + .05 with state divorce rates (excluding data from five not-reporting states: California, Georgia, Hawaii, Louisiana, Minnesota) (fig. 11.14).[19] Yet *across individuals, religious engagement predicts lower divorce rate.* In National Opinion Research Center General Social Surveys, actively religious individuals more often report being married or widowed and less often report being divorced or separated (fig. 11.15).

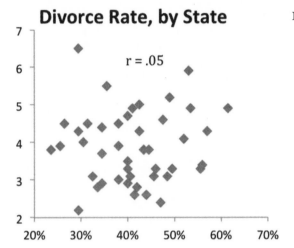

Divorce Rate, by State   FIG. 11.14

r = .05

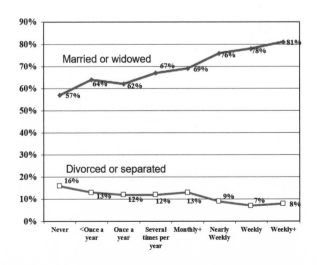

Marital Status, by Religious   FIG. 11.15

Attendance (n=52,545, NORC, 1972-2008)

Married or widowed

Divorced or separated

Teen Pregnancy and Birth

Across states, religious engagement predicts higher teen birth and pregnancy rates (figs. 11.16 and 11.17).[20] Using an eight-item measure of adult religious belief and practice from the Pew Forum's U.S. Religious Landscapes Survey, another research team found a stronger .73 correlation between state-level religiosity and teen (ages fifteen to nineteen) birth rate.[21]

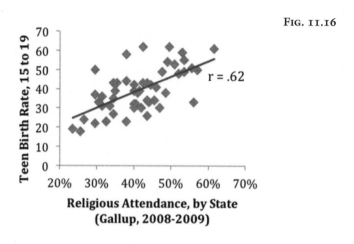

FIG. 11.16

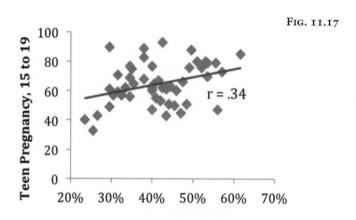

FIG. 11.17

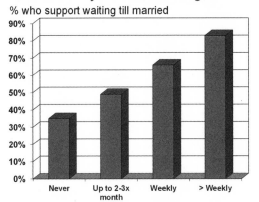

National Survey of Youth and Religion   FIG. 11.18

% who support waiting till married

Religious Attendance

National Longitudinal Study of   FIG. 11.19
Adolescent Health

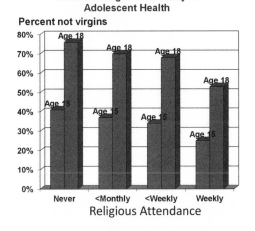

Religious Attendance

National Survey of Youth and Religion   FIG. 11.20

Percent "delayers"
(have not had sex and are in no hurry to)

Religious Attendance

Across individual teens, religious engagement predicts more support for "waiting till married," less sexual activity, and modestly fewer teen births. These figure 11.18 data come from the National Survey on Youth and Religion (a survey of a nationally representative sample of thirteen-to-seventeen-year-olds)[22] and the National Longitudinal Study of Adolescent Health.[23]

The latter study also found that religious engagement was not a predictor, among those sexually active, of using birth control at first or most recent sex. If religiously engaged teens are a) more sexually restrained, and b) not less likely to use birth control when sexually active, they should have somewhat fewer teen births. Indeed, religiously engaged teens have a slightly reduced risk of "ever being pregnant" (National Longitudinal Study of Adolescent Health: r = −.22) and of premarital pregnancy (a new meta-analytic review of 87 studies of adolescent religiosity and sexuality: r = −.16) (figs. 11.19 and 11.20).[24]

Two Exceptions to the Religious Engagement Paradox

One notable exception to the religious engagement paradox is the lower suicide rates of both more-religious countries[25] and individuals.[26] A second anomalous finding is Andrew Clark and Orsolya Lelkes' observation, from 86,701 respondents to the European Social Survey, that "people [both religious and nonreligious] are more satisfied in more religious regions," a finding they attribute to factors such as greater social capital and lower crime.[27]

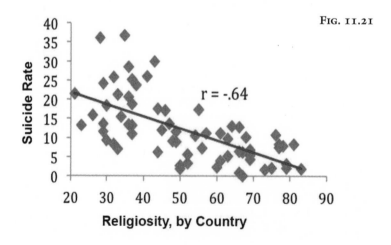

FIG. 11.21

Reflections on Aggregate versus Individual Data

In a 2018 chapter for the annual Sydney Symposium on Social Psychology, I offered these additional observations:

> So we are presented with strikingly paradoxical results. Various measures reveal a positive association between religious engagement and human flourishing across individuals, and a negative association across aggregate places. If you were to be plucked from where you live now and dropped into another country or state, and if you want your new place to embody the good life—the healthy, happy, crime free life—then hope for a secular place. Pray that it will be secular Denmark rather than religious Pakistan, or secular Vermont rather than religious Mississippi. Yet survey data from many countries (though especially the more religious countries) reveal that actively religious individuals are happier, live longer, smoke less, commit less crime, have lower risk of teen pregnancy, and so forth. For religion's apologists and critics there is a practical lesson here: If you want to make religion look good, cite individual data. If you want to make it look bad, cite aggregate data.

Angus Deaton and Arthur Stone have been independently struck by these paradoxical findings: "Why might there be this sharp contradiction between religious people being happy and healthy, and religious places being anything but?"[28]

And consider this: Similarly stunning individual versus aggregate paradoxes appear in other realms as well. As Ed Diener and I explain,[29] these realms include the following:

- *Politics. Low*-income states and *high*-income individuals have voted Republican in recent U.S. presidential elections (tinyurl .com/PoliticalParadox).
- *Happy welfare states and unhappy liberals.* Liberal countries and conservative individuals express greater well-being.[30]
- *Google sex searches.* Highly religious states, and less religious individuals, do more Google "sex" searching.[31]
- *Meaning in life.* Self-reported meaning in life is greatest in poor countries and among rich individuals.[32]

Sociologist W. S. Robinson long ago appreciated that "An ecological correlation is almost certainly not equal to its individual correlation."[33] But that leaves us wondering *why* religiosity correlates negatively with the good life across countries and positively across individuals. Surely there are some complicating factors.

Consider marriage, for example. Religiously active people are more likely to be married. And married people are happier and healthier. So is religion merely a proxy for the "real" marriage factor? (Or should we say that religion's encouragement of marriage is one of the social support mechanisms that mediates its effect?) Earlier I noted that the religiosity-longevity association occurs both with women and with men (and so is not just a tendency for women, who are more religious, to outlive men). Similarly, the religiosity-happiness association exists both among married and unmarried people.

With these preliminary observations, I leave the full unraveling of the religious engagement paradox to others from higher statistical pay grades. There is surely more sleuthing to come. Solving the paradox will likely involve controlling for those complicating factors.

One such factor is income. We might ask, for example, if the religiosity-happiness association is mediated by a third factor—income—which has some association with happiness. Looking first at individuals:

1. Richer individuals are happier than poor individuals.
2. Religiously engaged individuals tend to have *lower* incomes.
3. Despite their generally lower incomes, religious people express greater happiness.

Ergo, across individuals, income seems not to explain the religiosity-happiness correlation (religiously engaged folks tend to be happier, though poorer).

But what about the comparisons of religious versus more irreligious places (countries and states)? Less religious places also tend to be *affluent* places (think Denmark and Vermont). More religious places tend to be poorer places (think Pakistan and Mississippi). Thus when we compare less versus more religious places we also are comparing richer versus poorer places. And as Ed Diener, Louis Tay, and I observed from Gallup World Poll data, controlling for objective life circumstances, such as income, eliminates or even slightly reverses the negative religiosity–well-being correlation across countries.[34] Thus lower incomes do help explain the lower life quality in highly religious places.

Finally, a question to ponder: Which data—aggregate or individual level—tell the more important or the truer story? If wondering whether rich people are relatively more or less likely to vote Republican, should we take our clue more from the aggregate data (where poor states vote Republican) or the individual data (where Republican support is greater among rich folks)? Ditto for the data on religious engagement and human flourishing: Is the more important story told by the aggregate or individual data?

In the meantime, we have a moral to our story. When reporting and interpreting data on predictors of the good life be aware: aggregate and individual data may point to radically differing conclusions. Conclusions drawn from aggregate data—comparing nations and states—may offer different predictors of the good life than data drawn from where life is lived—at the level of the individual.

References

Australian Centre on Quality of Life. 2008. "The Australian Unity Well-being Index." Deakin University. http://acqol.deakin.edu.au/index_wellbeing/Survey_18.2.pdf.

Chida, Yoichi, Andrew Steptoe, and Lynda H. Powell. 2009. "Religiosity/Spirituality and Mortality. A Systematic Quantitative Review." *Psychotherapy and Psychosomatics* 78: 81–90.

Clark, Andrew E., and Orsolya Lelkes. 2009. "Let Us Pray: Religious Inter-actions in Life Satisfaction." Unpublished manuscript, Paris School of Economics.

Deaton, Angus, and Arthur A. Stone. 2013. "Two Happiness Puzzles." *American Economic Review* 103, no. 3: 591–97.

Diener, Edward F., Louis Tay, and David G. Myers. 2011. "The Religion Paradox: If Religion Makes People Happy, Why Are So Many Dropping Out?" *Journal of Personality and Social Psychology* 101, no. 6: 1278–90.

FiveThirtyEight.com. 2010. "Divorce Rates Higher in States with Gay Marriage Bans." January 12, 2010. https://fivethirtyeight.com.

Gallup, George, Jr. 1984. "Religion in America." *The Gallup Report*, no. 222.

Gearing, Robin E., and Dana Lizardi. 2009. "Religion and Suicide." *Journal of Religion and Health* 48: 332–41.

George, Linda K., Christopher G. Ellison, and David B. Larson. 2002. "Explaining the Relationships between Religious Involvement and Health." *Psychological Inquiry* 13: 190–200.

Gould, Stephen Jay. 1999. "Non-Overlapping Magisteria." In *Rock of Ages: Science and Religion in the Fullness of Life*. New York: Ballantine Books.

Hartford Institute for Religion Research. "Fast Facts about American Religion: How Many Religious Congregations Are There in the United States?" Accessed July 16, 2016. www.hartfordinstitute.org/research/fastfacts/fast_facts.html#numcong.

Headey, Bruce, Jürgen Schupp, Ingrid Tucci, and Gert G. Wagner. 2010. "Authentic Happiness Theory Supported by Impact of Religion on Life Satisfaction: A Longitudinal Analysis with Data for Germany." *Journal of Positive Psychology* 5, no. 1: 73–82. http://ftp.iza.org/dp3915.pdf.

Hitchens, Christopher. 2007. *God Is Not Great*. New York: Hachette Book Group.

Hummer, Robert A., Richard G. Rogers, Charles B. Nam, and Christopher G. Ellison. 1999. "Religious Involvement and U.S. Adult Mortality." *Demography* 36: 273–85.

Inglehart, Ronald. 1990. *Culture Shift in Advanced Industrial Society*. Princeton, N.J.: Princeton University Press.

King, Laura A., Samantha J. Heintzelman, and Sarah J. Ward. 2016. "Beyond the Search for Meaning: A Contemporary Science of the Experience of Meaning in Life." *Current Directions in Psychological Science* 25: 211–16.

Kost, Kathryn, and Stanley Henshaw. 2010. "U.S. Teenage Pregnancies, Births and Abortions: National and State Trends by Age, Race and Ethnicity." Guttmacher Institute. https://www.guttmacher.org/pubs/USTPtrends.pdf.

Lucero, S., K. Kusner, E. Speace, and W. O'Brien. 2008. "Religiosity and Adolescent Sexual Behavior: A Meta-Analytic Study." Paper presented at the 20th Annual Meeting of the Association for Psychological Science, Chicago.

MacInnis, Cara C., and Gordon Hodson. 2015. "Do American States with More Religious or Conservative Populations Search More for Sexual Content on Google?" *Archives of Sexual Behavior* 44, no. 1: 137–47.

———. 2016. "Surfing for Sexual Sin: Relations between Religiousness and Viewing Sexual Content Online." *Sexual Addiction and Compulsivity* 23, nos. 2–3: 196–210.

McCullough, Michael E., William T. Hoyt, David B. Larson, Harold G. Koenig, and Carl Thoresen. 2000. "Religious Involvement and Mortality: A Meta-Analytic Review." *Health Psychology* 19: 211–22.

Myers, David G. 2000. "The Funds, Friends, and Faith of Happy People." *American Psychologist* 55: 56–67.

Myers, David G., and C. Nathan DeWall. 2018. *Psychology*. 12th ed. New York: Worth.

Myers, David. G., and Edward F. Diener. 2018. "The Scientific Pursuit of Happiness." *Perspectives on Psychological Science* 13, no. 2: 218–25.

Newport, Frank, Dan Witters, and Sangeeta Agrawal. 2010. "Very Religious Americans Lead Healthier Lives." December 23. http://www.gallup.com/poll/145379/religious-americans-lead-healthier-lives.aspx.

———. 2012. "Religious Americans Enjoy Higher Well-Being." February 16. https://news.gallup.com/poll/152723/religious-americans-enjoy-higher-wellbeing.aspx.

Nonnemaker, James M., Clea A. McNeely, and Robert William Blum. 2003. "Public and Private Domains of Religiosity and Adolescent Health Risk Behaviors: Evidence from the National Longitudinal Study of Adolescent Health." *Social Science and Medicine* 57: 2049–54.

Oishi, Shigehiro, and Edward F. Diener. 2014. "Residents of Poor Nations Have a Greater Sense of Meaning in Life than Residents of Wealthy Nations." *Psychological Science* 25: 422–30.

Okulicz-Kozaryn, Adam, Oscar Holmes, and Derek R. Avery. 2014. "The Subjective Well-Being Political Paradox: Happy Welfare States and Unhappy Liberals." *Journal of Applied Psychology* 99, no. 6: 1300–1308.

Pelham, Brett, and Steve Crabtree. 2008. "Worldwide, Highly Religious More Likely to Help Others." Gallup. October 8. http://www.gallup .com/poll/111013/worldwide-highly religious-more-likely help-others. aspx.

Pelham, Brett, and Zsolt Nyiri. 2008. "In More Religious Countries, Lower Suicide Rates." Gallup. July 3. https://news.gallup.com/poll/108625/morereligious-countries-lower-suicide-rates.aspx.

Putnam, Robert D., and David E. Campbell. 2010. *American Grace: How Religion Divides and Unites Us.* New York: Simon & Schuster.

Rasmussen, Kyler R., and Alex E. Bierman. 2016. "How Does Religious Attendance Shape Trajectories of Pornography Use across Adolescence?" *Journal of Adolescence* 49: 191–203.

Regnerus, Mark D. 2007. *Forbidden Fruit: Sex and Religion in the Lives of American Teenagers.* New York: Oxford University Press.

Robinson, William S. 1950. "Ecological Correlations and the Behavior of Individuals." *American Sociological Review* 15: 351–57.

Schwartz, Shalom H., and Sipke Huismans. 1995. "Value Priorities and Religiosity in Four Western Religions." *Social Psychology Quarterly* 58: 88–107.

SSRC. 2009. "American Human Development Report 2008–2009." New York: Social Science Research Council.

Strayhorn, Joseph M., and Jillian C. Strayhorn. 2009. "Religiosity and Teen Birth Rate in the United States." *Reproductive Health* 6, no. 14: https:// reproductive-health-journal.biomedcentral.com/track/pdf/6/10.1186/ 1742-4755-6-14.

Wilson, David Sloan. 2003. *Darwin's Cathedral: Evolution, Religion, and the Nature of Society.* Chicago: University of Chicago Press.

———. 2007. "Beyond Demonic Memes: Why Richard Dawkins Is Wrong about Religion." *eSkeptic.* July 4. https://www.skeptic.com/eskeptic/ 07-07-04/.

Wilson, Edward Osborne. 1998. *Consilience.* New York: Knopf.

12

SMART AND SPIRITUAL

The Coevolution of Religion and Rationality[1]

LAURENCE R. IANNACCONE

Something akin to religion is essential for human progress. This something has biological roots and arose before humans acquired the cognitive capacities associated with behavioral modernity some 50,000 years ago.[2] No one-word label seems to suffice: "religion" is too narrow, "faith" too broad, and "spirituality" too vague. I will instead speak of our *spiritual sense*, using the term as shorthand for a powerful predisposition to embrace assertions that cannot be validated and find their primary expressions in shared narratives and rituals. This predisposition stands between instinct and reason, influencing both.

Where would we be without this inborn affinity for transcendent truths and sacred stories? Dead, or at least deprived of progress. Without a spiritual sense operating alongside our emotional impulses and rational calculations, we would be too smart for our own good, too adept at promoting our own interests, and too prone to do so at the expense of others. The cognitive capacities that distinguish us from other animals are immensely dangerous precisely because they are profoundly productive. Our genes cannot adapt fast enough to prevent us from using new technologies in socially harmful ways. Though we are by far the most social of all primates, social instincts cannot fully solve our problem. Something more flexible and far-reaching is needed.

The big question is not how the gifts of rationality have promoted human progress but rather how we've survived these "gifts" at all. The answer may lie in a spiritual sense. Without it, rationality is not just insufficient for human progress; it positively precludes such progress.

My argument stands secularization theory on its head, particularly the "Age of Reason" story most of us learned as children and still carry in our heads. The Age of Reason story goes like this:

> *In ancient times, people were too ignorant to properly distinguish reality from imagination. Swayed by fear and hope, they attributed natural phenomena to supernatural forces. The shackles of superstition remained strong until recent centuries. But as religion gave way to reason, fact was separated from faith, and science and technology took off, leading to unprecedented gains in wealth, health, and freedom.*

The story is false. But so too are the more sophisticated versions of secularization theory—not because they overstate the productive power of reason or the constraining power of religion, but because they under-state the dangers of reason and the role of religion in curbing those dangers.

Reason Alone Cannot Sustain Large Societies

Moral philosophers of the seventeenth and eighteenth centuries system-atically studied the costs and benefits of self-interest. Among them, it was David Hume and Adam Smith who most clearly showed that our prosperity depends both on rational self-interest and prerational moral sentiments. Economists lost interest in moral philosophy as they rebuilt their field in the image of physics and engineering. But more recent research in experimental economics, behavioral economics, game theory, biology, psychology, anthropology, and humanomics have forced even the most devoutly neoclassical economist to acknowledge that the wealth of nations rests on much more than rational calculation.[3]

Among great economists of the twentieth century, Friedrich Hayek was one of the first to fully embrace this insight, precisely because he rejected the physics-like mathematization of economics in favor of insights from philosophy, biology, psychology, and evolutionary anthropology. Hayek argued that the "least appreciated facet of human evolution" is that civilization depends on an *extended order* of human cooperation that "arose from unintentionally conforming to certain traditions and largely *moral* practices"—traditions and moral practices "which men tend to dislike, whose significance they usually fail to understand, [and] whose validity they cannot prove." Hayek states, "It is not our intellect that created our morals: rather, human interactions governed by our morals make possible the growth of reason and those capabilities associated with it." It is in fact a "fatal conceit" to believe that reason led us to the morals and traditions we so desperately need or that reason alone can ever sustain them. It would be more fatal still to base our morals on our evolved social instincts, since these are the *collectivist* instincts of hunter-gatherers whose survival depended on near-total sharing within the tribe and near-homicidal hostility toward outsiders.[4]

In short, we prosper and progress thanks to moral practices that "stand between instinct and reason—logically, psychologically, temporally." The key moral practices are those that support impersonal exchange and abstract property rights, moral practices that religions codify in lists like the Bible's Ten Commandments. Hayek concludes that we owe our success in part to "beliefs which are not true or verifiable or testable in the same sense as are scientific arguments and which certainly are not the result of rational argumentation"—beliefs transmitted through mystical and religious beliefs and "the main monotheistic" faiths in particular.[5]

Hayek's short and speculative observations about religion presaged recent claims by renowned scholars in sociology, anthropology, economics, and psychology. To get a feel for this growing literature, see the books of Stark (2001, 2005), Wright (2009), Wade (2009), Norenzayan (2013), McCloskey (2016), Henrick (2016), and Rubin (2017). Despite their varied methods, all these scholars argue that religions have played a key role in sustaining large-scale cooperation.

Nor Can Reason Alone Sustain Small Groups

Yet even these writers understate the dangers posed by rational self-interest in *small* groups. Game theory illustrates the severity and scope of the problem.

Start with the one-shot prisoner's dilemma, the simplest game-theoretic model of tension between group and individual interests. A purely rational player will always defect, raising his well-being at the expense of the other player. And since the same logic holds for both players, the net result harms both. Moreover, the perils of pure rationality extend far beyond the distinctive and somewhat perverse character of the prisoner's dilemma. Virtually all forms of collective action provide analogous incentives to defect or free ride, so that equilibrium outcomes are all but guaranteed to be inefficient and possibly even deadly, especially as the number of players and complexity of interactions grow.

There are, of course, game-theoretic solutions to many free-rider problems, including the seemingly counterproductive practices that I modeled in my work on sacrifice and stigma[6] and that anthropologists, evolutionary biologists, anthropologists, and psychologists have extensively documented in works on "costly signaling." But I challenge you to find a social system that consistently solves its free-rider problems *merely* through costly signaling, repeated play, trigger strategies, or other purely rational means. The same holds true for the surprisingly successful solutions to common resource problems documented by Elinor Ostrom and her associates (1990).

Even the most seemingly simple real-world interactions abound in complications. Consider the coordination game called *Battle of the Sexes*. Two players (Ann and Bob) must each choose one of two possible activities (such as viewing a romantic comedy versus an action film). Ann prefers the rom-com whereas Bob prefers the action film, but both would rather stay together than separately watch their favored films. Though each benefits from making the *same* choice, their relationship will surely be stressed by a series of one-sided outcomes. You might suppose that friends or family members will readily reason their way to simple solutions, such as flipping coins or alternating movie types. But if Ann finds rom-coms far more enjoyable than action films, she might well reason that her preferences should prevail more often than Bob's. This tempts a clever Ann to overstate her love of rom-coms and eventually leads even the most gullible Bob to question Ann's claims or overstate his own.

In the real world, almost every game-theoretic solution raises additional game-theoretic problems, including the (second-order) temptation to free ride on any system of monitoring and punishment designed to solve a (first-order) collective action problem. Moreover, almost every real-world analog of an idealized game or choice connects to countless other games and choices. We can agree to see the rom-com but must still decide on the particular day, time, venue, seats, snacks, and means of transportation. And who among us hasn't sought to advance their own interests by altering the game itself, arguing that tonight might be better spent dancing, shopping, strolling through the park, or simply staying home? As the saying goes, no plan of battle survives first contact with the enemy. Real-world "games" can lead to genuine battles when the stakes are high or the players are strangers.

Natural Selection Is Too Slow and Rigid

It's tempting to pass the entire problem off to Darwin. The evolutionary record provides countless examples of astonishingly complex adaptations that benefit offspring or kin at the expense of the individual. For the sake of argument, let us therefore assume that evolution can indeed provide genetic solutions to any social problem given enough time.

But time is precisely what we lack. Human capacities to learn and communicate yield innovation at rates that are all but instantaneous relative to the speed of natural selection. Many innovations are fitness enhancing for individual actors or individual groups yet extraordinarily dangerous for humanity. The atomic bomb is a standard example, but humans have pursued mass destruction with cannons, swords, spears, compound bows, saddled horses, stone axes, secret codes, and even the sound of drums.

Nor do our social instincts solve the problem, because as Hayek emphasized, those instincts evolved long before the era of large-scale societies. Our hunter-gatherer instincts encourage us to resent leaders and *hate* outsiders.[7]

And even if later mutations for greater sympathy or sociability have arisen, they can only be fitness-enhancing if they leave us with ample supplies of self-interest (followed by a sharply declining sympathy gradient that puts family next, friends thereafter, and mere acquaintances at much greater remove). Even if individuals did evolve a love for all mankind, that love would do little to guide the incredibly complex, largely impersonal, and ever-changing interactions that sustain our civilization.

Pure Rationality Can Destroy Civilizations

If hyper-sociability won't do the trick, what about hyper-rationality instead? Can the march of science in the light of pure reason lead humanity ever onwards and upwards? The technological progress of the past few centuries has already endowed us with powers traditionally ascribed only to gods. What happens as those powers grow greater still?

Insofar as we retain our ancient instincts, we risk the future depicted in *Forbidden Planet*, a 1950s sci-fi classic in which spacefaring humans discover a barren world formerly inhabited by the Krell—super-intelligent beings who mysteriously perished just as they were gaining complete control over energy and matter. Turns out the Krell destroyed themselves by unleashing technologies that fully empowered their primal passions. If science fiction isn't your style, feel free to restate the argument in terms of Plato's ring of invisibility, the game-theoretic risks of deterrence based on the threat of mutually assured destruction, or the warnings of world-renowned scientists.

Mind without heart may be even more deadly. Cold-blooded logic can easily lead to violence (note the relative success of rational choice models in explaining warfare and terrorism), and cold-blooded killers are far more lethal than their hot-blooded counterparts. Serious scientists worry about self-aware AI's enslaving humans to advance their super-human interests, or protect other life forms, or save us from our own self-destructive tendencies, or from simple indifference to the welfare of inferior beings.[8]

Perhaps our greatest danger lies in looking long and hard through the lens of science and (rightly?) concluding that there really is no reason to believe our lives have meaning, that moral distinctions have meaning, or that existence itself has meaning. What happens if we accept that our life-filled planet is nothing more than a low-probability bubble of transient complexity in an entropic universe racing toward oblivion? Why aim for anything beyond personal pleasure before our brief candles burn out? "Life's but a walking shadow . . . a tale told by an idiot . . . signifying nothing."[9] Nothing, absolutely nothing, really matters in the end, or even in the present.

If you find this sort of rational nihilism ridiculous or revolting, credit your spiritual sense.

The Special Properties of Our Spiritual Sense

Recall that *spiritual sense* is my label for a powerful nonrational predis-position to embrace assertions that cannot be validated and find their primary expressions in shared narratives and rituals. Stated more simply, we have a spiritual sense because we're wired for *sacred stories* and *tran-scendent truths*. We're wired for worldviews that encompass more than that which we see as normal and natural.[10] In fact, we find it almost impossible to limit our sense of reality to that which we can physically perceive or logically prove.

Our spiritual sense has special properties. It stands between instinct and reason, appealing to head and heart while exercising some influence over both. The sense is strongly *social*, activated by shared performance rather than individual experience, and essentially *content-free*, able to support almost any worldview. The resulting beliefs and feelings can be strong enough to constrain thoughts and actions, while remaining responsive to group-level change. A sense rooted in personal experience could not induce convictions that were simultaneously strong, variable, and socially determined.

Our spiritual sense is attuned to compelling narrative rather than logical proof. Some convictions come so naturally to humans that even the simplest stories can suffice; hence, almost any shared experience can create a sense of shared identity, and simple proverbs can convey shared values. Less intuitive themes require additional elements of compelling narrative, including repetition, public performance, emotional intensity, appeal to the senses, clear themes, colorful characters, and conflict.

Because sacred stories shape behavior, and because good storytelling takes both skill and effort, there is ongoing competition among stories and storytellers. Club and market models provide some insights regarding the group-level outcomes, and models of human capital and household production provide some insight into individual behavior.[11] Systems of shared belief will often support multiple equilibria. Hence, dominant faiths can vary widely across seemingly similar cultures, and new faiths can sometimes sweep through a single seemingly stable culture with remarkable speed. But in most places and eras, dominant worldviews change quite slowly, responding in more-or-less predictable ways to incremental changes in technology and the environment.

In practice, our spiritual sense helps to sustain all the following:

- Solutions to coordination problems that sacralize some choices over others, elevating those choices to sacred status. A mere location becomes holy ground and hence a place to congregate, trade, or govern. An ordinary day becomes a holiday, and hence a way in which to structure the pace of life. A randomizing mechanism such as the drawing lots becomes a revered method of divination and thus a way to seek guidance and settle disputes.
- Identity and obligations rooted in supernatural interpretations of real or imagined history. (As Tevye remarks in *Fiddler on the Roof*'s song about "Tradition," "Because of our traditions, every one of us knows who he is and what God expects him to do.")
- Reduced free-riding and enhanced self-control through stories of supernatural beings and forces that monitor, reward, and punish.

- The legitimacy that people routinely ascribe to the laws and leaders of their polity.
- Moral sentiments that bridge the logical leap from "is" to "ought."
- The great moral and material significance that people routinely attribute to their actions—significance that cannot be justified in terms of measurable outcomes.

Our spiritual sense probably evolved through some combination of individual selection, group selection, and gene-culture coevolution. A purely cultural, nonbiological process seems unlikely given that supernaturalism arises in all cultures, and given that the behavioral imperatives of supernaturalism vary so widely over time and space. Whatever the source, the key point is that a spiritual sense can curb the harmful consequences of rational self-interest.

Application: The Durability of Major Religions

Many scholars now argue that human progress has required nonrational constraints. Evolutionary biologists, anthropologists, and psychologists point to our uniquely strong social instincts, acquired through (biological) natural selection. Others, like Hayek, stress nonbiological moral traditions that constrain our biologically based ethnocentric instincts. Still others have focused on theologies that promote faith in "Big Gods"—powerful, all-seeing agents that punish harmful acts and reward prosocial behavior. The concept of a spiritual sense extends these insights.

An inborn affinity for shared and sacred stories helps explain the remarkable durability of major religious traditions—Hinduism and Judaism being two of the best examples. Stories supply entertainment, inspiration, information, and vicarious experience. Good stories outlive their original authors and audiences; great stories outlast entire cultures. Great stories are also highly adaptable, hence easy to update or project into other settings. (*Forbidden Planet* is a sci-fi adaptation of Shakespeare's *The Tempest*. Bernstein's *West Side Story* is *Romeo and Juliet* transported to the American inner city.)

Supernaturalism vastly widens the range of possible plots, and other sources of durability come from outside the story itself. Insofar as a shared supernatural story facilitates collective action (or enhances social stability, property rights, market exchange, self-control, moral restraint, etc.), the beneficiaries have incentives to promote the stories even if they themselves doubt their literal truth.

The durability of a successful religion depends not only on the adaptability of its stories but also on their number and scope. The Hebrew Bible consists largely of narrative books, most of which are themselves collections of stories. The four Gospel narratives of Jesus' life plus Luke's story of the apostles' subsequent acts make up more than half of the New Testament, and nearly all the remaining books are letters by Paul and other early church leaders addressed to individuals or individual congregations struggling with specific problems. The impersonal style and abstract arguments that we now associate with theology, philosophy, and science are all but absent. Sacred stories are no less central to other religious traditions, from the Epic of Gilgamesh to the Book of Mormon.

Successful religions convey their stories in countless ways—through prose and poetry, song and chant, music and dance, prayer and meditation, plays and paintings, rituals and recitations, feasts, holidays, architecture, and even styles of diet, dress, and speech. The net result is a spiritual system that can seem ageless while constantly changing. Core doctrines are rarely dropped but regularly reinterpreted; new teachings and technologies are added all the time.

A focus on sacred stories avoids biases that come naturally to Western scholars. We routinely equate religion with the big-God supernaturalism of Judaism, Christianity, and Islam. (Call it the "one God, one faith, one church" approach.) Our monotheistic orientation becomes problematic when studying Hinduism, Buddhism, or Greco-Roman paganism, more problematic still when talking about so-called "folk" religions, and nearly useless when talking about hunter-gatherer religion. By contrast, the sacred story approach highlights forms of expression and the faiths they sustain, forms and faiths that encompass far more than the worldviews of Abrahamic monotheism.

Application: The Sacred Side of "Secular" Politics

Consider the surprising failure of secularization theory—surprising because scientific progress truly has undermined the testable claims of every religion, technological progress truly has lessened the material needs that religions address, and historic trends plausibly point to a not-too-distant future when humans enjoy standards of living traditionally ascribed to paradise. Why have the theory's core predictions remained unfulfilled for more than two hundred years? Supernaturalism hasn't died; no major religious tradition has collapsed; knowledge of science predicts a person's religiosity less accurately than gender, race, and the religiosity of peers and parents; and religions remain a major source of both individual identity and social conflict.

An inborn affinity for shared and sacred stories can account for these predictive failures, because it implies that a religion will survive as long as it remains a primary source of sacred stories and transcendent truths. In practice, religions lose out to competing religions far more frequently than they fall prey to scientific progress.[12] No wonder religious leaders have so often traded their independence for established-church status, using their spiritual authority to legitimate any secular authority that suppressed their competitors.

There is, however, an important sense in which the United States and other Western democracies *are* secularized nations. The Constitution of the United States radically limited the federal government's capacity to support one religion or suppress others. But the secularization rested on a narrative that shifted the sacred source of legitimacy from the will of God to the will of the people. Viewing people as an entity is itself an act of faith; imputing a will to this entity requires still greater faith; and granting it sovereignty over millions of individuals smacks of outright irrationality. Yet as faiths go, this one has worked so well that you, and I, and almost every living American identify personally with the words "We the People . . . do ordain and establish this Constitution for the United States of America." We likewise share deep and abiding commitment to the "self-evident" "truth" that "all men are created equal"—self-evident only to those whose faith transcends the limits of ordinary logic and observation. The American system was always less secular than it seemed other ways as well. The combination of limited government, state rights, individual rights, religious freedom, and endless immigration spawned a vast array of religious institutions that complemented government—producing public goods, tackling social problems, promoting generalized trust, and helping to sacralize American life and government though holidays, hymns, rituals, novel interpretations of sacred texts, and much more.

Faith in government was all the more necessary in the Soviet Union, where religion was all but abolished. Soviet communism sacralized government as never before. As in Western democracies, legitimacy derived (in theory) from "the people." The opening sentences of the 1936 Constitution of the USSR declared that "all power belongs to the working people of town and country." But a state that sought to replace traditional governments, traditional economies, traditional religions, and even traditional families needed all the sacred support it could get.

Marxist-Leninism therefore established a system of "scientific-atheism" that mimicked Christianity. Soviet communism had it all: sacred writings; sainted founders; special holidays; rites of passage; new doctrines and elaborate systems of indoctrination; youth organizations; heresy trials; proselytizing; egalitarian ideals; faith-promoting art, music, literature, and drama; a new partitioning of humanity (bourgeois, capitalist, proletariat); and a prophetic eschatology (which included the dictatorship of the proletariat, the withering away of the state, and the creation of the New Soviet man).

Though the quasi-religious character of democracy and communism merit continued study, priority should go to the study of contemporary western liberalism. Over the past few decades, this faith (more properly termed democratic socialism) has become the dominant political ideology of the Western world. While its ultimate concerns have changed little since the 1800s, its immediate goals have steadily grown more comprehensive, its methods more focused on centralized governmental action, and its rhetoric more moralistic. Liberalism replaced the traditional tightly constrained mission of American government with a governmental commitment to address all the problems of society: poverty, injustice, racism, sexism, crime, worker exploitation, inequality, illness, addiction, illiteracy, hunger, homelessness, hatred, child abuse, sexual misconduct, environmental harms, and much more. It's only natural that a comprehensive, moralistic, and widely shared ideology should resemble a religious movement, and in late-nineteenth century America, its natural partner was the Social Gospel Movement, led largely by Protestant ministers. Contemporary American liberalism thus carries in its DNA the dualistic (good versus evil) worldview of New Testament Christianity and New Testament Christian commitment to equality, fraternity, nonviolence, charity, self-sacrifice, collective action, spreading the truth, and saving the world. But unlike the early Christians, who operated as a powerless minority sect within a Jewish state ruled by the pagan Roman Empire, contemporary liberalism enjoys strong support in politics, law, education, news media, entertainment media, medicine, high-tech industry, and most other elite sectors of society. Status akin to that of an established religion all but guarantees hostility toward all major competitors—be they political (Republicans), cultural (social traditionalists), or religious (evangelical Christians).

We need to better understand the quasi-religious character of contemporary liberalism, the ways in which its appeal is more spiritual than scientific, and the ways in which its stories convince our minds by first capturing our hearts. We need to catalog the myriad ways in which its stories are communicated—through novels, news, schooling, songs, art, theater, holidays, sermons, political discourse, movies, TV shows, and the like. We particularly need to appreciate the almost magical ways in which movies and other forms of video create a shared worldview: shared beliefs about what is good and feasible; shared identity; shared sets of (mostly fictional) heroes and villains; and shared history based on dramatizations that tend to be anecdotal, moralistic, and anachronistic. The rapid shift in opinion over homosexuality and gay marriage is a case in point, led by positive portrayals of a population whose existence was scarcely acknowledged in movies and television prior to the 1980s.

Summing Up

Humans are in many ways too smart for their own good. Without a spiritual sense standing between instinct and reason, we'd have killed ourselves off long ago or at least put an end to our progress. The sense remains essential for our continued progress, and it is in any case too deeply wired into our nature to disappear. Our spiritual sense can't be reduced to our primate social instincts, important as these are, nor can it be reduced to the ethnocentric egalitarianism that maximizes survival in hunter-gather societies. The sense is so nearly content-free that it can sustain almost any collection of shared convictions, even those that lead to group extinction. But this also means that the sense gives rise to content that varies greatly over time and place, providing the flexibility needed to constructively coevolve with the social and technological products of intelligence.

Our propensity to jointly embrace sacred stories and transcendent truths promotes collective action, moral imperatives, shared identities and customs, shared commitments, submission to authority, and belief that life has meaning. The phenomenon we call religion owes much to our spiritual sense, but so too do our economic and political institutions—not only those that ally themselves with religions but even those that suppress religions and promote atheism. Ignoring the faith-based foundations of political and economic systems is both foolish and dangerous.

Contrast these conclusions to those of the "new atheists." Science shows no sign of replacing the sacred, nor has our taste for transcendent truth declined in the face of increasing education, urbanization, industrialization, globalization, wealth, health, technology, or any of the other trends emphasized by secularization theory. Indeed, there is little evidence that a truly secularized society would be viable, much less beneficial. Deprived of faith-based morals, meaning, customs, and institutions, we would cease being recognizably human and soon cease being at all. Yet the dedicated atheists I've known are all sincere and thoughtful people seriously committed to doing good. I sympathize with their attempts to understand the world through the lens of science, and I agree that science offers scant support for supernaturalism. My principal complaint is not how readily they dismiss supernaturalism but rather how rarely they acknowledge that they themselves are living by faith. Indeed, the new atheists all advocate modern Western values that mirror the core values of early Christianity. There's nothing wrong with that. Atheists are human, and humans *must* live by faith. There is no other way to flourish and no other way for an intelligent species to survive.

References

Hayek, Friedrich A. 1988. *The Fatal Conceit: The Errors of Socialism*. Chicago: University of Chicago Press.

Henrich, Joseph. 2017. *The Secret of Our Success: How Culture Is Driving Human Evolution, Domesticating Our Species, and Making Us Smarter*. Princeton: Princeton University Press.

Iannaccone, Laurence R. 1992. "Sacrifice and Stigma: Reducing Free-Riding in Cults, Communes, and Other Collectives." *Journal of Political Economy* 100, no. 2: 271–91.

———. 1994. "Why Strict Churches Are Strong." *American Journal of Sociology* 99, no. 5: 1180–211.

———. 1998. "Introduction to the Economics of Religion." *Journal of Economic Literature* 36, no. 3: 1465–95.

Jenkins, Philip. 2011. *The Next Christendom: The Coming of Global Christianity*. 3rd ed. New York: Oxford University Press.

McCloskey, Deirdre N. 2016. *Bourgeois Equality: How Ideas, Not Capital or Institutions, Enriched the World*. Chicago: University of Chicago Press.

Norenzayan, Ara. 2013. *Big Gods: How Religion Transformed Cooperation and Conflict*. Princeton: Princeton University Press.

Ostrom, Elinor. 1990. *Governing the Commons: The Evolution of Institutions for Collective Action*. Cambridge: Cambridge University Press.

Rubin, Jared. 2017. *Rulers, Religion, and Riches: Why the West Got Rich and the Middle East Did Not*. Cambridge: Cambridge University Press.

Shultziner, Doron, Thomas Stevens, Martin Stevens, Brian A. Stewart, Rebecca J. Hannagan, and Giulia Saltini-Semerari. 2010. "Causes and Scope of Political Egalitarianism during the Last Glacial: A Multi-Disciplinary Perspective." *Biology and Philosophy* 25: 319–46.

Smith, Vernon L. 2007. *Rationality in Economics: Constructivist and Ecological Forms.* Cambridge: Cambridge University Press.

Smith, Vernon L., and Bart J. Wilson. 2019. *Humanomics: Moral Sentiments and the Wealth of Nations for the Twenty-First Century.* Cambridge University Press.

Stark, Rodney. 2001. *One True God: Historical Consequences of Monotheism.* Princeton: Princeton University Press.

———. 2005. *The Victory of Reason: How Christianity Led to Freedom, Capitalism, and Western Success.* New York: Random House.

Subrick, John R. 2015. "Religion and the Social Order: Lessons from Smith, Hayek, and Smith." *Journal of Markets and Morality* 18, no. 2: 309–29.

Wade, N. 2009. *The Faith Instinct: How Religion Evolved and Why It Endures.* New York: Penguin Press.

Wright, Robert. 2009. *The Evolution of God: The Origins of Our Beliefs.* Boston: Little, Brown.

13

THE ECONOMICS OF RELIGION IN DEVELOPING COUNTRIES

SRIYA IYER

"The number of micro-level social anthropological studies is continually growing. Many of these concentrate on what to the economist may appear odd aspects of society such as ritual and religion . . . and to which he pays little or no attention. For instance, an understanding of the complex of Hindu religious beliefs as they operate at village level . . . is directly relevant to the problem of developing India's economy."[1]

A major international study of over 230 countries, 2,500 censuses and surveys, released by the Pew Research Centre in 2012, showed that 84 percent (5.8 billion) of the world's population currently report a religious affiliation. The world's major religious groups are Christians (32 percent), Muslims (23 percent), Hindus (15 percent), Buddhists (7 percent), and Jews (0.2 percent).[2] The geographical distribution of adherents over time also revealed that while rich countries are getting more secular, the world overall is getting more religious. In less developed countries, we have seen rising incomes with economic growth, increasing inequality, the resilience of religion, and greater religious conflict over the past twenty years. So it seems important to think about how religion might contribute to human flourishing in these contexts more carefully.

The Economics of Religion

The economics of religion is a relatively new field of research in economics.[3] In this field, one can apply economic and statistical tools to evaluate the role of religion in society. This field evaluates economic theories that elucidate religious change and the socioeconomic attributes of religious communities. Economic studies of religion contribute to broader debates about religion in three ways: first, they link economics with religion; second, they examine nonmarket behavior, such as the role which norms, values, social capital, and "spiritual capital" may play in influencing human behavior; and third, they show how culture more broadly can affect economic systems.

Recent research in the economics of religion has examined spatial models of religious markets and evolutionary models of religious traits.[4] But it has also thought about examining causal influences on religious behavior, drawing both from research in the economic history of religion and contemporary development. This is also reflected in a wider literature on the role of institutions, which argues that there are various determinants of economic growth—be it physical capital, human capital, or population—but that institutions are the main reason that some countries are rich and others poor. These institutions may be political, legal, financial, or social. Among the latter, we can include religion, gender, race, and the family. The literature though has its limits, not least that most research in this area is concentrated on the United States and Europe. There is comparatively less research on the economics of religion in developing countries, especially countries like India, which is a selective subsample of broader research in the economics of religion. There is still a great need for studies on Latin America, Africa, the Middle East, and Asia.

The economic concern with religion dates back to Adam Smith, who first made reference to the church and competition between religions in *The Wealth of Nations* and in *The Theory of Moral Sentiments*.[5] Smith discussed three concepts which still resonate with economists—the role of competition, religious institutions including service provision, and religious pluralism. These early reflections are still themes that economists discuss today—the value of religious pluralism, the relationship between pluralism and religious participation, and the relationship between the church and the state. Smith pointed out an early concern that a monopoly religious organization could undermine a state, with implications for religious freedom and state repression of religion. This focus on religion continued a century later when Max Weber explored the Protestant ethic on capitalism.[6] Economists argue that Weber's work is particularly important to the study of religion and development because he was the first to attribute causality to the Protestant ethic. There are also critics of the Weber theory. Notably, a contemporary reinterpretation is that Protestantism encouraged human capital formation, literacy, and printing, which led to economic growth. For the developing world, Protestants' activities as missionaries contributed to democracy because they affected printing, the rule of law, corruption, and education.

Religion, Services, and Development

Religion affects economic development in several ways. First, religion directly affects norms of behavior; and through this, it affects economic growth and performance. Religion has the power to affirm contracts, reinforcing commitment and imposing sanctions against those who deviate from them. Religious norms may influence upholding the rule of law and corruption. The interaction between religious institutions and the state has consequences for religious freedoms and religious suppression. In some societies, women's roles and gender are affected by religious norms.

One study presents an overview of how interethnic complementarities in Indian medieval trading ports led to better institutions and cooperation, which minimized the chance of Hindu-Muslim conflict many centuries later.[7] It is in this context that my coauthored research in India is relevant.[8] The research asks: How do religious organizations provide and change their religious and nonreligious services in response to the competition for adherents and inequality? In this context, the research involved conducting, to the best of my knowledge, the first Indian economic survey of religious organizations, called the India Religion Survey, between 2007 and 2010, which focused on religious organizations' welfare service provision. Second, developing a theoretical economic framework drawing upon industrial organization and game theory to argue that the strength of religious beliefs may be related to inequality, religious competition, and nonreligious service provision.[9]

Our unique primary data were collected on 568 religious organizations, of which there were 272 Hindu, 248 Muslim, 25 Christian, and 23 Sikh and Jain organizations. The organizations were temples, mosques, churches but also ashrams, madrasas, and religious charities. The survey was conducted in seven major Indian states—Jammu and Kashmir, Uttar Pradesh, Gujarat, Karnataka, Madhya Pradesh,

West Bengal, and Maharashtra. The way the religious organizations were chosen was to randomly sample them from a listing of all religious organizations under the Registrar of Charities. To avoid the possibility that we might induce a common-method bias in the responses associated with the same person answering all the questions, we interviewed three people in each organization—typically a Trustee, Administrative Officer, and Financial Officer. We also made repeat visits and conducted semistructured conversations in order to understand the ethos of the organizations, to view services provided, and to deal with various statistical issues such as self-selection and endogeneity.

One of the questions the survey asked was, "Would you describe your organization as religiously Very Strong, Strong, Mild, or Very Mild?" Figure 13.1 below shows the responses on the strength of religious belief by religious affiliation.

Hindus and Muslims are more likely to describe themselves as very strong in their beliefs. Other religions are more likely to describe themselves as mild. As shown in figure 13.2, we also asked the organizations

FIG. 13.1 STRENGTH OF RELIGIOUS BELIEFS.[10]

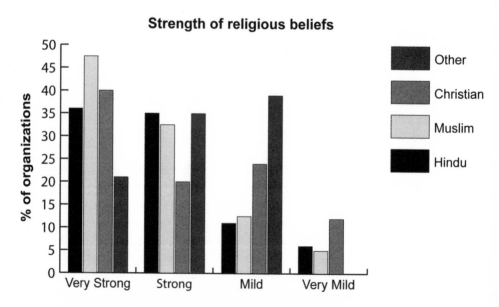

FIG. 13.2 RELIGIOUS SERVICES.[11]

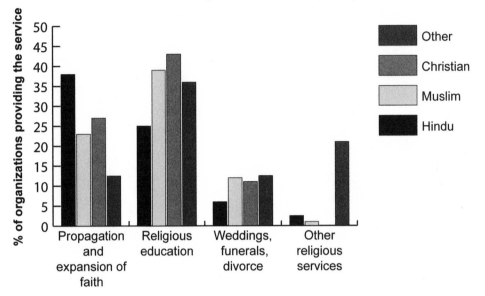

which religious services they provided, such as propagation of the faith, religious education; weddings, funeral, and divorce services; and others. Briefly, for the Hindus, expansion of the faith is most important. But for all minorities—Muslims, Christians, Sikhs, Jains—religious education is crucial. Another interesting aspect of these religious services was the manner in which technology and the media is increasingly being used to promote them. For example, many Hindu temples are using internet, video, and mobile phone technology to keep in touch with their congregations.

Moving on to nonreligious services, we define these as those services for which secular substitutes are available. Figure 13.3 shows that the most common nonreligious welfare services are education, health, food distribution, employment, childcare, and other services.

Some examples of these nonreligious services include English-language education and computer classes for younger devotees; book distribution and sari distribution, flood relief, blood donation and other medical camps where an individual can obtain a checkup and medicine for one rupee only; microfinance and cow-lending schemes to deal with adverse income shocks. Figure 13.3 shows the percentage of organizations by religion providing a particular welfare service. The

FIG. 13.3 Nonreligious welfare services.[12]

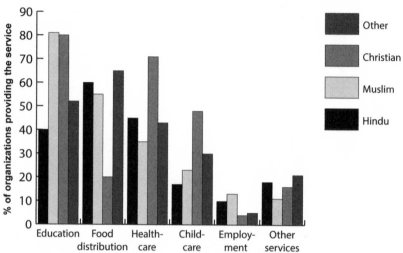

Non-religious service provision after 1991, by religion

religious variations are quite striking: Hindus are mainly providing food distribution (60 percent). The Muslims and Christians seem to provide the most education services (about 80 percent). The bottom line on our fieldwork revealed that all religions provide religious and nonreligious services. And there are important variations among the religious groups in the kinds of services they provide. Moreover, as religious institutions provide this insurance function, these networks might then determine the extent to which education or healthcare is taken up, especially where these services are less provided for by the state. These activities directly contribute to flourishing and welfare at the grassroots level.

An Economic Framework to Think about Religion

If we are interested to explore economic methods to study religion, then we need to think about our survey findings more theoretically as well. Iyer, Velu, and Weeks elucidate how religious organizations might differentiate themselves on the strength of religious beliefs, and the implications following from this for service provision, as applied to the context of a developing country like India.[13] Their economic model, drawn from the economics of industrial organization, emphasizes the dependence of the religious decision and the service decision on each other. This model is also particularly important in societies which have income inequality. The model suggests that one factor which pushes religious organizations toward more extremes is nonreligious service provision: religious organizations essentially product differentiate to minimize competition in service provision. This model and others that use theories from the economics of industrial organization are particularly applicable to religion in developing countries where inequality may be very high, and where the state cannot adequately provide services such as education and healthcare. The model also suggests that as religious organizations differentiate themselves more religiously, this then sets up the potential for greater conflict between them, which may be mitigated by the same organizations also providing more nonreligious services. The implication is that the same religious groups which may demonstrate underlying tensions among them, might also provide the welfare services which can serve to mitigate those tensions.

If it is useful to view these religious organizations through the lens of industrial organization and game theory, then we think of these organizations in the following economic model as follows: Religious organizations (*sellers*) act competitively in the market for nonreligious services to attract adherents (*buyers*) by differentiating themselves on their strength of religious beliefs (*location*) and by providing nonreligious services (*pricing*). Each organization is competing for adherents, possibly owing to political, monetary, or other benefits from having a large number of adherents. Each organization is making decisions about their strength of beliefs and the nonreligious services they provide, which we assume the poor will value more than the rich, because the latter already have them. Each adherent is also choosing membership of a religious organization based on their personal religiousness and the wealth benefits from membership of a religious organization. This leads to a classic game-theoretic problem in which organizations choose their religiousness and decide upon the nonreligious services provided, but they need to do this by taking into account each other's choices, while they are both competing for adherents. The authors also examine what happens to the solution when economic inequality across the population of individuals in the economy is added. In their work, the authors emphasize especially the dependence of the religious decision and the service decision on each other. What they find when solving the game-theoretic model mathematically is that in the presence of competition in the provision of nonreligious services, the religious organizations differentiate themselves religiously. Secondly, the provision of nonreligious services by the religious organizations increases when there is a change in economic inequality.

The first result comes about because organizations are differentiating themselves religiously in order to minimize how much they have to compete for providing nonreligious services. And when economic inequality is rising, then religious organizations provide more nonreligious services because the poor will use these more, and again the organizations are competing for more adherents among them. All this does suggest though that the whole area of applying models from industrial organization to the study of religion seems ripe for further research.

Iyer, Velu, and Weeks then use the India Religion Survey data to examine if these findings are also supported empirically in the data.[14] They examine if the strength of religious beliefs is chosen randomly by the organizations or not. One of the questions the organizations were asked was whether they provided a new service because other organizations in their immediate area provided a new service. Using statistical methods, they examine if this affected the strength of religious beliefs. In the postliberalization period in India (post-1991), inequality over the past twenty years may also affect the religious organizations' provision of education and health services. This effect can be tested statistically, while also controlling for other factors that might affect the outcomes. These factors may include the organization's age, adherents, expenditure, donations, employees, their location (if urban or rural), if they had formal networks with other organizations, communal riots, the state they are located in, and the religion they adhere to. The results show that organizations in India are differentiating themselves on the strength of religious beliefs and that this choice is not independent of each other's decisions. The results also show that religious competition matters, and that a change in the perception of inequality may be associated with religious organizations providing more education and health services.

The Economics of Religion and Human Flourishing

What is the future of the economics of religion in developing countries and what are the implications for human flourishing? It strikes me that emerging economies such as India are experiencing appreciable modern economic growth, yet this is coterminous with the increasing resilience of religious institutions. And it is this dichotomy between the sacred and the secular that epitomizes the puzzle of the relationship between religion and economic development. But for any economist seeking to engage with the study of religion, this is not for the fainthearted. There are still significant challenges to face. First, to understand the endogenous interactions between religion and economic variables; for example, is it religion which affects economic growth or economic growth that affects religion? Secondly, how much does this really matter? What are the techniques and methods needed to quantify these interactions? And thirdly, and as a consequence, how do we evaluate more widely the impact of religion on economic policy; or indeed the influence of economic policy on religion?

In assessing the current economics of religion research, it is very striking that there is much more scholarship on the economics of Islam than on the economics of Hinduism, Buddhism, Jainism, or Sikhism, so this is another area to explore more. One aspect to consider here is that within the economics of religion framework, the notion of "freedom of religion" is largely, though not exclusively of course, a Western phenomenon. In India, the Middle East, Tibet, or Indonesia, one is born into a religion and "choice" in this instance typically means giving up one's right to live within the community of one's birth. Practically speaking, then, people do not have a choice of religion. This implies that many people may practice a religion that they do not approve of, or which even harms their interests. For this reason, some models in the economics of religion sometimes fail to resonate with non-Western religions, precisely because of their neglect of social pressures. Other models, such as "club" models of religion, do better here.

One important dimension for developing countries especially is the role of social networks: for example, a well-established literature in related disciplines such as sociology has found social networks to be important for religion, religious conversion, and recruitment. It is here, among other areas, that economists of religion have yet to contribute significantly. The main areas which many existing studies do not examine is the role of network structure, the militancy of fundamentalists, and how fundamentalism might arise as a response to secularity or modernity.

Yet one theme that also comes up repeatedly in developing countries is the ability of religion not only to foster conflict, but equally to mitigate it and to foster cooperation. It is in this context that I am hopeful that the outcome of our survey of religious organizations in India will have considerable policy relevance. Based on primary survey data on Indian religious organizations collected between 2007 and 2010 spread across seven major states, our research shows that religious organizations are differentiating themselves on the strength of religious beliefs with respect to other organizations and are also providing higher education and health services in response to religious competition and as economic inequality increases in India. This is because it could be that as religious organizations are differentiating themselves more religiously, this sets up the potential for greater conflict between them, which could then possibly be mitigated by the same organizations also providing more nonreligious welfare services. I see this as a very *positive* role that many organizations are playing in their local communities by building social capital, addressing economic necessity, and contributing directly to human flourishing in these contexts.

References

Epstein, T. Scarlett. 1973. *South India: Yesterday, Today and Tomorrow.* Macmillan.

Iannaccone, Laurence. R. 1998. "Introduction to the Economics of Religion." *Journal of Economic Literature* 36, no. 3: 1465–95.

Iyer, Sriya. 2016. "The New Economics of Religion." *Journal of Economic Literature* 54, no. 2: 395–441.

———. 2018. *The Economics of Religion in India.* Cambridge, Mass.: Harvard University Press.

Iyer, Sriya, Chander Velu, and Melvyn Weeks. 2018. "Divine Competition: Religious Competition and Service Provision in India." Cambridge Working Papers in Economics. April.

Jha, Saumitra. 2013. "Trade, Institutions, and Ethnic Tolerance: Evidence from South Asia." *American Political Science Review* 107, no. 4: 806–32.

Pew Forum on Religion and Public Life. 2012. *The Global Religious Landscape.* Washington, D.C.: Pew Research Centre.

Smith, Adam. 1976. 1759. *The Theory of Moral Sentiments.* Edited by D. D. Raphael and A. L. Macfie. Oxford: Clarendon.

———. 1979. 1723–1790. *The Wealth of Nations: Books I–III.* With an introduction by Andrew Skinner. London: Penguin.

Weber, Max. 1904. *Die protestantische Ethik und der Geist des Kapitalismus* [The Protestant Ethic and the Spirit of Capitalism]. Translated by Talcott Parsons. London: Routledge.

14

ON BALANCE

AZIM F. SHARIFF

Science grows in the direction of the questions that we ask.[1] The potential for bias in our scientific knowledge doesn't come only from how we interpret what we find under the rocks that we turn over, but also from which rocks we choose. The scientific record is thus constantly getting warped and distorted by the questions we choose to ask and prioritize. The question posed by the symposium that begat this volume was *Does religion contribute to human flourishing?* It is, in a critical way, a half-baked question—focusing entirely on the potential positive effects of religion without addressing any of the consequences religion could have on the other side of the ledger. Half-baked questions tend to produce half-baked answers, and half-baked answers can often be devilishly misleading. In this particular case, asking whether religion contributes to human flourishing stacks the deck in terms of producing an affirmative answer that neatly paints religion in a positive light. After all, what is the null hypothesis? That religion does *nothing* good for humans? My colleagues in this volume blow away that null with gale-force winds, but even a soft breeze—a single tiny good consequence of religion—would have been sufficient to knock over this strawman. The challenge of this chapter is to raise that bar by broaching a fuller question: does religion contribute to human flourishing *on balance*? Does the good outweigh the bad?

As we will see as we dig into the research, there are at least half a dozen reasons why this is an unanswerable question. What determines what's good? Don't people hold different values? Aren't certain competing values incommensurable—how can we compare deleterious effects on violence to salutary effects on well-being? Don't values change? Don't religions change? Can you paint religion as a monolithic thing? What about the opportunity costs? Can you really add up good and bad as if you were doing double-entry bookkeeping? However, none of these preclude the value of reviewing the evidence on the generally agreed-upon positive and negative consequences wrought by studied forms of religion—even if these questions mean that the final tallying up must be done according to the values of the reader. The chapter, thus, seeks to stack up the data on the good and bad, divided into sections that represent a number of key values: prosociality, health, violence, bigotry, well-being, and finally, truth, science, and innovation.

Prosociality

My other chapter in this volume provides a snapshot of the psychological evidence on whether religion contributes to prosocial behavior—that is, behaviors like charity that benefit others, but are immediately costly to the self. I will not repeat this analysis here but will briefly summarize its (still tentative) conclusions. Research has demonstrated in many contexts that religions encourage believers to be more prosocial, both psychologically (motivating people to be more generous) and institutionally (providing structured opportunities to give). Though more investigation is needed, the research doesn't support the claim that the psychological motivation toward prosocial behavior that religion inspires is parochial—favoring only the ingroup. Instead, the data suggest that religiously inspired prosociality is universally directed toward ingroup and outgroup alike.

All that said, the evidence is mixed as to whether the religious are *more* generous than the nonreligious. Whereas the religious self-report higher levels of prosociality, studies that use behavioral measures fail to detect any difference. That religion could motivate believers to be more prosocial, but not make them more prosocial than nonbelievers is not a paradox. Instead, it simply alerts us to the obvious point that religion is not the only motivator toward prosociality. The religious and nonreligious subscribe to different justifications for ethical decision-making, with the former more motivated (on average) by deontological divine commandment, and the latter more motivated by consequentialism,[2] with some preliminary research showing the nonreligious to be more motivated by empathy.[3]

In sum, the evidence clearly points to a positive effect of religion on prosociality, but against it being the only—or even best—path to prosocial behavior.

Violence

Violence is endemic to human nature. Our ancestors were violent well before they were religious.[4] The question is how does religion interact with those violent tendencies; does it exacerbate our violent natures or suppress them? This is an area that deserves much more empirical investigation, but the current evidence suggests that religion has both an enhancing and a suppressive effect on violence—with plenty of room for nuance. This section will be divided into two parts—religion's impact on violence within groups, and its impact on violence between groups.

Within groups, religion has been credited with reining in violent behavior and increasing harmony and stability.[5] This may occur through proximate mechanisms by which the threat of supernatural punishments can reduce violations of cultural norms—including those against violence.[6] Religion can also suppress within-group violence via more distal effects such as via norms regulating monogamy. As Henrich, Boyd, and Richerson (2012) note, monogamous marriage norms flatten the naturally unequal distribution of mating opportunities. This in turn suppresses violence by reducing the number of unpaired men—who tend to engage in more risk-taking and violent behavior. Thus, the researchers underscore the functional value that certain religious ideas have for suppressing violence and thereby increasing the harmony and strength of their societies.

However, there are complications in concluding that the effect of religion on intragroup violence is uniformly positive. Recent cross-national research—including a longitudinal analysis spanning seventy years—has shown that as religion has declined, there has been a concurrent increase in homicide rates.[7] Importantly, however, this pattern has only occurred in countries with relatively low average IQ. In countries with higher mean cognitive ability, religious decline is associated with no change in homicide rates. That results differed on the basis of country-level intelligence reminds us that religions' effects can be context-dependent: what is positive in one time and place may not be so in another.

Moreover, there are other areas in which religion may exacerbate intragroup violence. For example, the traditional patriarchal structure of many religions has been implicated in the perpetuation of domestic violence—from wife-battering to child abuse to honor killings.[8] The specific role that religion plays in each of these examples may differ. For example, in some cases religious devotion and institutions may provide impunity from the punishments that would otherwise deter this violence. In other cases, religions may bolster ideologies that justify abuse and dissuade victims from avoiding it. And in still other cases, popular interpretations of religious scriptures may permit or even require the violence outright. In all cases, religions can play some role in facilitating violence against societies' most vulnerable.

Let us now turn to violence directed outside the group. The rise of new atheism in the mid-to-late aughts was partially in response to the Islamist terror attacks in the early part of that decade. While the role of religion in those attacks was complex and has spawned great debate, it is hard to discount completely. The research on what Atran and colleagues have called "The Devoted Actor" has shown two interacting roles by which religion can exacerbate violence: the commitment to sacred values and identity fusion with a larger collective.[9] Sacred values are understood to be ideas, objects, and lands that possess incalculable value such that they don't follow the same cost-benefit calculation as common, secular, profane values. Importantly, sacred values need not be religious. Democracy is considered by many to be a sacred value. Secularism itself may be considered a sacred value to many people in France. However, religions have been shown to increase sacralization.[10] The willingness to die and kill for these sacred values is only heightened by the fusion of one's own identity with those of a collective of like-minded group members that are also devoted to the same set of values. Fusion with these group members is enhanced through the rituals and language of "fictive kin" that are common among religions.[11] Again, religion is not the only means by which the Devoted Actor is animated, but religions have proved to be a particularly powerful key for unlocking this latent psychological profile, and in doing so, letting slip the dogs of war. Pinker (2011) implicates some of the same features of the Devoted Actor in the prolongation of the European Wars of Religion of the sixteenth and seventeenth century. Cutting your losses and suing for peace is easier when sacred values and shared identities are not at stake. He argues that a weakening hand of religion and a shift to wars fought more obviously for profane ends—such as land or economic advantage—lessened the ferocious persistence of the fighting forces. Among other factors, and in fits and starts, this led to a more peaceful world.

Can we compare the relative effects religion has on suppressing and encouraging violence? Doing so is difficult in part because we are comparing instances in which religion has exacerbated violence to counterfactual situations in which violence would have occurred sans religion. Perhaps civilizations would have been even more violent without religion. Perhaps civilizations would not even have been possible without religion, and our species would have remained in the (ultraviolent) bands of hunter-gatherers that preceded large settlements. Perhaps a better question to ask, then, is whether religion *today* perpetuates more violence than it suppresses. If religion were to disappear *today*, would the world be more peaceful?

Given the role of psychological and institutional innovations in expanding the power of secular institutions, such as surveillance and centralized police forces, the alternatives to religion's intragroup violence-suppressing features have never been stronger. Thus, religion's benefits in terms of reducing violence may be in the process of being obviated, at least in many parts of the world. However, these secular structures have also been effective at reining in the violence-enhancing effects of religion. Thus, religion's role in violence—both positive and negative—may be shrinking overall. From the perspective of violence, its absence may not be missed. Again, though, this is likely to be most true in the rich world. In areas where alternative institutions are less developed, the hypothetical removal of religion may neuter the effects it has on motivating people to fight and die, and remove the shield of impunity it offers to those who abuse those with less social power, but it may also unleash the intragroup violence that religion has been keeping in check. The context matters.

Bigotry

There is a rich correlational literature linking religiosity to various forms of bigotry including racism,[12] sexism,[13] and anti-LGBTQ attitudes.[14] As usual, the limitations of correlational designs circumscribe the conclusions that can be drawn. For example, a number of researchers have noted that the commitment to rigid, conservative, or authoritarian ideologies may serve as a third variable that complicates a simple causal story of religiosity's effects on prejudicial attitudes.[15] That is, ideological rigidity could lead to both religiosity and prejudice, while these latter two variables could conceivably share no causal relationship. Still, researchers have employed creative methods in order to investigate whether religion may have a causal impact. For instance, priming research has shown that the subliminal or supraliminal presentation of religious concepts increases benevolent sexism,[16] and increases the dislike of ethnic, national, and religious outgroups.[17]

Thus, the bulk of research points to religion being a negative and likely causal factor in perpetuating prejudicial attitudes. However, there are studies that offer some nuance to this picture. Several of these studies highlight why an overly coarse view of "religion" can be misleading. For example, Clobert, Saroglou, and Hwang (2015) found that priming Buddhist concepts reduced prejudice directed toward outgroups and did so for Christians and Buddhists alike. Preston and Ritter (2013) showed that priming "religion" caused people to be more parochial in their generosity—giving more to the ingroup—whereas priming "God" had the opposite effect, making them actually more generous to outgroup members than ingroup members. Ginges, Hansen, and Norenzayan (2009) conducted a priming study on Israeli Jews, asking them about their support for a Jewish suicide terrorist who killed nearly thirty Muslim worshippers at a mosque. Critically, prior to asking participants this question, the authors primed the participants by asking them about the (a) institutional aspect of their religiosity (how often do you attend synagogue?), (b) the devotional aspect of their religiosity (how often do you pray), or (c) no question (the neutral control condition). Respondents primed with synagogue attendance reported increased support for the suicide terrorist compared with the control condition (suggesting more negative attitudes toward Muslims), whereas those who were initially primed with prayer showed marginally less support for the terrorist than neutral (suggesting more positive attitudes toward Muslims, or at least less positive attitudes toward coalitional violence).

One of the most striking studies investigated how participating in the annual Islamic pilgrimage to Mecca—the Hajj—affected attitudes toward various outgroups.[18] Taking advantage of a lottery system in Pakistan that randomly assigned which of the many Hajj aspirants were permitted to actually take the oversubscribed pilgrimage, the authors found that among the subset who actually undertook the Hajj were not only more tolerant of those from other sects of Islam (with whom they had interacted with during the Hajj), but also of those from other religions, suggesting something more than a simple contact effect.

In sum, religion appears to enable bigotry, but the relationship is not necessarily direct or absolute. Aspects of religion appear to contribute to and benefit from conservative, system-justifying, status quo ideologies that reinforce inequities and divisions between groups. However, there are aspects of religions that could have the opposite effects. Thus, there are engines of both tolerance and intolerance within religion, and while the bulk of the data suggest that the balance is tilted toward the latter, proper cultivation could tip this balance toward something more supportive of human flourishing.

Well-Being

David Myers, one of the eminent experts in whether religion contributes to well-being, wrestles with just that topic in his chapter in this volume. He notes the intriguing Simpson's paradox in that religion is associated with less well-being at the country level but is associated with more well-being at the individual level. That is, the happiest countries, such as Norway and Finland, tend to be the *least* religious, but the happiest people, such as Ned Flanders, tend to be the *most* religious. But, as he reviews, it is indeed very well established that religion has positive effects on well-being at the individual level. He credits the effect to a combination of factors that are buoyed by religion: social support, enhanced meaning and purpose, impulse control, self-acceptance, and terror management.

Myers' own research on the boundary conditions of the religion-happiness link speaks to some of the mechanisms. Using Gallup data from nearly half a million people in 154 countries, he and his colleagues show that the religious-happiness link is strongest in countries where life circumstances are hard, or where religious people are in the majority.[19] Depending on how you measure it, the link is attenuated, absent, or in the reverse direction in places where life circumstances are relatively easy or where nonreligious people are in the minority. Stavrova, Fetchenhauer, and Schlösser (2012) find consonant results. Using World Values Survey and European Values Survey data, they find that the religion-happiness link is strongest in those countries where religion is socially dominant and embraced—and where the nonreligious are least tolerated. Moreover, they find mediational evidence suggesting that the greater respect and recognition afforded to the religious (compared to the nonreligious) in these more normatively religious societies partially explains their higher levels of well-being. Myers and Stavrova's findings thus join those of Clark et al. (in press), discussed in the prosociality section, in emphasizing that the effects that religion has—positive or negative—depend on the particular ecosystem in which they are embedded. What may contribute to human flourishing in one society, may do nothing in another, and may do the opposite in a third.

Health

Religion's connection to physical and mental health is probably the most researched of all the topics covered in this chapter. And, as discussed more extensively in VanderWeele's chapter in this volume, reviews of this research consistently point to a positive effect of religion on both physical[20] and mental[21] health. Researchers credit religion's salubrious effects to a host of factors, including the social support provided by religious communities, the psychosocial effects provided by religious teachings and meaning systems, the anxiolytic effects of religious rituals, and the clean living promoted by prescriptions about hygiene, exercise, and moderation in diet, alcohol, and other drugs.[22]

As with religion's effects on violence and well-being, there is evidence that the strength of these effects interacts with the social context. Stavrova (2016) found that religion's positive effects on health depend somewhat on person-culture fit. The relationship is the strongest in those countries where religiosity is most normative—that is, where it is common and socially desirable. In generally nonreligious places, the relationship tends to flatten, though it only significantly reverses in two countries (Albania and Moldova). As with Stavrova's well-being research discussed above,[23] these findings are suggestive that religion's positive effects on health rest in part on the social advantages afforded to the religious over the nonreligious in religiously devout communities. This explanation is supported by more recent research that examined the reported health of individuals across 258 U.S. counties (Stroope and Baker 2018). Though the more religious reported better health than the less religious everywhere, the gap was larger in more religious counties, whereas the gap was smallest in the less religious counties. Moreover, in the words of the authors, "the deleterious effects of religious contexts on nonreligious individuals'" health are considerably greater (50 percent larger) than the salutary effect of religious contexts on devout individuals' health."

In sum, there is considerable evidence showing how religion contributes to health in many positive ways. However these effects, like many we have discussed, depend on context. And part (though certainly not all) of the health superiority of the religious appears to have nothing to do with any benefit offered by religion, but rather with the health costs paid by the nonreligious for being outsiders to a believing majority.

Truth, Science, and Innovation

Many of religion's greatest recent critics lob their invective from positions in the House of Science.[24] They are agitated, at least in part, by the threat that religion appears to pose to more accurate beliefs grounded in science. Whether religion and science are in fundamental opposition remains heavily debated.[25] The *perception* that the two are incompatible appears to systematically vary across cultures—being more prominent in predominantly Christian countries than in predominantly Muslim ones.[26] However, there is at least some psychological evidence suggesting that this conflict exists at a fundamental implicit level, at least in research conducted in North America. One of my early studies with the esteemed editor of this volume found that offering people an argument for evolution depressed their religiosity, measured not only by self-report (which is highly susceptible to demand characteristics), but also implicitly.[27] Preston and Epley (2009) found that people hold scientific and religious explanations in a hydraulic fashion; when scientific explanations are described as weak, people implicitly compensate by increasing their esteem in religion. Likewise, when religion's explanatory power is bolstered, people implicitly compensate by downgrading their esteem in science. The researchers argue that though people need "ultimate explanations," those offered by science and religion are incompatible, and if doubt in science is sown, people don't react by living without an explanation, but they rush to an alternative one. Likewise, having a satisfying religious explanation leaves little motivation to find a new—and likely conflicting—scientific one. Thus religion can crowd out holding more accurate scientific beliefs. Given the cross-cultural differences in perceived science-religion incompatibility reported above, it is important to see if these effects are replicated in Muslim-majority populations.

In any case, if we grant that one of religion's great flaws is that it is not only incompatible with, but inimical to, an evidence-based mode of describing the material world, how much should that matter? In terms of human flourishing, how should that be weighed against the benefits and costs of religion in the domains outlined above? For some, there appears to be an *intrinsic* value to truth. They may believe that holding a false belief or maintaining a belief for any reason other than its consistency with evidence is a moral affront, even if it leads to no other harm. There is evidence, for instance, that people moralize rational thinking, that there are individual differences in the degree that people do so, and such moralization is indeed negatively related to religiosity.[28]

Of course, the religious may see an intrinsic moral value in faith. And even though these two groups may have very strong opinions about these respective values, adjudicating which ought—*in and of itself*—to be considered a better contributor to human flourishing can only be a matter of opinion.

However, there is also *extrinsic* value to factual truth. The applied returns on science, via the technologies that (usually) improve living standards, are good examples of ways in which a commitment to factual truth has contributed to human flourishing. There are obvious historical examples of religion interfering with scientific progress (e.g., the Catholic Church's inquisition of Galileo), and there are certainly other examples of religions contributing to scientific advancement (e.g., the direct financial investment of the Catholic Church into scientific activities, including those of Galileo in his earlier days). Today, however, the data suggest that religions retard scientific innovation. Bénabou and colleagues show that, at both the country and U.S. state level, religiosity is negatively associated with the production of patents per capita, and at the individual level, religiosity is negatively associated with a host of pro-innovation attitudes, including risk-taking, openness to new ideas, and the cultivation of independence and imagination in children.[29] Other research yields similar findings. Religiosity has been found to be associated with more negative values toward creativity, and religious people found their environments to be less creative.[30] Finally, Osiri, Houenou, and Stein (2019) examined a composite cross-national index of innovation—the Global Innovation Index[31]—which aggregates a number of innovation-related variables beyond simply patent production. Controlling for relevant variables, they found the Innovation Index and each of its subcomponents to be negatively related to measures of both religious affiliation and religious belief, though not religious attendance. Turning to specific scientific innovations that have or promise to contribute considerably to human flourishing, research finds that religiosity is negatively related to support for genetically modified foods,[32] nanotechnology,[33] and climate change acceptance and policies.[34] Granted all of these studies rely on correlational designs, however, research currently ongoing is using priming techniques to experimentally test for the causal effect.

In sum, though there are certainly incidents in which religion contributed to the pursuit of scientific truth and the fruits it can produce, the data tilt toward religion being an impediment.

Limitations and Conclusion

Every reader will certainly notice some topic that hasn't been discussed. What about civic participation? Women's rights? What about art? Space and practicality prevent covering every corner, but the topics above cover a substantial area of what comprises human flourishing. Nevertheless, there are other limitations.

One methodological complication that hovers over many studies in this body of research concerns response biases. Researchers have extensively documented that those reporting to be religious tend to be higher on self-enhancement—that is, the tendency to perceive oneself especially positively on culturally valued characteristics.[35] This has led to the concern that many of the relationships between religiosity and socially desirable constructs measured by self-report (e.g., happiness, some measures of prosociality and health) may be overstated since the religious would inflate their reports of well-being, prosociality, or health more than would the nonreligious. However, as my colleagues and I have discussed in more detail elsewhere,[36] the problem could be even worse. Since religiosity itself is socially desirable in most places, high self-enhancers might also be overreporting their religiosity. There is abundant evidence that people do so, for both religious attendance[37] and belief.[38] As a consequence, any relationship seen between socially desirable religiosity and any other socially desirable construct could largely or entirely be the product of a third variable: individual differences in self-enhancement and one's tendency to inflate one's responses on socially desirable matters. All of the correlations that solely involve self-report measures may simply be differentiating the high self-enhancers from the more accurate and honest responders. This concern highlights the need for behavioral measures and experimental designs, which of course have their own limitations. In general, however, this methodological concern should inspire more skepticism toward research painting religion in a positive light than that painting it in a negative one.

Many of the legitimate charges against religion involve big things that garner a lot of negative press and attention, such as child abuse scandals and terrorists. On the other hand, many of the positive things tend to be small and personal, such as the stress reduction of a religious ritual or the comfort from a religious community member, and thus fail to capture the same level of attention as religion's deleterious consequences. However, the challenge is further and potentially fatally complicated by the need to factor in counterfactuals. How would the world be today if religion had never existed? What grievous crimes or great creations have been preempted by the influence of religion? What utopia or dystopia might have been? Since we cannot run the tape again, I've argued above that the more tractable—and practical—question concerns the here and now.

One of the recurrent themes that has emerged in our brief review of the evidence is that though religions provide a complex stew of costs and benefits, the balance among these will vary—often systematically—on the place and time. A general trend emerges that as societies become more developed, religion's benefits decline. In turn, religiosity declines as well, and as it becomes less normative, it becomes less valuable to those who believe, and less of an impediment to those who don't. Given these dynamic effects, context can change quickly. Indeed, the feedback loops could work in the opposite direction as well, and one could readily imagine scenarios in which the appeal of religion resurges. See, for example, research showing how war increases religiosity,[39] and speculation about how an intensifying climate crisis could lead to more cultural "tightness," which is associated with religiosity.[40]

All of this complicates our original question even further, which now becomes something like *does religion contribute to human flourishing on balance, today, in this society? And in what ways so that we may be able to predict whether these benefits are likely to continue?* But if human flourishing is truly our goal, then it behooves us to understand *all* sides of this question: how religion contributes to human flourishing, but also how it detracts. And in what contexts. And how and why, such that we might best understand its current role and its trajectory. That way, we may at least try to cultivate it to achieve the best ends of our species and spare us its indulging our worst.

References

Acar, S., M. A. Runco, and U. Ogurlu. 2018. "Creativity and Religiosity: A Reanalysis with Regional Predictors." *Creativity Research Journal* 30, no. 3: 316–21.

Anderson, J., and Y. Koç. 2015. "Exploring Patterns of Explicit and Implicit Anti-Gay Attitudes in Muslims and Atheists." *European Journal of Social Psychology* 45, no. 6: 687–701.

Atran, S. 2016. "The Devoted Actor: Unconditional Commitment and Intractable Conflict across Cultures." *Current Anthropology* 57, S13: S192–S203.

Atran, S., H. Sheikh, and A. Gomez. 2014. "Devoted Actors Sacrifice for Close Comrades and Sacred Cause." *Proceedings of the National Academy of Sciences* 111, no. 50: 17702–3.

Bénabou, R., D. Ticchi, and A. Vindigni. 2015a. *Forbidden Fruits: The Political Economy of Science, Religion, and Growth* (No. w21105). Cambridge, Mass.: National Bureau of Economic Research.

———. 2015b. "Religion and Innovation." *American Economic Review* 105, no. 5: 346–51.

Brenner, P. S. 2011. "Identity Importance and the Overreporting of Religious Service Attendance: Multiple Imputation of Religious Attendance Using the American Time Use Study and the General Social Survey." *Journal for the Scientific Study of Religion* 50: 103–15.

Burn, S. M., and J. Busso. 2005. "Ambivalent Sexism, Scriptural Literalism, and Religiosity." *Psychology of Women Quarterly* 29, no. 4: 412–18.

Clark, C. J., B. Winegard, J. Beardslee, R. Baumeister, and A. F. Shariff. In press. "Declines in Religiosity Predicted Increases in Violent Crime—But Not among Countries with Relatively High Average IQ." *Psychological Science*.

Clingingsmith, D., A. I. Khwaja, and M. Kremer. 2009. "Estimating the Impact of the Hajj: Religion and Tolerance in Islam's Global Gathering." *Quarterly Journal of Economics* 124, no. 3: 1133–70.

Cohen, R., C. Bavishi, and A. Rozanski. 2016. "Purpose in Life and Its Relationship to All-Cause Mortality and Cardiovascular Events: A Meta-Analysis." *Psychosomatic Medicine* 78, no. 2: 122–33.

Cooperrider, D. L. and Whitney, D. 2001. "A Positive Revolution in Change: Appreciative Inquiry." *Public Administration and Public Policy* 87: 611–30.

Cox, D., R. P. Jones, and J. Navarro-Rivera. 2014. "I Know What You Did Last Sunday: Measuring Social Desirability Bias in Self-Reported Religious Behavior, Belief, and Identity." *Public Religion Research Institute* 2: 57–58.

Coyne, J. A. 2016. *Faith versus Fact: Why Science and Religion Are Incompatible*. New York: Penguin Books.

Dawkins, R. D. 2006. *The God Delusion*. London: Transworld.

Diener, E., L. Tay, and D. G. Myers. 2011. "The Religion Paradox: If Religion Makes People Happy, Why Are So Many Dropping Out?" *Journal of Personality and Social Psychology* 101, no. 6: 1278.

Ecklund E. H., D. R. Johnson, C. P. Scheitle, K. R. W. Matthews, and S. W. Lewis. 2016. "Religion among Scientists in International Context: A New Study of Scientists in Eight Regions." *Socius: Sociological Research for a Dynamic World* 2: 1–9.

Funk, C., and B. A. Alper. 2015. "Religion and Views on Climate and Energy Issues." *Pew Research Center* 22. https://www.pewresearch.org/internet/wp-content/uploads/sites/9/2015/10/PI_2015-10-22_religion-and-science_FINAL.pdf.

Gaunt, R. 2012. "'Blessed Is He Who Has Not Made Me a Woman': Ambivalent Sexism and Jewish Religiosity." *Sex Roles* 67, nos. 9–10: 477–87.

Gervais, W. M., and M. B. Najle. 2018. "How Many Atheists Are There?" *Social Psychological and Personality Science* 9: 3–10.

Glick, P., and S. T. Fiske. 2001. "An Ambivalent Alliance: Hostile and Benevolent Sexism as Complementary Justifications for Gender Inequality." *American Psychologist* 56, no. 2: 109.

Glick, P., M. Lameiras, and Y. R. Castro. 2002. "Education and Catholic Religiosity as Predictors of Hostile and Benevolent Sexism toward Women And Men." *Sex Roles* 47, nos. 9–10: 433–41.

Gómez, J. M., M. Verdú, A. González-Megías, and M. Méndez. 2016. "The Phylogenetic Roots of Human Lethal Violence." *Nature* 538, no. 7624: 233–37.

Hadaway, C. K., P. L. Marler, and M. Chaves. 1993. "What the Polls Don't Show: A Closer Look at U.S. Church Attendance." *American Sociological Review* 58, no. 6: 741–52.

Haggard, M. C., R. Kaelen, V. Saroglou, O. Klein, and W. C. Rowatt. 2018. "Religion's Role in the Illusion of Gender Equality: Supraliminal and Subliminal Religious Priming Increases Benevolent Sexism." *Psychology of Religion and Spirituality* 11, no. 4: 392–98.

Hajjar, L. 2004. "Religion, State Power, and Domestic Violence in Muslim Societies: A Framework for Comparative Analysis." *Law and Social Inquiry* 29, no. 1: 1–38.

Hall, D. L., D. C. Matz, and W. Wood. 2010. "Why Don't We Practice What We Preach? A Meta-Analytic Review of Religious Racism." *Personality and Social Psychology Review* 14, no. 1: 126–39.

Hansen, I. G., and A. Ryder. 2016. "In Search of 'Religion Proper' Intrinsic Religiosity and Coalitional Rigidity Make Opposing Predictions of Intergroup Hostility across Religious Groups." *Journal of Cross-Cultural Psychology* 47, no. 6: 835–57.

Henrich, J., M. Bauer, A. Cassar, J. Chytilová, and B. G. Purzycki. 2019. "War Increases Religiosity." *Nature Human Behaviour* 3, no. 2: 129–35.

Henrich, J., R. Boyd, and P. J. Richerson. 2012. "The Puzzle of Monogamous Marriage." *Philosophical Transactions of the Royal Society B: Biological Sciences* 367, no. 1589: 657–69.

Hossain, F., B. Onyango, A. Adelaja, B. Schilling, and W. Hallman. 2004. "Consumer Acceptance of Food Biotechnology: Willingness to Buy Genetically Modified Food Products." *Journal of International Food and Agribusiness Marketing* 15, nos. 1–2: 53–76.

Jackson, J. C., and M. J. Gelfand. 2019. "Could Climate Change Fuel the Rise of Right-Wing Nationalism?" *Conversation* (Boston, Mass.). Accessed November 30, 2019. https://theconversation.com/could -climate-change-fuel-the-rise-of-right-wing-nationalism-123503?utm _medium=amptwitter&utm_source=twitter.

Johnson, D. 2016. *God Is Watching You: How the Fear of God Makes Us Human*. New York: Oxford University Press.

Johnson, M. E., C. Brems, and P. Alford-Keating. 1997. "Personality Correlates of Homophobia." *Journal of Homosexuality* 34, no. 1: 57–69.

Johnson, M. K., W. C. Rowatt, L. M. Barnard-Brak, J. A. Patock-Peckham, J. P. LaBouff, and R. D. Carlisle. 2011. "A Mediational Analysis of the Role of Right-Wing Authoritarianism and Religious Fundamentalism in the Religiosity–Prejudice Link." *Personality and Individual Differences* 50, no. 6: 851–56.

Johnson, M. K., W. C. Rowatt, and J. LaBouff. 2010. "Priming Christian Religious Concepts Increases Racial Prejudice." *Social Psychological and Personality Science* 1: 119–26.

Kiper, J., and R. Sosis. 2016. "Shaking the Tyrant's Bloody Robe: An Evolutionary Perspective on Ethnoreligious Violence." *Politics and the Life Sciences* 35, no. 1: 27–47.

LaBouff, J. P., W. C. Rowatt, M. K. Johnson, and C. Finkle. 2012. "Differences in Attitudes toward Outgroups in Religious and Nonreligious Contexts in a Multinational Sample: A Situational Context Priming Study." *International Journal for the Psychology of Religion* 22, no. 1: 1–9.

Levin, J. S. 1994. "Religion and Health: Is There an Association, Is It Valid, and Is It Causal?" *Social Science and Medicine* 38, no. 11: 1475–82.

Li, S., M. J. Stampfer, D. R. Williams, and T. J. VanderWeele. 2016. "Association of Religious Service Attendance with Mortality among Women." *JAMA Internal Medicine* 176, no. 6: 777–85.

Mercier, B., S. R. Kramer, and A. F. Shariff. 2018. "Belief in God: Why People Believe, and Why They Don't." *Current Directions in Psychological Science* 27, no. 4: 263–68.

Mikołajczak, M., and J. Pietrzak. 2014. "Ambivalent Sexism and Religion: Connected through Values." *Sex Roles* 70, nos. 9–10: 387–99.

Nason-Clark, N. 2004. "When Terror Strikes at Home: The Interface between Religion and Domestic Violence." *Journal for the Scientific Study of Religion* 43, no. 3: 303–10.

Norenzayan, A., A. F. Shariff, W. M. Gervais, A. K. Willard, R. A. McNamara, E. Slingerland, and J. Henrich. 2016. "The Cultural Evolution of Prosocial Religions." *Behavioral and Brain Sciences* 39, E. doi: 10.1017/S0140525X14001356.

Osiri, J., B. Houenou, and R. Stein. 2019. "A Cross-Country Study of Innovation and Religiosity." https://ssrn.com/abstract=3451502.

Piazza, J., and J. F. Landy. 2013. "'Lean Not on Your Own Understanding': Belief That Morality Is Founded on Divine Authority and Non-Utilitarian Moral Thinking." *Judgment and Decision Making* 8, no. 6: 639–61.

Pinker, S. 2012. *The Better Angels of Our Nature: Why Violence Has Declined.* New York: Penguin.

———. 2018. *Enlightenment Now: The Case for Reason, Science, Humanism, and Progress.* New York: Penguin.

Preston, J. and N. Epley. 2009. "Science and God: An Automatic Opposition between Ultimate Explanations." *Journal of Experimental Social Psychology* 45, no. 1: 238–41.

Recker, D. 2017. "Faith, Belief, and the Compatibility of Religion and Science." *Zygon 52*, no. 1: 212–31.

Rios, K., and Aveyard, M. 2019. "Science–Religion Compatibility Beliefs across Middle Eastern and American Young Adult Samples: The Role of Cross-Cultural Exposure." *Public Understanding of Science* 28, no. 8: 949–57. https://doi.org/10.1177/0963662519869815.

Saslow, L. R., R. Willer, M. Feinberg, P. K. Piff, K. Clark, D. Keltner, and S. R. Saturn. 2013. "My Brother's Keeper? Compassion Predicts Generosity More among Less Religious Individuals." *Social Psychological and Personality Science* 4, no. 1: 31–38.

Scheufele, D. A., E. A. Corley, T. J. Shih, K. E. Dalrymple, and S. S. Ho. 2009. "Religious Beliefs and Public Attitudes toward Nanotechnology in Europe and the United States." *Nature Nanotechnology* 4, no. 2: 91–94.

Sedikides, C., and J. E. Gebauer. 2010. "Religiosity as Self-Enhancement: A Meta-Analysis of the Relation between Socially Desirable Responding and Religiosity." *Personality and Social Psychology Review* 14, no. 1: 17–36.

Seybold, K. S., and P. C. Hill. 2001. "The Role of Religion and Spirituality in Mental and Physical Health." *Current Directions in Psychological Science* 10, no. 1: 21–24.

Shariff, A. F., A. B. Cohen, and A. Norenzayan. 2008. "The Devil's Advocate: Secular Arguments Diminish Both Implicit and Explicit Religious Belief." *Journal of Cognition and Culture* 8: 417–23.

Sheikh, H., J. Ginges, A. Coman, and S. Atran. 2012. "Religion, Group Threat and Sacred Values." *Judgment and Decision Making* 7, no. 2: 110.

Smith, T. B., M. E. McCullough, and J. Poll. 2003. "Religiousness and Depression: Evidence for a Main Effect and the Moderating Influence of Stressful Life Events." *Psychological Bulletin* 116: 614–36.

Ståhl, T., M. P. Zaal, and L. J. Skitka. 2016. "Moralized Rationality: Relying on Logic and Evidence in the Formation and Evaluation of Belief Can Be Seen as a Moral Issue." *PLoS ONE* 11, no. 11: e0166332. https://doi.org/10.1371/journal.pone.0166332.

Stavrova, O., D. Fetchenhauer, and T. Schlösser. 2013. "Why Are Religious People Happy? The Effect of the Social Norm of Religiosity across Countries." *Social Science Research* 42, no. 1: 90–105.

Van Assche, J., Y. Koç, and A. Roets. 2019. "Religiosity or Ideology? On the Individual Differences Predictors of Sexism." *Personality and Individual Differences* 139: 191–97.

VanderWeele, T. J., S. Li, A. C. Tsai, and I. Kawachi. 2016. "Association between Religious Service Attendance and Lower Suicide Rates among US Women." *JAMA Psychiatry* 73, no. 8: 845–51.

Whitehouse, H., and J. A. Lanman. 2014. "The Ties That Bind Us: Ritual, Fusion, and Identification." *Current Anthropology* 55, no. 6: 674–95.

Wunsch-Vincent, S., B. Lanvin, and S. Dutta. 2015. *The Global Innovation Index 2015: Effective Innovation Policies for Development* (No. id: 7491).

NOTES

1 Meanings and Dimensions of Flourishing
Miroslav Volf, Matthew Croasmun,
Ryan McAnnally-Linz

1 On the role of individual "dreams" in privatized visions of the good life, see Rosa 2019, 17–26, as well as Volf and Croasmun 2019, 24–28.
2 For a sketch of such an argument, see Volf 2019.
3 For an argument for such "pagan" polytheism see de Benoist 2018. For a popular advocacy of national gods, see Harari 2018, 127–39.
4 On axial transformations, see Bellah and Joas 2012. See also Volf 2016.
5 For a recent argument that religion has a legitimate place in the modern university, see Wolterstorff 2019.
6 See, for example, MacIntyre 1988; MacIntyre 1990.
7 We have invited scholar-practitioners of many of the world's religions (along with proponents of non-religious philosophical traditions) to artic-ulate their visions of flourishing life through the lens of this formal account. Their responses demonstrated exactly this tension between, on the one hand, finding that their vision of flourishing spanned all three dimensions and, at the same time, finding occasional places where their tradition would push back on the formal structure itself. ("Joy and the Good Life Across Traditions," symposium at Yale Divinity School, February 14–16, 2018.)
8 Wolterstorff 2007.
9 All figures created by Matthew Croasmun.
10 After World War II and in the wake of discovery of unpublished text of early Marx, interpretations of Marx's theory developed which highlighted praxis and free play of creative activity within the dialectical movement of history.
11 Huxley 2014.

12 Huxley 2014, 238.

13 Huxley 2014, 220.

14 Huxley 2014, 237.

15 Bentham 1970, 11. Indeed, not only Bentham, but *any and all* of the so-called "hedonistic" utilitarian thinkers are committed to a vision of flourishing that reduces to the affective. See, for instance, the recent work of Peter Singer.

16 Volf and Croasmun 2019, 149–85.

17 Love can be taken to be the ground of the creation of an entire new world (Rom 8:35, 39; 1 Cor 13). For love as an affective state of longing, see Phil 4:1. Peace is described as an internal state in Phil 4:7; "living peaceably" is commended in Rom 12:18. Paul's readers are commanded to rejoice time and again (paradigmatically in Phil 4:4). The fact that this command can be stated "rejoice *always*" gives the sense that this joy can be imagined as a continual state to which the believer can always return.

2 Virtues, Vices, and the Good Life
Celia Deane-Drummond

1 I would like to thank Mary Ann Meyers for the kind invitation to take part in the Advanced Symposium on Human Flourishing at Harvard University from November 29–December 1, 2018, colleagues at the symposium for helpful feedback, and also Adam Cohen for his support.

2 Evans 2018.

3 Taylor 2007.

4 Deane-Drummond 2017; Deane-Drummond and Fuentes 2017.

5 Deane-Drummond 2019.

6 Nussbaum 2001, 302.

7 Nussbaum 2001, 301.

8 Spikins et al. 2010; Spikins 2015.

9 Spikins et al. 2010, 305.

10 Spikins 2015, 60–67.

11 Spikins et al. 2010, 309.

12 Spikins et al. 2010, 309.

13 Aquinas 1968, Qu. 58.1.

14 Miner 2015, 71n1.

15 Miner 2015, 73.

16 Aquinas 1966, 1a, Qu. 25.3.

17 Aquinas 1974a, 2a2ae, Qu. 30.2.

18 Aquinas 1966, 1a, Qu. 21.3.

19 Klimecki et al. 2014, 873–79.

20 Peterson 2017, 232–57.

21 Aquinas 1974a, 2a2ae, Qu. 30.1.

22 Aquinas 1974a, 2a2ae, Qu. 30.1.

23 Aquinas 1974a, 2a2ae, Qu. 30.1.

24 Aquinas 1974a, 2a2ae, Qu. 30.3.

25 Aquinas 1974a, 2a2ae, Qu. 30.4.

26 Aquinas 1974a, 2a2ae, Qu. 30.4.
27 Aquinas 1974a, 2a2ae, Qu. 30.4.
28 Darwin 2004, 132–60.
29 Mead 1940, 402–5.
30 Knauft 2011, 203–25.
31 Whitehead 2002.
32 Kim and Kissel 2018, 45.
33 Sela, Shackelford, and Liddle 2016, 197–216.
34 Martens 2015, 133–50.
35 Boyd 2017.
36 Aquinas 1972, 2a2ae, Qu. 40.
37 Aquinas 1972, 2a2ae, Qu. 40.1.
38 Aquinas 1972, 2a2ae, Qu. 40.1.
39 Aquinas 1972, 2a2ae, Qu. 40.2.
40 Aquinas 1965, 2a2ae, Qu. 123.5.
41 Aquinas 1974a, 2a2ae, Qu. 29.2.
42 Heath 1972, 197.
43 Aquinas 1974b, 2a2ae, Qu. 66.8.
44 Aquinas 1974b, 2a2ae, Qu. 68.8.
45 Aquinas 1972, 2a2ae, Qu. 40.3.
46 Aquinas 1969, 1a2ae, Qu. 105.3.
47 Heath 1972, 193.
48 Deane-Drummond et al. 2016, 115–51.

3 *Status Viatoris* and the Path Quality of Religion
Jonathan Rowson

1 In Rowson 2017 I define Spiritual Sensibility as "a disposition towards reality characterized by concern for the fullness of life and experienced through simultaneous intimations of aliveness, goodness, understanding and meaning. Those glimpses of wholeness and integration have a texture that is at once emotional, ethical, epistemic and existential—the feeling of being alive, the conviction that something matters, the intuition that the world makes sense, and the experience that life is meaningful respectively" (5).
2 I develop this case for transformative education in response to social and ecological crises more fully in a recent essay, Rowson 2019.
3 Pieper 1977, 1.
4 Williams 2014.
5 Batchelor 2016.
6 Mascolo and Fischer 2015, 149.
7 Kegan 1983, 43–45.
8 Foster and Moran 1985.
9 Bronner 2011, 77.
10 Sachs 2017.
11 Quoted in Mesle 2008, 87.
12 Dale 2014.

4 Spiritual Well-Being and Human Flourishing
Tyler J. VanderWeele

1 VanderWeele 2017a, 2017b, 2018.
2 VanderWeele 2017a, 2017b, 2018; Koenig, King, and Carson 2012; Idler 2014; Iannaccone 1998; Wilcox and Wolfinger 2016; Johnson 2011; Johnson et al. 2001; Krause 2012; Strawbridge et al. 1997; Li et al. 2016a, 2016b; Fruehwirth, Iver, and Zhang 2018; VanderWeele et al. 2016; Hummer et al. 1999; Chida, Steptoe, and Powell 2009; Putnam and Campbell 2012; Shariff et al. 2016; Lim and Putnam 2010; Chen and VanderWeele 2018.
3 VanderWeele 2017c.
4 VanderWeele 2017a, 2017b.
5 Aquinas 1948; Vatican 2000; Westminster 2014. Here and throughout I will speak mostly in reference to Christianity, but many of the remarks, I believe, may be more broadly applicable.
6 VanderWeele 2017c. Flourishing, as an abstract verbal noun, might be understood as "the state in which all aspects of a person's life are good"; flourishing, as a gerund or present participle, might be understood as "living in a state in which all aspects of a person's life are good."
7 John Paul II 1984.
8 Aquinas 1948.
9 Aquinas 1948; Vatican 2000; Curry et al. 2018.
10 Fowler and Christakis 2010.
11 Carroll and Shiflett 2001; C. Schmidt 1885; A. J. Schmidt 2001; Woods and Canizares 2012.
12 Cohen and Johnson 2017.
13 Cavanaugh 2009.
14 Volf 2015; Goodman 2014.
15 Aquinas 1948; Vatican 2000.
16 Paloutzian and Ellison 1982.
17 Peterman et al. 2002; Koenig 2008.
18 VanderWeele, Long, and Balboni, in press.
19 VanderWeele 2017c.
20 VanderWeele 2017a, 2017b, 2018; Koenig, King, and Carson 2012; Idler 2014; Iannaccone 1998; Wilcox and Wolfinger 2016; Johnson 2011; Johnson et al. 2001; Krause 2012; Strawbridge et al. 1997; Li et al. 2016a, 2016b; Fruehwirth, Iver, and Zhang 2018; VanderWeele et al. 2016; Hummer et al. 1999; Chida, Steptoe, and Powell 2009; Putnam and Campbell 2012; Shariff et al. 2016; Lim and Putnam 2010; Chen and VanderWeele 2018.

5 Religion and Human Flourishing in the Evolution of Social Complexity
Harvey Whitehouse

1 E.g., Paul-Labrador et al. 2006; but see also Sloan and Bagiella 2002.
2 Malhotra 2010; but see also McKay and Whitehouse 2015.
3 Rossano 2012.
4 Aronson and Mills 1959.
5 Sosis 2004.
6 Henrich 2009.
7 Wiltermuth and Heath 2009.
8 Curry et al. 2018.
9 Whitehouse 2011.
10 Legare et al. 2015; Hermann et al. 2013.
11 Watson-Jones et al. 2014; Watson-Jones, Whitehouse, and Legare 2016.
12 Atkinson and Whitehouse 2011.
13 Whitehouse 1995, 2000, 2004.
14 Whitehouse 1992, 2002, 2018.
15 Whitehouse and Lanman 2014.
16 Swann et al. 2012.
17 Whitehouse et al. 2014; Whitehouse 2018.
18 Jong et al. 2015; Kavanagh et al. 2018.
19 Jackson et al. 2018.
20 Newson, Buhrmester, and Whitehouse 2016.
21 Buhrmester et al. 2018.
22 Swann et al. 2010.
23 Whitehouse 2004.
24 Whitehouse and Lanman 2014.
25 Whitehouse 2004.
26 Whitehouse et al. 2017.
27 Atkinson and Whitehouse 2011.
28 Whitehouse and Hodder 2010; Whitehouse et al. 2013.
29 Whitehouse and Lanman 2014.
30 Whitehouse 2004.
31 Whitehouse et al. 2019b.
32 Gantley, Bogaard, and Whitehouse 2018.
33 Whitehouse 2018.
34 Whitehouse and McQuinn 2012; Whitehouse 2018.
35 Barker 2009.
36 Watts et al. 2016.
37 Turchin et al., forthcoming.
38 Jaspers 1953.

39 Turchin et al. 2015.
40 Turchin et al. 2018.
41 Mullins et al. 2018.
42 Whitehouse et al. 2019b; Turchin et al. 2018b.
43 Norenzayan 2013.
44 Watts et al. 2015.
45 Raffield, Price, and Collard 2017.
46 Baumard et al. 2015.
47 Whitehouse et al. 2019b.
48 Whitehouse et al. 2019a.
49 Curry, Mullins, and Whitehouse 2019.
50 Curry et al. 2019.

6 The Next Generation
Dominic D. P. Johnson

1 Dawkins 2006, 222.
2 In defining religion, I follow Cohen (Introduction) as simply "the broad sense of faith traditions," and focus on component "religious beliefs and behaviors"—more tangible individual traits—rather than religion, *per se*, for the reasons articulated by (Barrett 2017). In defining flourishing, or "well-being," I agree with VanderWeele in recognizing that this can be defined in many ways, beyond commonly employed material metrics such as wealth or health, to include "a much broader range of states and outcomes, certainly including mental and physical health, but also encompassing happiness and life satisfaction, meaning and purpose, character and virtue, and close social relationships" (VanderWeele 2017, 8148). As will become clear, however, the purpose of this chapter is to deliberately focus down on one specific subset of this larger range, exploring to what extent religion may promote flourishing as defined by biological or "Darwinian" fitness (via the metrics of survival and reproductive success).
3 Hitchens 2007; Dawkins 2006; Dennett 2006.
4 For these and many other examples, see Birkhead, Wimpenny, and Montgomerie 2014; Davies, Krebs, and West 2012.
5 Trivers 1972; Standen and Foley 1989.
6 Johnson 2016; Norenzayan 2013.
7 Searcy and Nowicki 2005; Johnstone 1997.
8 Zahavi 1975.
9 E.g., Sosis and Alcorta 2003; Sosis 2003b; Sosis 2006; Cronk 2005.
10 Trivers 2011; Gigerenzer and Brighton 2009; Cosmides and Tooby 1994.
11 Gigerenzer 2002; McKay and Dennett 2009; Johnson et al. 2013.
12 Haselton et al. 2009; Gigerenzer and Brighton 2009; Cosmides and Tooby 1994; Kenrick and Griskevicius 2013.
13 Von Hippel and Trivers 2011; Fiske and Taylor 2013; Gigerenzer 2002.
14 Foster and Kokko 2009. See also Haselton and Nettle 2006.
15 Johnson 2009; Johnson, Lenfesty, and Schloss 2014; Wilson 2002.

16 For reviews of evolutionary theories of religion, see Bulbulia et al. 2008; Wade 2009; Norenzayan and Shariff 2008; Bering 2010; Schloss and Murray 2009; Wright 2009.

17 Technically, Darwinian fitness is *only* reproductive success, since traits that lead to successful reproduction are all that genes "care" about, not survival per se. However, I add survival here because (a) organisms have to at least survive to reproductive age, and (b) in humans, adaptations for survival are important for long periods of life before, during, and after reproduction. Many adaptations clearly aid survival, even if natural selection only operates via reproduction itself.

18 Darwin 1871, 82.

19 For alternative conceptions of flourishing, see VanderWeele 2017.

20 Darwin 1871; Johnson 2016. See also Wilson 2002; Norenzayan 2013; Bering 2010.

21 Andrews, Gangestad, and Matthews 2002; Sosis 2009; Tinbergen 1963.

22 Dawkins 2006; Bulbulia 2008.

23 Adapted from Wilson 2005.

24 For a review, see Bulbulia et al. 2008.

25 Wilson and Sober 1994.

26 Tom Bartlett, "Dusting Off God," *Chronicle of Higher Education*, August 13, 2013.

27 West, El Mouden, and Gardner 2011.

28 Pinker 2012; Dawkins 1976.

29 Williams 1966; Andrews, Gangestad, and Matthews 2002.

30 Johnson, Price, and Takezawa 2008; Johnson and Kruger 2004.

31 See discussions in Sosis 2009, 2003a; Wilson 2006.

32 Creanza, Kolodny, and Feldman 2017; Mesoudi 2011.

33 Norenzayan et al. 2016; Shariff, Norenzayan, and Henrich 2009.

34 Brewer et al. 2017.

35 Koenig et al. 2005.

36 Rowthorn 2011.

37 Norris and Inglehart 2004.

38 Dawkins 2006, 222.

39 Tinbergen 1963.

40 Mayr 1961; Tinbergen 1963; Scott-Phillips, Dickins, and West 2011.

41 Davies, Krebs, and West 2012, 2.

42 Curry, Mullins, and Whitehouse 2019; Wright 1994.

43 Volf, Croasmun, and McAnnally-Linz, chap. 1.

44 E.g., Purzycki et al. 2016; Shariff and Norenzayan 2007; Ruffle and Sosis 2007. For a meta-analysis of priming studies, see Shariff et al. 2016.

45 Johnson and Reeve 2013; Whitehouse and Lanman 2014; Sosis and Handwerker 2011.

46 Shah and Toft 2006; Sosis 2011; Atran and Ginges 2012; Whitehouse and McQuinn 2013.

7 Religions Help Us Trust One Another
Adam B. Cohen

1 Hall et al. 2015.
2 Blais et al., in press.

8 Religion's Contribution to Prosociality
Azim F. Shariff

1 Kelly, Kramer, and Shariff 2018.
2 See a meta-analysis by Sedikides and Gebauer 2010.
3 Kelly, Kramer, and Shariff 2018.
4 Sedikides and Gebauer 2010, 19.
5 There is now mounting evidence for the overclaiming of religiosity, both in terms of religious practice (Cox, Jones, and Navarro-Rivera 2014; Hadaway, Marler, and Chaves 1993) and religious belief (Gervais and Najle 2016).
6 Saslow et al. 2013.
7 Piazza and Landy 2013.
8 Richard, Bond, and Stokes-Zoota 2003.
9 Shariff et al. 2016.
10 Billingsley, Gomes, and McCullough 2018; Van Elk et al. 2015.
11 White et al. 2019. Full disclosure: six studies were run in total. In the one study that produced inconsistent results, participant reports revealed that they had misunderstood the experimental paradigm. Correcting for those errors revealed the results to be in line with the other five.
12 Stark (1996) has famously argued that early Christians were able to recruit new members to their group by extending their benevolence to non-Christians.
13 Ginges et al. 2020.
14 Note that we were predicting null effect for the interactions in both studies. Null effects are harder to support than a positive effect since there are other reasons—such as methodological problems and underpowered samples—why an effect may be absent. Neither are a large concern here. The methodology was sufficient to elicit the two main effects, suggesting that it is "working" to capture condition-based differences in generosity. Moreover, we had a very well-powered study: 828 participants in the first study and 1157 in the second. Thus, if an interaction of any meaningful size really did exist, our design should have been sufficient to pick up on it. Moreover, Bayes factors provide support for no difference between the priming effect between ingroup and outgroup targets in both studies.
15 Ginges et al. 2020.
16 Ginges et al. 2020.

9 Religion's Contribution to Population Health
Christopher G. Ellison

1 Levin 2016.
2 For review, see Oman 2018.
3 Koenig, King, and Carson 2012; Koenig, McCullough, and Larson 2001.
4 Koenig and Shohaib 2014; Levin and Prince 2013.
5 Hummer et al. 2004; Idler 2011.
6 Enstrom and Breslow 1988; Flannelly et al. 2002; Phillips 1975.
7 Durkheim 1951 (1897).
8 Ellison, Burr, and McCall 1997; Pescosolido and Georgianna 1989.
9 Bruce et al. 2017; Gillum et al. 2008; Hummer et al. 1999; Idler et al. 2017.
10 Hummer et al. 1999; Rogers, Krueger, and Hummer 2010.
11 Ellison et al. 2000; Hill et al. 2005.
12 Hill, Saenz, and Rote 2020.
13 Brenner 2011.
14 E.g., Krause 2006a.
15 Hill et al. 2006, 2016; Idler and Kasl 1997.
16 E.g., Cozier et al. 2018; Gillum and Ingram 2006.
17 Hill, Bradshaw, and Burdette 2016.
18 Koenig, McCullough, and Larson 2001; Koenig et al. 2012.
19 Schieman, Bierman, and Ellison 2013; Smith, McCullough, and Poll 2003.
20 E.g., Ellison and Flannelly 2009; Miller et al. 2012.
21 Ellison 1991; Lim and Putnam 2010.
22 Hill and Pargament 1997; Idler et al. 2003; Krause 2008a; Pargament 1997.
23 Lin and Ensel 1989; Pearlin et al. 1981.
24 Ellison and Henderson 2011.
25 Ellison and Henderson 2011.
26 Ellison et al. 2008; Gillum 2005; Gillum and Holt 2010.
27 Enstrom and Breslow 1988; Phillips 1975; Troyer 1988.
28 E.g., Benjamins and Brown 2004.
29 Ellison and Henderson 2011.
30 Ellison and George 1994.
31 Billingsley 1999; Krause 2008a; Taylor et al. 2000, 2017.
32 E.g., Krause 2006a, 2008a.
33 Ellis 1962.
34 Ellison and Burdette 2012; Schieman, Bierman, and Ellison 2010; Schieman, Pudrovska, and Milkie 2005; Schieman et al. 2017.
35 E.g., Krause 2008b.
36 E.g., Krause 2003; Sethi and Seligman 1993.
37 E.g., Krause 2006b.
38 Pargament 1997; Pargament et al. 2000.
39 Ano and Vasconcelles 2005; Pargament et al. 1988, 2000.
40 E.g., Hill and Pargament 2003.

41 Brenner 2011.
42 Idler et al. 2009.
43 Flannelly 2017; Park 2017.
44 E.g., Ellison et al. 2019.
45 Ellis 1962.
46 Berger 1967.
47 Exline et al. 2011, 2014; McConnell et al. 2006.
48 Flannelly 2017; Uecker et al. 2016.
49 Pargament 2002.
50 Bradshaw and Ellison 2010; Ellison, Schieman, and Bradshaw 2014.
51 Ross and Mirowsky 2006.
52 E.g., Ellison, Schieman, and Bradshaw 2014; Krause 2008a.
53 Ellison, Schieman, and Bradshaw 2014; Krause 2008a.
54 Lu and Yang 2020.
55 Hayward and Elliott 2014; Upenieks, Foy, and Miles 2018.
56 Stroope and Baker 2018.
57 E.g., Ellison et al. 2009; Krause 2008b.
58 Ellison and Xu 2014.
59 Hout and Fischer 2014.
60 Schwadel 2011.
61 Baker, Stroope, and Walker 2018.
62 Hill, Bradshaw, and Burdette 2016.
63 McEwen 1998.
64 E.g., Hill et al. 2014.
65 Bruce et al. 2017.

10 Offender-Led Religious Movements
Byron R. Johnson

1 VanderWeele 2017a, 2017b, 2018.
2 Grammich et al. 2012; Melton and Ferguson 2016.
3 Stark 2008.
4 Koenig, King, and Carson 2012.
5 Johnson 2011; Johnson and Jang 2012.
6 Johnson et al. 2000a, 2000b, 2001; Ellison 2007a; Ulmer et al. 2010, 2012; Jang and Johnson 2001, 2011.
7 Lee et al. 2016, 2017.
8 Johnson 2004, 2006, 2018a, 2018b.
9 Johnson 2011, 2012; Johnson and Jang 2012; Duwe and Johnson 2013.
10 Putnam and Campbell 2012; Cnaan and Boddie 2001; Krause and Hayward 2013, 2014a, 2014b; Krause et al. 2014.
11 Johnson, Thompkins, and Webb 2006; Johnson and Wubbenhorst 2017; Wydick, Glewwe, and Rutledge 2013, 2017; Glewwe, Ross, and Wydick 2017.

12 Brooks 2007; Pagano et al. 2015; Johnson et al. 2015; Stark 2015.
13 Hallett et al. 2016.
14 Johnson et al. 2016, 2017; Jang and Johnson 2017.
15 Young et al. 1995.
16 Johnson et al. 1997.
17 Johnson 2004.
18 The InnerChange Freedom Initiative (IFI) is a reentry program for prisoners based on the life and teachings of Jesus Christ. Inmates begin the program eighteen to twenty-four months before their release date and continue for an additional twelve months once they have returned to the community.
19 Johnson 2006.
20 Johnson 2011.
21 Duwe and King 2013.
22 Duwe and Johnson 2013.
23 Kerley, Matthews, and Blanchard 2005.
24 Kerley, Matthews, and Schulz 2005.
25 Duwe and Johnson 2016.
26 Carleton 1971.
27 Louisiana Department of Corrections 2015.
28 Nellis 2010.
29 Rideau 1985.
30 All photos except figure 10.5 are the author's.
31 Johnson 2011.
32 Hallett et al. 2016.
33 Hallett et al. 2017.
34 Duwe et al. 2015.
35 Jang et al. 2018.
36 Jang et al. 2017.
37 Hallett et al. 2016.
38 Johnson 2017.
39 Cruz et al. 2018; Maslin 2018.
40 https://www.1843magazine.com/features/can-religion-solve-el-salvadors-gang-problem.
41 Nouwen 1979.
42 *Gates v. Collier*, 501 F.2d 1291 (5th Cir., 1974), was a landmark case decided in U.S. federal court that brought an end to the trusty system and the flagrant inmate abuse that accompanied it at Mississippi State Penitentiary in Sunflower County, Mississippi.
43 Hays et al. 2018.
44 Ronel and Elisha 2011.
45 Braithwaite 2005.
46 Johnson et al. 2016.

11 Some Big-Data Lessons about Religion and Human Flourishing
David G. Myers

1 This essay draws content from my chapter, "Religious Engagement and Living Well," in *The Social Psychology of Living Well*, ed. Joseph P. Forgas and Roy F. Baumeister (New York: Routledge, 2018).
2 Gould 1999, 601.
3 Gallup 1984.
4 All figures are the author's creation.
5 Newport et al. 2010, 2012.
6 Headey et al. 2010, 2.
7 Hartford Institute for Religion Research.
8 Myers and DeWall 2018, 474.
9 Hitchens 2007.
10 D. Wilson 2003, 2007.
11 E. Wilson 1998.
12 Schwartz and Huismans 1995.
13 Putnam and Campbell 2010.
14 Pelham and Crabtree 2008.
15 Australian Centre on Quality of Life 2008.
16 Myers 2000.
17 SSRC 2009.
18 Chida, Steptoe, and Powell 2009; George, Ellison, and Larson 2002; Hummer et al. 1999; McCullough et al. 2000.
19 FiveThirtyEight.com 2010.
20 Kost and Henshaw 2010.
21 Strayhorn and Strayhorn 2009.
22 Regnerus 2007.
23 Nonnemaker, McNeely, and Blum 2003.
24 Lucero et al. 2008.
25 Pelham and Nyiri 2008.
26 Gearing and Lizardi 2009.
27 Clark and Lelkes 2009, 1.
28 Deaton and Stone 2013, 595.
29 Myers and Diener 2018.
30 Okulicz-Kozaryn, Holmes, and Avery 2014.
31 MacInnis and Hodson 2015, 2016; Rasmussen and Bierman 2016.
32 Oishi and Diener 2014; King, Heintzelman, and Ward 2016.
33 Robinson 1950, 467.
34 Diener, Tay, and Myers 2011.

12 Smart and Spiritual
Laurence R. Iannaccone

1 Thanks to the many colleagues who commented on early versions of this essay, including Jean-Paul Carvalho, Sabiou Inoua, Hillard Kaplan,

Douglas Norton, and Avner Seror. I especially thank Deirdre McCloskey for her detailed comments on each draft and Rodney Stark for his extraordinary insights and personal encouragement.

2 For a summary of the distinction between behavioral modernity and anatomical modernity, see Wikipedia, s.v. "Behavioral Modernity," accessed November 10, 2019, https://en.wikipedia.org/w/index.php?title=Behavioral_modernity &oldid=923817461.

3 For an introduction to the new field of humanomics, see Smith and Wilson 2019.

4 To read these quotes in context, see Hayek 1988, 6, 21, 23.

5 Hayek 1988, 36–37. See Smith (2007) for an extensive treatment of the limitations of what Hayek called "constructivist rationality." See Subrick (2015) for an incisive summary of Hayek's thoughts on religion and the social order and the related thoughts of Adam Smith and Vernon Smith.

6 Iannaccone 1992, 1994.

7 Shultziner et al. 2010, 123–24.

8 There are many other scenarios seriously entertained by serious scientists that suggest ways in which "progress" can be fitness-reducing for *Homo sapiens*. Indeed, many scientists who seriously believe that the Fermi paradox (which asks why no other technologically advanced species appears to exist with fifty-plus light years of the solar system) is best answered the hypothesis that intelligent life is so destructive as to remain vanishingly rare. See Wikipedia, s.v. "Fermi Paradox," accessed November 11, 2019, https://en.wikipedia.org/w/index.php?title=Fermi_paradox&oldid= 924091281.

9 *Macbeth* 5.5.24–28.

10 As Richard Hooker wrote centuries ago, "Man doth seek a triple perfection: first a sensual . . . ; then an intellectual . . . ; lastly a spiritual and divine, consisting in those things whereunto we tend by supernatural means" (Hooker, *Of the Laws of Ecclesiastical Polity* 1.11.4 [1593]).

11 Iannaccone 1998.

12 The rapid, continuing growth of evangelical Protestantism, Mormonism, Adventism, and the Jehovah's Witnesses in Africa, Asia, and Latin America is a striking contemporary example (Jenkins 2011).

13 The Economics of Religion in Developing Countries
Sriya Iyer

1 Epstein 1973, 6.

2 One of the more interesting findings of the study was that as many as 16 percent of respondents had no formal reported religious affiliation, which made them the third largest group in their sample.

3 Iannaccone 1998; Iyer 2016.

4 See Iyer 2016 for an overview.

5 Smith 1976, 1979.

6 Weber 1904.
7 Jha 2013.
8 Iyer 2018.
9 See Iyer, Velu, and Weeks 2018 for a more technical presentation of the model and findings.
10 India Religion Survey, 2010.
11 India Religion Survey, 2010.
12 India Religion Survey, 2010.
13 Iyer, Velu, and Weeks 2018.
14 Iyer, Velu, and Weeks 2018.

14 On Balance
Azim F. Shariff

1 To paraphrase Cooperrider and Whitney 2001.
2 Piazza and Landy 2013.
3 Saslow et al. 2013.
4 Gómez et al. 2016.
5 Norenzayan et al. 2016.
6 Johnson 2016.
7 Clark et al., in press.
8 Hajjar 2004; Nason-Clark 2004.
9 Atran 2016; Atran, Sheikh, and Gomez 2014; see also Kiper and Sosis 2016, for similar arguments.
10 Sheikh et al. 2012.
11 Whitehouse and Lanman 2014.
12 Hall, Matz, and Wood 2010.
13 Burn and Busso 2005. Importantly, religiosity consistently tends to be associated with benevolent sexism, rather than hostile sexism, half of Glick and Fiske's (2001) ambivalent sexism construct (Burn and Busso 2005; Gaunt 2012; Glick, Lameiras, and Castro 2002). Whereas hostile sexism represents the outright derogation of women, benevolent sexism represents a gendered but reverent and protective view of women.
14 Anderson and Koç 2015; M. E. Johnson, Brems, and Alford-Keating 1997.
15 E.g., Hansen and Ryder 2016; M. K. Johnson et al. 2011; Mikołajczak and Pietrzak 2014; Van Assche, Koç, and Roets 2019.
16 Haggard et al. 2018, see n1.
17 Johnson, Rowatt, and LaBouff 2010; LaBouff et al. 2012.
18 Clingingsmith, Khwaja, and Kremer 2009.
19 Or both; Diener, Tay, and Myers 2011.
20 Levin 1994; Li et al. 2016.
21 Smith, McCullough, and Poll 2003; VanderWeele et al. 2016.
22 Cohen, Bavishi, and Rozanski 2016; Levin 1994; Seybold and Hill 2001.
23 Stavrova, Fetchenhauer, and Schlösser 2013.
24 E.g., Coyne 2016; Dawkins 2006; Pinker 2018.

25 E.g., Coyne 2016; Recker 2017.
26 Ecklund et al. 2016; Rios and Aveyard 2019.
27 Shariff, Cohen, and Norenzayan 2008.
28 Ståhl, Zaal, and Skitka 2016.
29 Bénabou, Ticchi, and Vindigni 2015a, 2015b.
30 Acar, Runco, and Ogurlu 2018.
31 Wunsch-Vincent, Lanvin, and Dutta 2015.
32 Hossain et al. 2004.
33 Scheufele et al. 2009.
34 Except nuclear energy; Funk and Alper 2015.
35 Sedikides and Gebauer 2010.
36 Mercier, Kramer, and Shariff 2018.
37 Brenner 2011; Cox, Jones, and Navarro-Rivera 2014; Hadaway, Marler, and Chaves 1993.
38 Gervais and Najle 2018.
39 Henrich et al. 2019.
40 Jackson and Gelfand 2019.

INDEX